ADVANCE PRAISE FOR

Transforming Campus Life

"Higher education is witnessing the emergence of more integrative forms of working, living, and learning that have the potential to transform universities and colleges. This book comes at the right time, offering insightful reflections on religious diversity and spiritual exploration in multiple dimensions of campus life. It is a valuable source of analysis and ideas for anyone interested in a more integrative future for higher education and, ultimately, a wiser world."

David K. Scott, Chancellor, University of Massachusetts Amherst

"*Transforming Campus Life: Reflections on Spirituality and Religious Pluralism* is a long-awaited and much-needed compilation of essays discussing the new and difficult terrain of religious diversity, spiritual expression, and multifaith gatherings occurring on our college and university campuses today. With candor and clarity, *Transforming Campus Life* delves into the complexities that emerge when profoundly different communities of faith seek to understand one another, dialogue with one another, and even share in interfaith worship. Because we are breaking new ground as we learn to meet the divergent and sometimes contradictory needs of different faith communities, case studies and successful models are needed as maps to guide our journey. *Transforming Campus Life* offers the theoretical underpinnings of our work as well as stories and concrete examples to support and strengthen our efforts."

Andrea Ayvazian, Dean of Religious Life, Mt. Holyoke College

"In *Transforming Campus Life: Reflections on Spirituality and Religious Pluralism*, Vachel W. Miller and Merle M. Ryan have produced an edited volume of stories related to spirituality on college campuses that covers a wide assortment of topics, programs, and types of institutions. Readers will appreciate the variety in tone and topic of the chapters, which range from the very personal to the conceptual and theoretical. This is an important resource for anyone struggling with the complexity of addressing the spiritual needs of college students, and is especially useful for student affairs courses or professional development seminars on the topic of college students and their experiences."

Patrick Love, Associate Professor,
Higher Education Program, New York University

Transforming Campus Life

Studies in Education and Spirituality

Peter L. Laurence and Victor H. Kazanjian, Jr.
General Editors

Vol. 1

PETER LANG
New York • Washington, D.C./Baltimore • Bern
Frankfurt am Main • Berlin • Brussels • Vienna • Oxford

Transforming Campus Life

Reflections on Spirituality and Religious Pluralism

EDITED BY
Vachel W. Miller
and Merle M. Ryan

PETER LANG
New York • Washington, D.C./Baltimore • Bern
Frankfurt am Main • Berlin • Brussels • Vienna • Oxford

Library of Congress Cataloging-in-Publication Data

Transforming campus life: reflections on spirituality and religious pluralism /
edited by Vachel W. Miller and Merle M. Ryan.
p. cm. — (Studies in education and spirituality; vol. 1)
Includes bibliographical references.
1. College students—Religious life—United States. 2. Universities and
colleges—United States—Religion. 3. Religious pluralism—United States.
4. Religion—Study and teaching (Higher)—United States—History.
I. Miller, Vachel W. II. Ryan, Merle M. III. Series.
BL625.9.C64 T73   200'.88'375—dc21   2001023990
ISBN 0-8204-5253-X
ISSN 1527-8247

Die Deutsche Bibliothek-CIP-Einheitsaufnahme

Transforming campus life: reflections on spirituality and religious pluralism /
ed. by Vachel W. Miller and Merle M. Ryan.
–New York; Washington, D.C./Baltimore; Bern;
Frankfurt am Main; Berlin; Brussels; Vienna; Oxford: Lang.
(Studies in education and spirituality; 1)
ISBN 0-8204-5253-X

Cover art by Walter Chestnut
Cover design by Lisa Dillon

The paper in this book meets the guidelines for permanence and durability
of the Committee on Production Guidelines for Book Longevity
of the Council of Library Resources.

© 2001 Peter Lang Publishing, Inc., New York

Printed in the United States of America

Contents

Part Two   Spirituality and Leadership: Self and Organizational
                    Transformation

Part Three   Integrating Spirituality into Learning and Life on Campus

Introduction

VACHEL W. MILLER AND MERLE M. RYAN

Conversations can change things. They can change what we value, and how we understand and represent our worlds. With this book, we hope to energize a new conversation among student affairs professionals and everyone concerned with the quality and meaning of campus life. This conversation is about the depth dimension of our shared learning and working, about our religious commitments and identities, about the limitations of familiar patterns, and the possibility of creating more hospitable spaces on campus for the human spirit.

For several decades now, religion and spirituality on campus have been understood as auxiliary to the real work of teaching and research. Especially in public institutions, religion has been kept at arm's length as a private matter that easily creates tension and anxiety when brought into public space. This book challenges that separation. It argues that an appreciation and constructive engagement with religious faith and spirituality is not only possible, but critical for the full development of students, for leadership and organizational change, and for rethinking higher education as a wellspring of positive change in the world.

Transforming campus life, from our perspective, is not about turning the campus into a temple or church, mosque or ashram. It is not about retreating to the premodern university controlled by denominational orthodoxy. But it is about challenging the academic orthodoxies that dismiss religious identity and religious insight as extraneous to learning and community life. It is about challenging conventional patterns of organization in higher education that maintain fragmentation, disconnection, competition, and ecological irresponsibility. It is about creating new patterns, new models, and new conversations that illuminate the horizon of possibility. It is about trusting that our deep desires for celebration, companionship, service, self-understanding, and justice are worthy, viable, and within reach, once we learn to reach out to each other.

In one sense, this book is a field report from people on the forefront of transformational work in student affairs. In several chapters, student affairs and religious life leaders speak of their experience developing new groups and programs that integrate religious identity and spiritual exploration into many aspects of campus life. Other chapters have been written by administrators and scholars examining the epistemological, cultural, and organizational dimensions of these issues. They inquire into the difficulties we experience talking together about religion and spirituality in the academy, and they suggest alternative approaches to leadership and learning.

More than perhaps any other group, student affairs professionals are well situated to address issues of religion and spirituality on campus, and student affairs can take a guiding role in transformational work with students, with the campus community, and with the larger world. It is our hope that this book can serve as a resource for those interested in finding new ways to bring religious and spiritual questions into dialogue with their practice—be that practice counseling, administering, advising, ministering, coordinating, or teaching.

Many of the contributors to this book were participants in a conference held in June 2000 at the University of Massachusetts Amherst. Entitled "Going Public with Spirituality in Work and Higher Education," the conference focused on spirituality in public organizations. It followed the landmark gathering hosted by the Education as Transformation Project in the fall of 1998. The Education as Transformation Project continues to support the work of colleges and universities across the country in developing multifaith spaces and finding new vocabulary for dialogue about religious pluralism and spirituality. The leaders of that project, Peter Laurence and Victor Kazanjian, also serve as editors of a new series on spirituality, of which this book is the first volume.

In assembling our roster of contributors for this book, we attempted to include diverse perspectives along a number of dimensions: race, gender, culture, spiritual orientation, religious affiliation, and institutional position. We were eager to include new voices that do not usually find a place in the professional literature. Thus, the book includes writing by graduate students and young professionals, alongside work by authors with more established careers. We also have attempted to include authors from diverse settings—from large public universities to religiously affiliated colleges—to illustrate both the unique aspects of the questions at hand, as well as the themes common across institutional type.

This volume does not focus on bringing specific religious perspectives to bear on campus life issues. While theological insights and religious interests from various traditions clearly inform several of the chapters, the book as a whole is primarily oriented toward broadening and deepening spaces for reflection and action across a wide spectrum of campus life. Reflecting our own identities and professional networks as editors, the book includes a number of Christian perspectives and lacks representatives from the rich array of religious and spiritual traditions present on college campuses across this country and across the world.

Clearly, there is a vast amount of room for further conversation. In the future, issues addressed here from a particular religious point of view or spiritual orientation might be examined from other perspectives. We would heartily encourage, for example, further reflections on questions such as these: how might we approach campus leadership from Muslim, Buddhist, or Native American perspectives? What is the meaning of civility and ecological responsibility from Bahá'í or Hindu perspectives? How do agnostic or fundamentalist students approach dialogue on religious identity and multiculturalism? This book is meant to help open space for these questions and others that matter to our integrity as learners, leaders, and educators.

CONTEXTUAL NOTES

To introduce some of the issues found in this volume, we briefly review the history of religion and spirituality at the University of Massachusetts Amherst. As at most American colleges and universities of the late nineteenth century, religious life was at the core of campus life at the university. From the beginning students were required to attend daily devotions as well as Sunday worship services: "A conscious effort was made to mold the student character according to the classic American model of 1869: sober, hard working, God-fearing."[1] Two of the early college presidents also served as chaplain to the university and students were required to attend Sunday afternoon Bible class at their homes. The College Christian Union (the precursor to the YMCA) was organized shortly after the college opened. Members of this group met on Saturday nights for Bible readings, hymn singing, and debates. Two of the debate topics certain to offer possibilities for lively debate were "Is College life detrimental to the cultivation of Christian character?" and "Does the Bible sanction polygamy?" Unfortunately, there is no information as to which side prevailed in these debates![2]

As early as 1922, questions were being raised about the role of religious education in the academy. An annual report from that time acknowledged the growing tension: "We all admit the importance of religious education, and yet we find it difficult to agree upon a plan which will be effective and still not offend religious beliefs or differences. This is especially true, of course, in a state institution."[3] Religious life on the campus was predominantly Protestant until 1946 when the priest of the local Catholic church and the rabbi assigned to work at the college were officially recognized and given office space. From that time until the 1990s, these three groups were the only recognized chaplaincies on the campus.

In 1995 religious diversity was finally recognized and given a place on the campus. A new Religious Affairs Committee was established that was inclusive of all faith groups. For the first time, both traditional religious faiths and evangelical groups were put on the same footing. About twenty different groups are now represented on the committee. The Religious Affairs Committee has fostered an atmosphere of collegiality among the recognized chaplains. The members of this committee collaborate on programming and freely discuss issues and concerns with one another.

Although the university is a public institution that abandoned religious life for many years, it has recently recognized that diversity also includes religion. The chancellor has established a Counsel on Community, Diversity, and Social Justice that is comprised of representatives from many constituencies. For the first time, two chaplains sit on this campus-wide group and work on social justice issues. This recognition has been critical to fostering the return of religious and spiritual life to campus. Over the past year, that return has gained momentum: students have shown great interest in lectures on science and religion; introductory world religion courses are overflowing; the Going Public with Spirituality conference was successful; a five college faculty dialogue group has formed to focus on teaching and contemplative modes of knowing; workshops on mindfulness in various dimensions of campus life are being planned with support from the Nathan Cummings Foundation; future conferences are being imagined. This book has emerged, in part, from these efforts. It is our hope that it sparks further conversations elsewhere.

OVERVIEW OF CONTENTS

The first section of the book focuses on issues of religious pluralism and spirituality in student life. Concerned with the consequences of secularization in higher education, Judy Raper, Associate Dean of Student Life at Lyndon State College, sketches the spiritual profile of today's students and the spiritual dimension of persistent student life problems such as substance abuse. Based on her qualitative research into students' spiritual and religious experience on campus, she questions who is served by silence on matters of the spirit and suggests ways to engage students in new conversations. Jennifer Walters, Dean of Religious Life at Smith College and former Ombuds for student affairs at the University of Michigan, chronicles her work on a committee that examined the relationship between student affairs and student religious organizations. She reviews the history of that relationship at Michigan and the legal requirement of institutional neutrality toward religion. Her chapter provides insight into students' perceptions of institutional support for religious groups and important contexts for understanding religious diversity at public institutions. Peter Laurence, Director of the Education as Transformation Project, and Victor H. Kazanjian, Jr., Dean of Religious and Spiritual Life at Wellesley College, offer insight into the work of the Education as Transformation Project, which serves colleges and universities throughout the country in their efforts to address the role of religious pluralism and spirituality in higher education. The essay includes, among other things, some examples of multifaith worship spaces now being created on college campuses, and the "moments of meaning" project, which opens a rich window for the exploration of the role of spirituality in the teaching and learning process. Ora Gladstone, Associate Director of the Hillel Foundation at Brandeis University, discusses the challenges and joys of forming a religious pluralism and spirituality (RPS) group in the unique context of Brandeis, a Jewish-sponsored, nonsectarian university. She highlights several innovative programs and events initiated by the RPS group to create a more spirit-friendly campus environment. Marie McDemmond, President of Norfolk State University, Arthur Jackson, Vice President of Student Affairs at Westfield State College, and Jacqueline Curtis, Special Assistant to the President at Norfolk State University, describe the role of spirituality at Historically Black Colleges and Universities (HBCUs). They point out that HBCUs take the support of students' spiritual development as central to their mission, in service to the ongoing struggle for social justice in the African American community.

The next group of chapters in this section offers further insight into the integration of religious diversity and spirituality into student life. Directors of the Self Knowledge Symposium Foundation—Mary Alice Scott, Georg Buehler, and Kenny Felder—describe the origins and operation of their model of transformative work with students across generational, organizational, cultural, and religious boundaries. Grounded in perennial spiritual principles and powered by students' commitment to self-understanding, the Self

Knowledge Symposium emphasizes the transformative value of action coupled with deep personal reflection. Further possibilities for the constructive engagement with religious difference on a college campus are offered by Margaret L. Causey, RSCJ, Professor of World Religions and Director of the Duchesne Center for Religion and Social Justice, and Richard A. Berman, President of Manhattanville College. They describe their college's comprehensive approach to integrating issues of religious diversity into the fabric of campus life. At Manhattanville College, exploration of religious identities and commitments complements discussion of cultural and political issues and connects the college community internally and externally. Reflecting on questions of diversity from the perspective of a campus minister, Leon Tilson Burrows, Protestant chaplain at Smith College, discusses the development of the Ecumenical Christian Church on his campus. Working with students to create a more socially inclusive and spiritually uplifting worship community, he considers how struggles for social justice have influenced contemporary liturgical practice.

The second main section of the book focuses on the role of spirituality in leadership and in the daily life of the campus community. Sarah Stockton, independent writer and former academic advisor, reports on a qualitative research project investigating faculty and staff attitudes about religious and spiritual dialogue on a west coast campus. She found that participants were wary of initiating conversations about religion and spirituality in an academic environment. Exploring the theme of bias against Christian vocabulary and practices, she notes that, in the words of one study participant, it has become "cool to meditate and weird to pray." She reflects on her own experience in student affairs and suggests avenues for beginning dialogue on religious issues. Based on their experience at Catholic colleges for women and men, Kathleen E. Allen, Associate Professor in the Department of Educational Leadership at the University of St. Thomas and Gar Kellom, Vice President for Student Development at St. John's University, articulate the importance of spiritual development as the cornerstone of leadership development. They analyze organizational barriers to the spiritual development of staff, offer practical suggestions for integrating spiritual growth into leaders' work, and suggest how "soul work" connects with change on larger social levels. Margaret A. Jablonski, Dean of Campus Life at Brown University, explores feminist spirituality as a framework for challenging dominant patterns of academic life and creating more connective leadership practices. Guided by her own leadership experience in multiple roles, she identifies opportunities for bringing spiritual depth into the leader's everyday actions, noting that "the future of our field depends upon the full integration of mind, body and spirit in the work that we do." Gil Stafford, President of Grand Canyon University, articulates the meaning of vulnerable leadership as a paradigm for living spirituality in positions of responsibility. He advocates a willingness to "empty the self" for others in the face of relentless demands on leaders' energy and attention. Grounded in the relational theology of Dietrich Bonhoeffer, Stafford's approach to leadership strives to create a "web of sociality" as an alternative to hierarchy and disconnection. The final chapter in this section provides a powerfully personal reflection on the intersections of spirituality and professional life in student affairs. Katja Hahn d'Errico, Director of Student Businesses at the University of Massachusetts Amherst, writes about her spiritual journey through doctoral study, cancer, and family tragedy. Her chapter provides a window into the role of healing, self-knowledge, and spiritual growth in organizational life and teaching.

The final section of the book explores new spaces for religious pluralism and spirituality in campus life. Joel Grossman, Coordinator of the Health Promotion Program at the University of Massachusetts Boston, describes his innovative approach to helping students realize their mental health and improve their study skills. Appreciating mental clarity as a divine gift available to everyone, his chapter makes a valuable connection between spirituality and learning. Fan Yihong, doctoral candidate at the Center for International Education at the University of Massachusetts Amherst, describes the formation and operation of a student-run learning community based on a student's desire to create connections among his peers and the community. This case study suggests how learning communities can break free of traditional academic boundaries and create new spaces of wholeness and meaning. Patricia Martin, Dean of Career Development at Mt. Hood Community College, discusses issues of conflict in higher education and student affairs. With insights from the Christian and Hindu traditions, she explores how religious ideas can offer innovative approaches to conflict transformation. The fundamental causes of incivility on campus are addressed by Jane Fried, Professor of Higher Education at Central Connecticut State University. Fried points out that competition and discord on campus are often rooted in a positivist epistemology and unidimensional system of valuing. As an alternative, she discusses the connective and affective rationalities prevalent in student affairs work. Dialogue between these positivist and affective rationalities will be necessary for the integration of academic and student life. The environmental consequences of our modern, positivist ways of knowing are explored further in the chapter by Alberto Arenas, Assistant Professor at the Center for International Education in the School of Education at the University of Massachusetts Amherst. He suggests practical strategies for realizing a new vision of eco-justice for higher education, and he calls for the renewal of care for the human communities and natural environments that support all of life on campus.

ACKNOWLEDGMENTS

This project grew out of the collaboration of Vachel Miller and Margaret Jablonski on a graduate course on spirituality and education at the University of Massachusetts Amherst. Jablonski, interested in developing a book on spirituality in student affairs, assembled an initial group of authors to contribute. To our surprise, the project found a home in both the Studies in Spirituality Series at Peter Lang and the New Directions in Student Services series at Jossey Bass. The latter volume, edited by Jablonski, is a cousin to this one.

We would like to thank Peter Laurence for his faith in our work and his generous assistance throughout the process. We are also grateful to University of Massachusetts Amherst Chancellor, David K. Scott, for enthusiastically supporting the Going Public with Spirituality conference and engaging in continuing conversations about the role of spirituality in a more integrative age.

Vachel would also like to extend his gratitude to the following people: to Clark, for kindness and modeling spiritual leadership without using the word; to Tom and Ron and all my friends at CSB/SJU and Crestone for practicing and teaching wisdom; to Richard, for making the cups that hold the tea; to Sarah for bringing such beauty with her; and to Mom and Dad, for the prairie, your love, and your encouragement to write.

Merle would like to thank Vachel for taking care of the many required details that were necessary for the editing of this book. She would also like to thank her children, Donna, Billy, and Kristen, for their ongoing love and support; to Mom and Dad who taught me so much and whose unconditional love and support have brought me to where I am; and to my friends and colleagues who have inspired me by incorporating their own spirituality into both their personal and professional lives.

ENDNOTES

1. Harold Whiting Carey, *The University of Massachusetts: A History of One Hundred Years* (Amherst, MA: Trustees of the University of Massachusetts, 1962).
2. Ibid., 44.
3. Massachusetts Agricultural College, *Annual Report* (Amherst, MA: Trustees of the University of Massachustts, 1922).

PART ONE

*Religious Pluralism and Spirituality
in Campus Life:
Issues and Approaches*

1. "Losing Our Religion": Are Students Struggling in Silence?

Judy Raper

As far as I can remember, what disappointed me during my first year at Harvard was not the absence of a specifically Christian worldview. Such disappointment would have been significantly perverse on my part, to say the least: one of the reasons I had chosen Harvard was to broaden my outlook. Nor was it the failings of any particular professor, most of whom were capable and congenial enough. It was rather a certain intellectual climate that I can now best characterize as the absence of a sense of mystery.
—Brother John, alumnus of Harvard University[1]

Spirituality played an integral role in the early American college. While religion was the only acknowledged medium through which to experience spirituality, it cannot be denied that those who pioneered higher education believed the spiritual development of undergraduates was a worthy component of a college's mission. Not only were most students preparing for the clergy, but their professors were likely to be ministers.[2] The chapel was the center of campus life, used for both morning prayers and discipline.[3]

By the end of the eighteenth century the Enlightenment took hold of American higher education.[4] The central role that religion had played among the early settlers was challenged by thinkers such as Thomas Jefferson and Benjamin Franklin, who believed that humanity no longer needed to depend on tradition as ultimate authority. As the Scientific Age was ushered in, these views became widespread among both educated and uneducated Americans.[5] In the decades following the Enlightenment, the influence of religion on American higher education dissipated until it was negligible. As those in sophisticated, intellectual circles began to question long-held truths about the physical world, the philosophy of science gradually preempted faith. Institutions of higher education, originally founded to perpetuate Puritan thinking, became secularized.

Few would argue the point that the secularization of colleges and universities marked an era of progress in higher education. In fact, in 1654 Harvard's president Henry Dunster questioned the practice of infant baptism and was given no choice but to resign.[6] Further, one of Harvard's admissions requirements was that "everyone shall consider the main end of this life and studies to know God and Jesus Christ which is eternal life."[7] Yale stipulated that "if any student shall profess or endeavor to propagate a disbelief in the divine authority of the Holy Scriptures and shall persist therein after admonition, he shall no longer be a member of the college."[8] To question Christian doctrine between 1636 when Harvard was founded and the dawn of the Enlightenment would have been to risk serious consequences, including expulsion. The form of indoctrination that occurred in the early life of the university did not allow students or faculty to think critically—now considered the hallmark of an effective liberal education. What is shocking, however, is that such a transformation in higher education occurred without much resistance or outcry. Given that secularization was so embraced at the time of its inception, it is not terribly surprising that we have never given much thought to what secularization may have cost us. Nevertheless, I believe this transformation demands closer scrutiny.

By focusing exclusively on religion, those who pioneered higher education did not fully attend to the spiritual needs of their students. Students who questioned religious doctrine were forced to remain silent or risk severe consequences. Psychologist William Perry, among others, argues that faith cannot grow unless doubts can be voiced, acknowledged, and embraced.[9] The environment of the early American college did not allow doubters and nonbelievers the opportunity to publicly explore their beliefs, values, and questions. However, there was in those days recognition that higher education must address the needs of the spirit as well as the mind even if those efforts fell short. This recognition is clearly lacking today, and I would contend that the lack of attention given to spiritual and religious issues has dearly cost our students and institutions.

In this chapter I will explore the possible reasons behind the silence in the academy on matters of the spirit and the impact this silence has had on today's generation of college students. I will also address the reasons this silence must be broken and offer suggestions for reintroducing religion and spirituality into campus life.

WHY THE SILENCE IN THE ACADEMY?

Given our history, it is ironic that in contemporary higher education spirituality is treated as a taboo topic.[10] It seems that spirituality is often confused with religion, and undoubtedly some of the tension around this topic stems from legalism: "The principle of separation of church and state has become so engrained that people say those words and diffuse any interest in the topics of spirituality and religion when nothing needs to be diffused."[11] John Butler contends in *Religion on Campus* that silence on this topic stems from the separation of church and state being taken to an unnecessary extreme.[12] Secularization was a critical step forward in higher education, but unfortunately the intentions of those who pioneered this movement have been, at least in part, misunderstood. The intention of America's founders to curtail state religion has been transformed into something entirely different so that today, religion, spirituality, and the "divine" are mentioned publicly only with great reservation.[13]

Religious and spiritual issues do not enjoy great respect academically. The raising of eyebrows among scholars in the academy regarding religious issues has relegated the discussion of spiritual matters to residence hall rooms, the chapel, and off-campus gatherings. Religious and spiritual inquiries are not considered to be intellectual endeavors; consequently, they receive little respect and attention in the academy. John Dixon states:

> As scholars we aren't permitted to think about divine or sacred things. We are permitted to observe that other people think there are Gods or a God and we can study what they do or think. We can take them seriously on our own terms; we cannot take them seriously on their own terms.[14]

Perhaps the greatest benefit of secularization was the recognition of religious perspectives other than Protestantism. This transformation should have allowed non-Protestant students to openly acknowledge and explore their beliefs without fear of negative consequences. Students who had been forced to live on the periphery of the academic community should have been able to join the circle to share and explore their belief systems.

It is ironic that secularization has instead progressed to a point where there is nearly total silence on the topics of religion and spirituality in the academy. Even as universities become increasingly diverse in regard to ethnicity and religion, public expression of this diversity is taboo. As George Marsden writes in *The Soul of the American University,* "Pluralism as it is often conceived of today seems to be almost a code word for its opposite, a new expression of the melting-pot ideal. Persons from a wide variety of races and cultures are welcomed into the university, but only on the condition that they think more or less alike."[15] Silence about religious diversity seems to be higher education's response to the mandate to create an inclusive community: in order to accommodate all belief systems, we profess to believe in nothing. At a time when students' religious and nonreligious values and attitudes should be most deeply probed, they are instead largely ignored and even discounted. Thus, our value-neutral approach to the accommodation of religious diversity is numbing not only to the spirit, but to the mind as well.

I am doubtful that anyone who recognizes the need to attend to the spiritual condition of students would advocate a return to our past. However, the religious roots of higher education demand attention and reflection. As Ernest Boyer once remarked, "Education for what purpose? Competence to what end? At a time in life when values should be shaped and personal priorities probed, what a tragedy it would be if the most creative movements were pushed to the fringes of institutional life."[16]

THE SPIRITUAL MAKE-UP OF GENERATION X

In discussing the impact of silence on religious and spiritual matters on college students, it is important to develop an understanding of who this generation is psychologically, politically, morally, and spiritually. It should be noted that for purposes of this essay, characteristics and relevant research highlighted here primarily reflect traditional-aged college students (18–22 years old).

Defining generations is something done with frequency in the United States. We are preoccupied with arriving at a set of common characteristics that define a group of people born in a particular period of time. The current generation of young people appears to be a generation that lacks a specific identity and consequently can be difficult to understand. In fact, this generation's common characteristics are so difficult to grasp that it is often referred to as "Generation X," a generation without an identity. A recent student body president at Emerson College described the situation like this: "Our generation hasn't had any defining moment to really galvanize us. The hundred-day Gulf War wasn't enough to do that. We didn't have the Vietnam War. We don't have a shared identity. There isn't anything holding us together or moving us."[17]

So what is it that we do know about this generation? We know that they have been disappointed and have endured far too many broken promises. Many of them have watched the commitment their parents made to love and honor "till death do us part" deteriorate. When President Clinton's presidency was jeopardized by scandal, I watched with curiosity the detachment and disinterest of students on the campus where I was studying at the time. As I began to inquire into their apparent apathy, I discovered they were not disappointed in Clinton personally, because they had not carried any expectations—a government that cannot be trusted cannot disappoint.

In a 1993 undergraduate survey, administered by Arthur Levine, the most frequently cited political and social events that had shaped students' lives included the Gulf War, the Challenger explosion, the Exxon *Valdez,* and the Rodney King trial. In general the students surveyed thought they were living in a troubled time in which intractable problems were multiplying and solutions were growing more distant. They shared a sense that their generation would be called on to fix everything and were torn between a desire to do well and to do good.[18]

Certainly, this generation has grown up in an age when technology is advancing more quickly than in any prior period in history. Today's students cannot remember record albums or a time when ATMs or fast food drive-through windows did not exist. Unlimited information is available at their fingertips via the World Wide Web. They have access to hundreds of cable channels on television and prepare many of their meals in a microwave oven. Furthermore, given the increasing popularity of distance learning, students can now obtain college degrees without ever having to step inside a classroom.

We also know that students today seem to be bringing more emotional and psychological issues to college campuses than previous generations of college students. A recent survey conducted among chief student affairs officers at 586 two-year and four-year colleges by the Carnegie Council supports this claim. Six out of ten chief student affairs officers (60 percent) report that undergraduates are using psychological counseling services in record numbers and for longer periods of time.[19] Eating disorders have increased at 58 percent of the institutions surveyed. Classroom disruption increased at a startling 44 percent of colleges; drug abuse increased at 42 percent; alcohol abuse increased at 35 percent of campuses. Concurrently, gambling has grown at 25 percent of the institutions, and suicide attempts have risen at 23 percent.[20]

The results revealed in this survey create an alarming picture of a generation that is lonely, hopeless, and self-destructive. Based on their research, Levine and Curreton describe the psychological climate among undergraduates in stark terms:

> The effect of the accumulated fears and hurts that students have experienced is to
> divide and isolate them. Undergraduates have developed a lifeboat mentality of
> sorts. It is as if each student is alone in a terrible storm, far from any harbor. The
> boat is taking on water and believed to be in imminent danger of sinking.[21]

Mistrust of government, authority, and institutions combined with feelings of isolation have today's students running from institutional religion in droves to seek out their own form of spirituality.[22] Reflecting on this trend, Tom Beaudoin comments, "we GenXers commonly feel free to pick and choose the 'best' from various religion or spiritual traditions."[23] Increasingly, young people are taking a consumer approach to religious practice.[24] This consumer orientation is not unlike the relationship this generation claims it desires to have with institutions of higher education. Increasingly, students are seeking a relationship with their colleges and universities that is similar to one they would have with a bank or other place of business.[25]

Today's students may lack a place of deep belonging. Beaudoin goes on to say, "People are sensing a real absence in their lives." Many in this generation "grew up in a fractured family situation" and still have "very ambivalent" familial relations.[26] They also have very little experience with institutional religions.

One could conclude that the attraction of a personalized and eclectic approach to spirituality is not unlike the soaring popularity of third-party political candidates. Traditional, mainstream approaches to government, family, and religion have failed in the eyes of many of today's college students. In the same way that absentee parents can unwittingly foster rugged individualism and self-reliance in children, so can the failures of institutional religion foster a sense of mistrust, cynicism, and self-seeking.

It is not surprising that a generation that has suffered profound disappointment, possesses a consumer mentality, and lacks meaningful connection with others seeks to feed its emptiness on whatever works to satisfy in the moment and caters to individual needs and values. That this quest to feed spiritual hunger can occur in an environment that does not acknowledge or give voice to the journey of the spirit can create a more desperate and even self-destructive path for young people.

THE COSTS OF SILENCE

I have examined the possible reasons for silence around religious and spiritual matters in the academy. I have also painted a picture of today's college students' moral, emotional, and spiritual make-up. This backdrop begs the question, how does the academy's silence and seeming indifference influence a generation that is seeking spiritual fulfillment through an eclectic, consumer-minded approach and often without the benefit of community? What are the intellectual, psychological, and spiritual costs to this silence? Why should these matters be of concern to the academy at all?

For student affairs professionals who are responsible for "out of the classroom" learning, a cornerstone of the profession's deeply held values and beliefs is holistic student development.[27] A student's spiritual wellness is just as vital to growth and change as cognitive, social, and physical wellness. To ignore this aspect of development is to act as if the essence of a student does not exist. By ignoring students' spiritual journeys, students are left to struggle with the universal questions that live inside all of us without the context of community support and challenge.

Furthermore, there are intellectual costs to excluding spiritual and religious exploration from the academy. In doing so, the critical thinking that educators continuously advocate as an important component in other areas of higher education is nullified. This neglect allows students to assume that the beliefs with which they were raised are superior truths. It permits them to act on commitments resulting from indoctrination instead of informed reflection. How is it in higher education that we are content to allow the most deeply felt values and beliefs of students to go unexamined?

There is another cost to silence in the academy on spiritual matters that is rarely acknowledged, but I believe wholeheartedly is connected to this silence—and that is substance abuse. It seems impossible to look at the troublesome picture of today's students painted in the 1997 Student Affairs Survey and not suspect a spiritual connection to vexing problems. Year after year college presidents assert that substance abuse is the most pressing problem on our college campuses leading to violence, suicide, unprotected sex, and academic failure.[28] Educators typically address these issues as behavioral problems and respond with increased preventative education and punitive measures. Regardless of the effort, time, and resources put toward potential solutions for the issue of substance abuse on college campuses, the problem continues to escalate. Why have our best intentions and efforts failed?

In the 1998 CORE Alcohol and Drug Study that is conducted annually at campuses nationwide, the primary reason cited by students for drinking was to "break the ice."[29] Research has repeatedly shown it to be true that we drink to feel comfortable connecting with other people. The desire for

connection (a spiritual craving) can only be realized when under the influence of a substance. I believe, as do many that have studied addiction, that
abuse of substances is a spiritual impulse. Though the journey might be
dangerous and self-destructive, it reflects the same seeking of fulfillment
one might search out in a church, synagogue, or on a peaceful mountaintop.
It is undoubtedly no coincidence that the most successful program for ad-
dicts, Alcoholics Anonymous, is spiritual in nature.

When Derek Bok, former Harvard president, was asked what adjective
best describes today's students, he replied "emptiness."[30] While their paths
may at times be self-destructive, students are undeniably searching for
meaning, a sense of belonging, identity, connection, and purpose. If the emptiness Bok speaks of leads to paths that produce emotional and psychological problems, it would seem that the recovery of a spiritual perspective
would be the most obvious cure.[31] How do we begin to address the isolation
and the hopelessness that students are experiencing?

James Fowler developed a widely known and respected theory regarding the stages of faith development. According to his theory, the age range
of traditional college students represents the most critical passage in the
faith journey. It is at this juncture when dualistic thinking is challenged by an
increased capacity to think critically and long-held beliefs and values are
called into question.[32] For many of our students these long-held beliefs are
rooted in religion and/or spirituality. It is as if the volume has been turned up
on those universal questions that we all struggle with to make meaning in
our lives: "Why am I here? Is there a God? Why do people suffer? What
should my role be in the suffering of others and how do I make sense of
tragedy?"

How do students interpret our silence on these matters? Consider for a
moment what it must be like to struggle with life's most daunting questions
in silence. Could we be contributing to the very meaninglessness and emptiness we hope to alleviate through higher education?

It is essential that we critically and thoughtfully reflect on the state of
higher education. It is our responsibility to prepare students not only for
careers, but also for lives that are fulfilling and purposeful. One administrator described today's students as "damaged goods" arriving with more
burdens than did students in the past.[33] This is undoubtedly true, making it
imperative that we seek to connect with our students on an emotional and
spiritual level. We must attend to the spiritual condition of our students and
seek to reach the heart and soul as well as the mind.

Listening to the Students

Not only do many of us in higher education view the exploration of faith as anti-intellectual and politically risky given our constitutional separation of church and state, but there are also many who claim that this topic is not of concern to students. At times I have questioned the priority of spirituality in the lives of students. In my work, much of my time is spent in judicial hearings. During these meetings, I often find myself asking students what matters to them, a question based on genuine curiosity about their passions. The empty stares which often greet me when I pose this question leave me wondering if students have any concern whatsoever regarding matters of the spirit.

In the fall of 1998 I pursued my curiosity by conducting qualitative research for my dissertation. Like many researchers, my interest in my subject matter was rooted in personal experience. I was raised in a devoutly Christian home in a small midwestern town in Indiana. I attended a large public university of over 30,000 students. I went to college expecting to grow spiritually, and, at the time, my definition of growth was tied to my tradition of religion. As I encountered students, faculty, and staff members whose beliefs, religiously and otherwise, differed greatly from my own, I entered a state of spiritual confusion and crisis. I began to deeply question all of the beliefs and values I held dear for so long, and I had no sense that any of my peers or the faculty struggled with these same questions. It is no coincidence that I began to drink heavily. In fact, I binged on a nightly basis after years of total abstinence.

The only person who ever confronted me about my drinking was a student affairs administrator. She spoke to me of her concern about my physical health and bad judgment. At the time I was not sure if I was more afraid of someone finding out about my excessive drinking or nobody noticing at all. That she had noticed was something for which I was somewhat grateful, but her words failed to touch me in any meaningful way. My drinking was merely a symptom of a spiritual crisis. How could I have possibly explained to her that I was drinking because I was no longer sure God existed?

While my story may be different from many of today's college students who have had less experience with institutional religion, the story of spiritual struggle is not unique. For purposes of my research, I sought out students who wished to speak about their religious and spiritual lives and the role of spirituality on campus. Most of the students I interviewed attended a medium-sized, public institution in New England where the number of students claiming a religious identity was well below the national average.

What I discovered surprised me. There were many more students with a desire to be interviewed about this topic than I had time to interview. Furthermore, once students began discussing their spiritual lives, their desire to speak about this matter was so great that I had difficulty bringing many of the interviews to a close. Some of the students I interviewed I knew well and others I did not know at all. Nevertheless, my prior relationship with these students did not seem to have any impact on the depth of their sharing.

Regarding the silence on religious matters in the academy, one student had this to say:

> Being a public university, we are obligated to not be taking any side in a religious debate. As I've said before and continually say, I know that spirituality is not a matter specifically related to any one religion in particular or even religion in general. But the fact of the matter, as I see it, is that a lot of people, here at least, do see the two to be linked and would rebel against any attempt at shaking the status quo as far as religion goes.

In a similar spirit another student said:

> Why should religion be left at the door? It shouldn't be a barrier between people like race shouldn't be a barrier, but if it's something you carry with you all the time, why don't we talk about it? Why do people generally ignore it and how can we get past that?

Warren Nord states in *Religion and American Education,* "A totally secular education—one that ignores religion—is profoundly illiberal."[34] Why are we afraid to talk about the narratives that have shaped our students' lives? How can we allow students to graduate without ever having conversed with them about why they are here, about purpose, truth, God, spirituality, and religion? How can we talk about "educating the whole student" while ignoring the essence of our students? One student said, "my spirituality is so vital to me. I think about it everyday, but I have no idea who to talk with about it." Another one said, "when you come to college any religion gets buried inside you. College fosters academics and social relationships but it doesn't foster spiritual growth at all." How sad that at a time when we should be cultivating the spirit of our students, we are instead suppressing it with our silence.

Clearly there were some students who appeared grateful for a secular environment in which religion was not discussed freely. One said, "I believed in God all my life because I was expected to. I don't believe in God anymore and college has made me comfortable with my non-belief. College helped me get out from under the weight of my religion." Another student said, "one day I will come back to my religion. At college I want to explore another side of myself and that means putting religion aside for now. I think going to Mass hindered my creativity." Though these students have found relief in a secular world, the alternative paths they are forging are spiritual in nature. While it may be a relief to get out from under the "weight" of one's religion, it also forces the exploration of alternative ways of making meaning.

Based on my experiences, I am convinced that it is educators who fear and avoid "God talk"—not students. Given that we know traditional-aged students are at the most critical juncture in their faith journey, how can we justify ignoring spirituality and religion? Our lack of courage in discussing matters of the spirit minimizes the role of spirituality in our students' lives and shortchanges the educational process.

Recently I had to confront my own fears around "God talk" at the small public institution in Vermont where I am currently employed. The civil union law passed by the Vermont legislature, permitting gays and lesbians to file for civil unions, has divided not only the state but our campus as well. As I probed the values and beliefs of the students expressing the most vehement anti-civil union rhetoric, I discovered their values and beliefs were largely rooted in religion. I decided to organize a series of open forums and hall discussions encouraging "civil discourse" on civil unions. During the first forum, whenever the conversation moved in the direction of religion, I found myself growing uncomfortable. As a Christian and an educator, I wanted everyone to know that not all Christians were opposed to civil unions. I tried to talk louder and more frequently than those Christian students expressing opposition to the new law. In short, I effectively silenced some of the students in attendance.

In the aftermath of that first forum, I had to do a lot of soul searching about how tolerant I truly was and how open to "God talk." I clearly had an agenda the students upended, and when they did I became angry and defensive. A trusted faculty member said to me, "It is not important what is said. What is important is that the conversation is allowed to happen."

Respecting the spiritual and religious journeys of our students is not easy. It is not predictable nor something for which we can prepare an agenda or syllabus. It will change us and take us in unexpected and even frightening directions. Our struggle will mirror that of the students. Yet I believe it is that struggle which is at the heart of a liberal education.

BREAKING THE SILENCE

Percy Walker writes in *The Moviegoer*, "The search is what anyone would undertake if he were not sunk in the everydayness of his life. To become aware of the possibility of the search is to be on to something. Not to be on to something is to be in despair."[35] We all struggle to make sense of the world. We all search for the meaning we cannot live without. As Nietzche once said, "He who has a *why* to live for, can bear almost any *how.*"[36] Which of us has not looked up on a clear, starry night and asked, "who made all of this?" Which of us has not, when faced with personal tragedy, asked ourselves, "why me?" or "who decides what happens to me?" It is not the answers to those questions that matter. It is the asking.

Emmanuel Kant asserts there are three questions we should ask ourselves in relationship to our spiritual beliefs: What can I know? What can I do? (and) What can I hope? It occurs to me that these are perhaps the most important questions we can ask ourselves as educators. What can I know, do, and hope to contribute to the kind of learning experience that I have wanted for myself and I envision for my students? I am not at all certain the answers matter nearly as much as the questions.

WHAT CAN WE KNOW?

James Carse writes, "Every step on our journey adds to what we know, but it also reveals there is no end to knowing."[37] Although I ultimately chose higher education as a career, I admit it took me some time to come to the place where I value and love learning for its own sake. For a long time, I found the classroom to be a place where ideas were used as a way to compete with fellow students instead of as a way to connect. Unfortunately, we have yet to find a better way of measuring student learning than giving grades. Too often the desire to get good grades turns classrooms into battlefields instead of learning communities. I believe that to effectively impart knowledge to our students, we must focus less on what we know and more on what we do not know.

This suggestion, I admit, might be hard for academicians and student affairs educators to take. Professors are not tenured because their students love them. Professors, more often, are tenured because of groundbreaking research and publications. We are rewarded in the university community for what we know. I am not certain at all, however, that this should be the goal of higher learning. Why is it that being open to the possibility that one might be wrong about something implies weakness? Robert Nash writes, "like each one of you, I am a fallible interpreter whose life is an ongoing, lived interpretation, and whose 'ultimate' direction is unsure."[38] I am much more likely to trust someone who admits to being unsure than someone who claims to possess the truth.

I have known professors I would consider brilliant. They were well read, worldly, engaged in learning, and yet they understood that what they knew was vulnerable and open to interpretation. They viewed the acquisition of knowledge not as a destination, but as a journey. I have also studied with professors who I suspected might be brilliant, but whose egos seemed to reside in their knowledge. There was not enough room in the classroom for their ego and my learning. Their "brilliance" seemed to fill the room and close off all the space that should have been left for real learning.

I would suspect one fear regarding the exploration of religion and spirituality is a fear of evangelism. If educators broach this topic in residence hall lounges or the classroom, isn't it likely that someone who believes she possesses the truth will trample on another's tradition or beliefs? If it is true, as William Perry[39] asserts, that faith cannot grow in the absence of questions and doubts, educators must work to create community around questions. Not knowing is the essence of the faith journey. Believing one has discovered the "Truth" abruptly ends the journey. There is nothing to do with one's remaining time but attempt to bring others to the "Truth." Educators must encourage the exploration of multiple ways of making meaning and that exploration begins with the admission that none of us has a monopoly on the absolute truth.

Of course, I want students to have beliefs and values to which they are committed. In fact, I hope they have something in which they believe so strongly that they would be willing to give their lives. However, I equally wish for students that they would be as open to and excited by the unknown as they are by what is known. Knowledge should not be a closed door, but an open, spacious, and inviting room. Students can grow to love learning only when they recognize how much they have to learn. When knowledge becomes a possession rather than a quest, it destroys itself. When knowledge is about certainty rather than mystery, it destroys the learner. Perhaps one of the students involved in my research said it best:

> My spirituality is my walk, journey or search to find meaning in life that is greater than teaching and social constraint, but is a personal belief. It may concur with some interpretations of divinity, but this is an evolving personal interpretation, not a public one. My meaning in life includes service, love, and acceptance. I do not believe that I will achieve knowledge of the ultimate truth. However, the journey and the questions I ask are valuable and are definitely honorable. I believe that most people have trouble honoring the journey, especially when the journey is another's.

Those of us who are educators must "honor the journey." We would not expect anyone to deny his or her ethnic identity. We encourage students who are gay, lesbian, bi-sexual, or transgender to explore their sexuality and identity and take pride in it. With regard to race and sexual orientation, the cost of silence has become clear. Why is it that our understanding stops at religious differences?

We can no longer ignore the consequences of stifling rather than encouraging the spiritual journeys of our students. In their own way and in their own voices our students are asking that we honor their journeys into the unknown. This can be done only through the cultivation of questions. It can be accomplished only if we, as educators, can become comfortable with the words, "I don't know."

WHAT CAN WE DO?

Dorothy Soelle asserts in her book *Thinking About God* that whether or not we believe in God is not what is important. What matters is how we act on our belief. Does our belief in a higher power lead us to responsible action?[40]

I realize that I have levied numerous criticisms at higher education throughout this essay. I have accused the academy of neglecting the spiritual condition of its students, and I do consider this aspect of development one of the most ignored in higher education. I am aware, however, that there are institutions and educators around the country who are making a sincere attempt to nurture spiritual growth.

An example of a powerful and successful program comes from Boston College. Each year at Boston College, the chaplain, Anthony Penna, coordinates a program called "Forty Eight Hours," a weekend retreat for in-coming college students. The program aims to give first-year students the opportunity "to think and talk about their lives before college, their lives at college, and the lives they dreamed of living after college."[41] The day's agenda is organized by older students and includes discussions about such matters as Ignatian spirituality, alcohol abuse, and opportunities for volunteerism. Throughout the retreat students are given numerous opportu-nities for quiet reflection. The retreat ends with a "covenant walk" during which students walk down to the beach in small groups to discuss their plans for the remainder of the year and ways to reconnect with each other. The idea for this walk comes from John Dacey, whose research suggests that students are more likely to engage in change if they share their aspira-tions with each other.[42]

Another example of engaging students in conversation about purpose and meaning can be found in the classroom at Middlebury College. A course entitled "The Search for Meaning" is designed to "facilitate the search for meaning" and "attempts to integrate the spiritual, intellectual, emotional and physiological dimensions of life."[43] Students are introduced to readings such as *The Interrupted Life, The Road Less Traveled, Man's Search for Meaning,* and *The Unbearable Lightness of Being* among others. Top-ics for class discussions include literature, psychotherapy, personal phi-losophy, being, separation, the longing for community, death, and gender. As I read through this class syllabus, I could not help but think how revolu-tionary it would be if every new student had the opportunity for this kind of critical dialogue with peers and professors.

Residential life staff programming can also play a role in opening dia-logue about spirituality and religion. Resident assistants are generally re-quired to do a specific number of programs and often operate from a wellness model that ensures they are programming in diverse areas. Spirituality ap-pears in many of these models. Programs typically offered in this area (from my experience) include meditation, relaxation, and other mind/body topics. One of the students I interviewed said that he believed many of his peers did not engage in religious conversation on campus because it was as if "religion had become a bad word." Addressing spirituality in the form of mind/body programming is seen as safe and nonoffensive. While I am not discounting the validity of such programming, RAs and residential life staff should be encouraged to push the envelope, and with the help of faculty and other staff, initiate conversations that allow students to publicly and hon-estly explore their faith and the faith of others. Panels of college and com-

munity members that represent diverse backgrounds of faith can be powerful vehicles for initiating such conversation.

Another important way to engage students in thinking and talking about
meaning is by connecting them to work related to social justice. The tension
between doing good and doing well that Levine and Cureton attribute to this
generation is not unique or new, and it is certainly a struggle of the spirit.[44]
Probably each of us at some time or another has weighed our desire for
personal comfort against our desire to serve and even sacrifice for others.

Getting students involved in service work brings them face-to-face with
the questions that must haunt us all if we ever hope to bring about real
change. "Why is there suffering? Why do some people have so much and
others have so little? What does it mean to be compassionate? What are the
limits of my compassion? What does social justice have to do with my
beliefs about a higher power?" Further, we must join with students in these
endeavors and reflect on them as well. It is through reflection that students
have the opportunity to give voice to the questions that inevitably arise when
confronted with the faces of suffering.

I have suggested that the classroom, educational programming, and
service work are critical ways by which to enrich and expand the spiritual
journeys of our students. Still this is not enough.

The search for meaning must infiltrate every aspect of the academic
experience. Just as we cannot hope to find a remedy to binge drinking by
having one department address the issue, we cannot engage students in a
genuine search for meaning unless we find a way to involve the entire
campus community in the process. Such involvement means that career
centers must focus on more than job placement and students' choice of
major. They need to engage students in conversations about choosing a
calling and purposeful work. Student activities staff must do more than
involve students in leadership. They need to help students work toward
personal definitions of leadership, ponder the implications of leadership, and
consider issues such as personal responsibility and the importance of using
our gifts for the common good. Our athletic programs need to expand the
criteria by which they hire coaches to include not only winning percentages,
but the willingness of coaches to mentor their athletes and recognize that
athletes are students first and foremost.

Only when the campus as a community embraces the notion that a
spiritual path is critical to intellectual and emotional growth will we truly
honor our students' journeys.

What Can We Hope?

I believe there is no more important question we can ask ourselves than, "what can I hope?" I admit that as I have grown up in this profession I have lost much of my idealism and have become more aware of my own limitations and the realities of university life. This change, however, only increases my urgency to act in a way which gives my work meaning and purpose. Each of us has a choice when we examine all of the ways that higher education falls short of its mission and purpose. We can blame, complain, or perhaps, worst of all, simply go through the motions of doing our jobs—or we can look at the academy we claim to love and choose hope.

There is no doubt that our institutions of higher learning house bright minds and creative individuals, and I firmly believe that most students desire more from their education than increased earning potential. It is our responsibility to give them more. It is our responsibility to push the limits of our students' imaginations, to uncover their hopes, and to explore with them the mysteries that we often wait too long to ponder.

The dominant principle of campus life in the pre-sixties universities was *in loco parentis* (in place of parents). In those days students who violated curfew would arrive back at their dorms only to be greeted by a disapproving housemother. That same housemother might be found another day baking cookies for the students she had grown to love, holding the hand of a homesick new student, or attempting to heal a heart broken by a failed romance.

Following the upheaval of the 1960s, *in loco parentis* was replaced with a more progressive philosophy that emphasized student responsibility. While standards for student behavior did not go by the wayside, administrators began to take a more hands-off approach in an effort to become less parental, thereby encouraging increased autonomy.

In theory this approach seems appropriate, but I wonder if our abandonment of *in loco parentis* has become an excuse to abandon our students. There are questions we might begin to ask ourselves: How much of our workday is spent engaging in meaningful dialogue with students? Have we become more concerned with establishing boundaries than building bridges?

David Hoekema writes in *Campus Rules and Moral Community*: *In Place of In Loco Parentis:*

The typical college proclaims its lofty goal of building responsible citizens and
nurturing the sense of moral and social accountability only in the first few pages of
the catalogue, while its actions carry another message which might be summarized
thus: "We have excellent scholars for our faculty, maintain a good library, and fill
the flower beds for parents' weekend; and we sincerely hope that the students will
turn out all right."[45]

We must do more than hope. We must act, but our actions should begin
with hope. Just as all new parents have hopes and dreams for their newborn
children, we must have great hopes for our students.

I hope that we can learn to see the divine in our students and honor
them for their sanctity. I hope that we can find the courage to break down
the barriers that have become obstacles to creating meaningful relationships with students. I hope we can become more willing to inquire about
their values, beliefs, dreams, and, most importantly, their questions. I hope
we can put agendas and egos aside and become as willing to express the
unknown as we are to profess the known.

The landscape of higher education is dramatically different than it was
200 years ago. Further, despite advances that have made previously time-
consuming, labor-intensive tasks easier to perform than ever, students find
themselves busier than ever. In the fast-paced world of higher education,
which not only reflects but also often leads cultural and societal change, it
is difficult to slow down enough to talk and reflect about the essence of
one's existence, that which gives life meaning.

To borrow a metaphor from the addiction field, I believe that faith,
meaning, and spiritual seeking is the elephant in the room that we all know
exists but nobody talks about. Our refusal to acknowledge its existence
comes at a great cost. While the daily lives of today's students would be
unrecognizable to students of two centuries past, the need to make meaning and find purpose in life has been constant.

Although there are no clear solutions for ending the silence and starting
a spiritual conversation in the academy, we must begin to stress the importance (and I would argue necessity) of acknowledging, honoring, and nurturing our students' spiritual lives. Only then will we be able to offer an
education that fosters a sense of awe, mystery, curiosity, purpose, and even
delight. Only then will we be able to offer the kind of education that not only
informs, but also transforms, our students' lives.

ENDNOTES

1. Kelly Monroe, *Finding God at Harvard* (Grand Rapids, MI: Zondervan Publishing House, 1996), 309.
2. Frederick Rudolph, *The American College and University: A History* (Athens, GA: University of Georgia Press, 1991).
3. Ernest Boyer, *College: The Undergraduate Experience in America* (New York: Harper and Row, 1987).
4. Warren Nord, *Religion and American Education* (Chapel Hill, NC: The University of North Carolina Press, 1995).
5. George Marsden, *Religion and American Culture* (San Diego: Harcourt Brace Jovanovich, Publishers, 1990).
6. George Marsden, *The Soul of the American University* (New York: Oxford University Press, 1994).
7. Warren Nord, *Religion*, 65.
8. Ibid., 84.
9. William Perry, *Forms of Intellectual and Ethical Development in the College Years* (New York: Holt, Rinehart and Winston Inc., 1970).
10. James R. Collins, James C. Hurst, and Judith Jacobson, "The Blind Spot Extended: Spirituality," *Journal of College Student Personnel* 28:3 (1987): 274–276.
11. Ibid., 275.
12. John Butler, *Religion on Campus: New Directions for Student Services* (San Francisco: Jossey-Bass Publishers, 1989).
13. James R. Collins, James C. Hurst, and Judith Jacobson, "The Blind Spot," 274–276.
14. John Dixon, "What Should Religion Departments Teach?" *Theology Today* (January 1990): 364–372.
15. George Marsden, *Religion and American Culture,* 432.
16. Ernest Boyer quoted in Warren Nord, *Religion and American Education* (Chapel Hill, NC: The University of North Carolina Press, 1995), 95–96.
17. Arthur Levine and Jeannette S. Cureton, *When Hope and Fear Collide: A Portrait of Today's College Student* (San Francisco: Jossey-Bass, 1998).
18. Ibid.
19. Ibid.
20. Ibid.
21. Ibid., 96.
22. David Elkins, L. James Hedstrom, J. Andrew Leaf, and Cheryl Saunders, "Toward a Humanistic Phenomenological Spirituality," *Journal of Humanistic Psychology* 28:4 (1988): 5–16.
23. Thomas Beaudoin, *Virtual Faith: The Irreverent Spiritual Quest of Generation X* (San Francisco: Jossey-Bass, 2000).

24. Richard Cimino and Don Lattin, *Shopping for Faith: American Religion in the New Millenium* (San Francisco: Jossey-Bass, 1998).
25. Levine and Cureton, *Hope and Fear*, 96.
26. Beaudoin, *Virtual Faith.*
27. Patrick Love and Donna Talbot, "Defining Spiritual Development: A Missing Consideration for Student Affairs," *NASPA Journal*, 37:1 (Fall, 1999): 361–375.
28. Henry Weschler, "Alcohol and the American College Campus," *Change* (July/ August, 1996).
29. CORE Institute, *CORE Alcohol and Drug Survey* (Carbondale, Illinois: Southern Illinois University, 1998).
30. Kelly Monroe, *Finding God,* 6.
31. Elkins, Hedstrom, Leaf, and Saunders, "Toward a Humanistic," 7.
32. James Fowler, *Stages of Faith; The Psychology of Human Development and the Quest for Meaning* (New York: Harper and Row, 1981).
33. Anne Matthews, *Bright College Years: Inside the American Campus Today* (New York: Simon and Schuster, 1993).
34. Warren Nord, *Religion and American Education.*
35. Percy Walker, *The Moviegoer* (New York: Ballantine Books, 1960).
36. Frederick Nietzche in *Man's Search for Meaning,* Victor Frankl (Boston: Beacon Press, 1992), 109.
37. James Carse, *The Mysticism of Ordinary Experience* (New York: Random House, 1994), xi.
38. Robert Nash, *Faith, Hype and Clarity: Teaching about Religion in American Schools* (New York: Teachers College Press, 1999), 20.
39. William Perry, *Intellectual and Ethical Development.*
40. Dorothy Soelle, *Thinking About God: Introduction to Theology* (Philadelphia: Trinity Press International, 1990).
41. Charlotte Bruce Harvey, "48 Hours," *Boston College Magazine,* Spring (1996), 46–51.
42. Ibid.
43. Thomas H. Naylor and William Willimon, *The Abandoned Generation: Rethinking Higher Education* (Grand Rapids, MI: Wm Eerdsmans Publishing Co., 1995).
44. Levine and Cureton, *When Hope and Fear Collide.*
45. David Hoekema, *Campus Rules and Moral Community: In Place of In Loco Parentis* (Lanham, MD: Rowman and Littlefield, 1994), 126-127.

2. Student Religious Organizations and the Public University

JENNIFER L. WALTERS

My aim is to reflect on the historical roots and the present challenges of student religious organizations in public universities through the prism of my recent experience as the chair of an inquiry into the role of student affairs in supporting these organizations at the University of Michigan.[1] Though the University of Michigan has a unique historical relationship with religious organizations and campus ministries, it is not so unique in some of the tensions, difficulties, and misunderstandings experienced by faculty, student affairs staff, and students in managing religious pluralism on a public campus. The path between supporting the development of the whole student and honoring the public university's obligation to constitutional principles governing free speech and the relationship between religion and the state is thorny. However, since the challenges before the University of Michigan are shared, at least in part, by other institutions, then a close look at Michigan's experience may help others interested in making colleges and universities more hospitable environments for spirituality and religion.

When I was asked to chair a committee or "task team" on the role of student affairs in supporting student religious organizations at the University of Michigan, I accepted the invitation with some trepidation, given the circumstances. A formerly innovative and active program supporting student religious activity at the university had, by the time the task team was formed, nearly expired for lack of support. What in the 1960s and 1970s had been a robust Office of Religious Affairs with full-time professional and administrative staff, had been hewn to a skeletal 16-hour-a-week part-time liaison for ethics and religion/religious counselor in the Office of Counseling and Psychological Services. The appointment of the task team coincided with the retirement of the liaison, the last institutional remnant of a vibrant and memorable history of partnership between religious leaders and the university, and members of the religious community were angry and sad.

The task team was appointed, in part, because there had been a number of recent complaints from student religious organizations involving access to meeting space and allegations of discrimination. In addition, while the senior leadership of the Division of Student Affairs acknowledged the significance of spirituality in students' lives and development, they also wanted guidance about student affairs' appropriate role within a public university. Lodged within this charge is the key question: While student affairs professionals may acknowledge and even share in the religious commitments and spiritual journeys of students, what is permitted and appropriate support within a public university context? It is this question that I aim to answer in this chapter.

CAMPUS RELIGIOUS ORGANIZATIONS IN HISTORICAL CONTEXT

The University of Michigan has a complex and unique history of collaboration with religious organizations. Among public institutions of higher learning in the late nineteenth and early twentieth centuries, the University of Michigan was "conspicuous as a center of experimentation" in the arena of religious activity.[2] Gabriel Richard, a Catholic priest, and John Monteith, a Protestant minister, founded the university in 1817. By 1888, the University of Michigan and Harvard College were the largest institutions of higher education in the country. In its earliest days the largest and most prosperous student organization on campus was the Michigan Christian Association, the first of its kind in any college.[3] University President James Burrill Angell advocated the development of a private endowment to support the association. Students were attracted to the University of Michigan because, unlike denominational colleges, there were no chapel requirements and fewer restrictions on students. Historian Howard Peckham quotes a *Harper's Weekly* report from July 1887:

> Students [at the University of Michigan] are allowed the widest freedom consistent with sound scholarship in pursuing the studies of their choice.... No religious tests are imposed, but devotional exercises are held at stated times, which no one is compelled to attend against his choice, but all are welcome.[4]

By that time, the Michigan Christian Association had changed its name to Students Christian Association (SCA) and changed its charter so as to include women as members.

In the 1920s and 1930s, the SCA held regular sessions where faculty, including John Dewey, gave speeches and led discussions about civic engagement, social ethics, and the nature of community. During these years, the SCA began to provide what we would now recognize as student affairs programming: the freshman handbook, student housing, job placement, a student directory, used book exchanges, and lectures on sex hygiene.[5] This blending of roles among religious and student services professionals also occurred at other public universities as administrators began to accept increasing responsibility for religious life on campus.[6] In addition to the University of Michigan, the earliest public institutions to do this were Iowa State College, Florida A&M College, and Kentucky State College.

The University of Michigan's Lane Hall, a spacious campus building, was the campus center for religious organizations and activity. In the aftermath of the Great Depression, however, the SCA could no longer maintain the building and gave it to the university with the understanding that the university would take responsibility for "a program that will tend to encourage student interest and study in the broader aspects of religious education and properly coordinated student activities in religious and allied fields."[7] The meaning of this charge remains vague (and at times contested), though given the fairly homogeneous student body (with few Catholic or Jewish students on campus), this blurring of roles between religious activity and student affairs was not immediately thought to be problematic.

After World War II, with an expanded and increasingly diverse student body and the nascent professionalization of student affairs work, universities and colleges around the country rapidly began to assume responsibility for programs and services formerly carried out by religious professionals and student organizations. In response, campus religious groups and professionals hustled to address the needs of this new wave of college students and confront the challenges of religious pluralism on campus. In 1938, by one account, about two hundred full-time professionals were employed by religious organizations for campus work throughout the United States; by 1953 there were over one thousand.[8]

As the student population became more diverse in race, class, gender, and religion, campus ministries that had largely been the possession of Protestant denominations were no longer workable as Catholic and Jewish students began attending public universities in larger numbers. Multifaith and ecumenical cooperation, "while never enthusiastic,"[9] was now imperative, particularly for the Protestant ministries. However, with the proliferation of campus religious organizations, these ministries had become increasingly conservative and concerned to pass on their unique traditions. This made cooperation immensely difficult. Some historians suggest that concern for preserving tradition undermined the effectiveness of the ministries in relationship to university administrations and their collective influence gradually diminished.

In the 1950s, university administrations claimed a more active role in creating and facilitating relationships between the university and the religious resources available to it. At Michigan the Regents instituted an Office of Religious Affairs.[10] Similar coordinating offices were instituted at Ohio State and the University of Minnesota and other universities during this era. This office at Michigan was to be the agent for coordination and communication between the university and religious groups. It was charged to provide programs for students and consultant services to the campus "for the stimulation of religious thought and activity."[11] Furthermore, the coordinator was to encourage all efforts toward the understanding and appreciation of the various faiths represented on the campus and to provide counseling to students with faith concerns. Thereby the locus of action and accountability shifted from religious groups and their professionals toward the university administration.

This shift toward public university administrations taking an active role in religious programming was short-lived. During the late 1960s and early 1970s, some campus religious organizations focused less on preserving their traditions and became loci of activism and agitation for social and institutional change, thus challenging university authority and endangering their relationships with sponsoring denominations.[12] The tension between the university administration, students, and campus ministers who harbored and assisted student protesters strained the respect that had sustained collaboration. This was also a time of academic and institutional change on many public university campuses with social and intellectual shifts and steep reductions in federal funding. When the University of Michigan began to expand the campus in the north end of Ann Arbor, the Regents enthusiastically supported a proposal to sell several acres to the Association for Religious Counselors (ARC), an independent association of campus ministry professionals, to develop an interfaith student center for religious organizations and activity. While this decision shows the university's acknowledgment of students' spiritual needs, it also suggests a growing reticence to provide services to religious student organizations and a desire to re-privatize responsibility for religious activity. Since this project was not a town-gown collaboration and it coincided with an economic recession, the religious counselors failed to raise the money to purchase the land and the project died.

The next thirty years were characterized by gradual downsizing of the programs and staffing offered by the University of Michigan to student religious groups. Several university committees during that time recommended that issues of values and religion be given a higher profile, but by 1978, the Office of Religious Affairs was reduced to one program director and an administrative assistant with a corresponding reduction in budget and office space. A number of institutional and cultural forces contributed to the decline of this office. Court decisions cautioning public universities to untangle their administrations from sanctioned religious activities, reduced federal funds for universities, conflicts with religious groups over the politics and policies, and the increasing importance given by students to other social group identities along lines of race, ethnicity, gender, and sexual orientation all contributed to the gradual reduction of the program. But perhaps the most important factor was the lack of a powerful patron or advocate in the university's president or vice president of student affairs. In 1993, the Office of Ethics and Religion was reduced to a single 16-hour per week position known as the "Liaison for Ethics and Religion."

While the variety and number of registered student religious organizations at the University of Michigan had ballooned to sixty groups (out of 800-plus student organizations) with a collective membership of over 10,000 students, the staff resources targeted to support these organizations had diminished.[13] What had, at its peak, been an innovative model program among public universities, by end of the twentieth century found itself no longer equipped to provide leadership on its own campus or anywhere.

LISTENING TO STUDENTS

I wish the university would do more to let students know that religion is a vital part of a person's life. — Christian student

Sometimes my group will have to pray in hallways while people pass by. The campus is my home; I want to be able to pray in my home and feel a community feeling of reverence. — Muslim student

The task team was composed of student affairs staff, several academic administrators and faculty, undergraduate and graduate students, and campus ministry professionals. This was a theologically diverse group informed by several religious traditions. Our members were Muslim, Hindu, Baptist, Episcopalian, Buddhist, Unitarian, United Church of Christ, non-denominational Christian, and one who was active in several faith communities.[14] The team members also embodied different social identities by race, gender, sexual orientation, country of origin, ethnicity, age, education, and university affiliation.

The task team devoted most of our time talking with students about their experiences and concerns. But first we attempted to root ourselves in our own particular spiritual journeys. During the first couple of meetings as a team we talked together about how we got to where we are from where we started. In other words, we shared, in an abbreviated fashion, our spiritual autobiographies and reflected on key events in our own college experiences that shaped our sense of purpose and meaning.

This process, though seemingly "off-task," was key in setting the groundwork for the kind of listening we needed to do with students. It is in the particularity of our own experience that we mostly deeply connect with others, and it was my hope that given the little bit of time we had to work together, our task team would listen not just to our students' words but to their lives—what they communicated with their actions and omissions. This sharing of personal stories by task team members also set a precedent for the way we would work together from many different vantage points to craft a common vision that could inform and influence the university's administration.

We conducted interviews with student representatives from a cross-section of the university community. In addition to a significant amount of background reading and consultations with the Association of Religious Counselors (ARC), the university's general counsel, and various offices within student affairs, the team took special care also to review university policies relating to students and religious activity. Finally, we held a series of six "open-house" sessions during a two-week period after spring break with more than sixty representatives of twenty-three different student organizations, including the Association of Religious Counselors.

Staying in conversation with this group was critical, not only because they are the most articulate and organized group of advocates for student religious concerns on campus, but because of the University of Michigan's long history of collaboration with campus ministers. The association's affiliation with the university has been formalized over the years so that its members have a university e-mail address, borrowing privileges at the libraries, and a university card identifying them as a "sponsored affiliate" of the University of Michigan community. In addition, the interim Vice President of Student Affairs and I met with the group-at-large as well as the officers on several occasions. With the loss of the Ethics and Religion program, this partnership with the university was on the verge of disintegrating. It was my hope that by providing ARC with multiple opportunities for input, this partnership with the university might be revitalized.

Qualitative researchers recognize that one of the most effective ways to get to the heart of what matters to people is to invite them to tell their story. When team members met with students, we brought a list of prepared questions to ask of them about themselves and their organizations, such as the following: Why do you participate in your organization? What contribution does your organization make to the community? Where do you get funding for your activities? Who helps you navigate the university system? How do you publicize your activities? Have you collaborated with other student religious organizations? What kind of support would you like to have from the university?

Task team members were also encouraged to let the conversations run where the students took them, rather than be constrained by the list of questions. It is true that we wanted to collect information, but we also wanted to leave room for students to direct the inquiry toward topics of greatest concern to them. One of the most rewarding aspects of this process for team members was to listen and watch the conversation unfold among students as they learned about each other's differences, discovered shared concerns, and began to tell their own stories. These sorts of opportunities are rare, and the students took full advantage of the chance to learn a bit more about one another and themselves in a more diverse religious and ethnic context than they customarily find themselves.

At one open-house gathering, the first four students who arrived knew each other because they were members of the Christian groups that sometimes work together. As they began to talk, they spoke in a kind of code in the relaxed way one talks with those with whom one shares a set of beliefs and assumptions. They did not so much converse as give short speeches to nodding heads. This continued in response to the interviewer's questions until a Jewish man and a Hindu woman joined the group. What had been assumed among the students could no longer be assumed. The students' body postures changed; they leaned forward in their chairs. The Christian students began to listen more—even to each other. They spoke more softly, their sentences more open-ended, inviting response rather than agreement.

Students stopped directing their comments to the interviewer and began asking questions of each other.

Through these focus groups we learned that despite the great variation in the sorts of religious and spiritual activities available on campus, most students join these groups for quite similar reasons: a desire to cultivate a spirituality or a connection to God, a longing for community and a feeling of being "at home," an opportunity to develop leadership skills, a need for help in dealing with social pressures to engage in sexual activity and drug use, a wish to be valued for something other than performance or achievement. One student said, "Students focus a lot on getting spending money to keep up with their friends. Being in my [religious] group helps me stay focused on my values." Others said that being in a religious organization meant that their parents didn't worry about them as much. They felt that belonging to a religious group helped bridge the gap between home and school, particularly for out-of-state and international students. We also learned that while students felt that the university community was tolerant of religious diversity, they think it should be more so.

THEORETICAL CONTEXT

Religion is a part of me. I don't want to proselytize in my papers but I want to acknowledge my faith at school. — Christian student

Student development and social identity theory informed the task team's interpretation of our findings. Sharon Parks suggests that the central task of young people in their college years (18 to 23 years old) is the formation of a dream—a task—to which they can devote themselves and around which they can begin to organize their values and energies.[15] She writes, "in adolescence, all the precursors of a sense of agency are brought to the test of finding tasks with real meaning in the adult world."[16] Most developmental models view change as a movement toward self-differentiation, integration, and complexity in thought and behavior. Socio-environmental models or "college impact theories" tend to identify sets of variables which may influence student change. While researchers and student affairs professionals may approach young adult development differently, virtually everyone acknowledges that some sort of positive change occurs in most students. Colleges and universities, therefore, strive to facilitate readiness for development through student encounters with various bodies of knowledge and modes of inquiry, as well as training in critical thinking, and the evaluation of alternative ideas and courses of action.[17]

The university is a community of experimentation and imagination. One of the important facets of student development and student learning is the capacity to recognize complexity and to deal with it constructively. To that end, the university provides opportunities for students to test ideas and beliefs and practice new roles.[18] The university provides opportunities for critical self-awareness through occasions to "explore, understand, appreciate, and assess the many aspects of culture that make up our social background, including our ethnicity, social class, gender, geographic region, sexual orientation, exceptionality, age, and religion or mode of spirituality."[19] As students explore aspects of self-identity, they also wrestle with questions of significance and meaning.[20] The study of religion and participation in religious groups are two frameworks within which students may ask themselves questions about what matters to them and to what they are willing to devote their lives.

Increasingly, religious faith and spirituality are being scientifically legitimated as significant elements of a person's psychology, social group identity,[21] and behavior. Recent studies conclude that religious involvement or affiliations are strong correlates and, in some cases, determinants of political preference, sexual activity, criminal behavior, social support, marital happiness, and even attitudes toward the environment.[22] One study discovered positive relationships between religious attitudes, religious practices, and health behaviors of adolescents.[23] Over 79 percent of the 1999 entering undergraduate class at the University of Michigan report a religious preference and over 59 percent said they pray or meditate every week.[24] And yet, public colleges and universities (and, indeed, academe itself) are just beginning to problematize religious affiliation and identity as an element of the social matrix within which dynamics of maturity, intimacy, identity, difference, power, and privilege play out.

Student affairs professionals coordinate opportunities to explore diversity through a number of offices and programs that support multiple student identities across race, gender, ethnicity, sexual orientation, and physical ability. Yet, despite statistics suggesting that the majority of students themselves say that spirituality and religion are important to them, public universities have chosen to leave religious and spiritual activities largely to religious denominations and the students themselves with a minimum of collaboration. Shoestring budgets and concerns to preserve their own traditions or to maintain theological purity make multifaith and ecumenical collaboration by religious groups difficult on many campuses. Opportunities for students to experience the richness and challenge of religious experiences and practices different from their own are rare. Some conversation occurs in academic courses and the most intense experience across religious difference occurs in university residence halls. Even university administrators who are knowledgeable about and sympathetic toward students' spiritual development feel constrained by the murky parameters governing the separation of church and state, unsure of what kind or level of support or activity is appropriate. Nevertheless, our task team heard from students a need for the university's assistance in providing more opportunities to explore the religious aspect of their cultural identities outside of the classroom.

WHAT'S "PERMISSIBLE" AND WHAT'S "APPROPRIATE" ON A PUBLIC CAMPUS?

Public universities have a unique responsibility to abide by constitutional principles guiding the relationship between the state and religion, yet *how* to execute this responsibility appropriately is not always clear. The substance of this responsibility has evolved over the last century via challenges in the U.S. Supreme Court, particularly over the last sixty years. In the first thirty years of the twentieth century, many public universities reflected the hegemony of a Protestant ethos with requirements to attend chapel services, the largely Protestant student body, and dominance of Christian student groups, (e.g., the Student Christian Association at Michigan). In the 1950s, Christian political power resulted in the amendment of the nation's pledge of allegiance to include the phrase "under God."[25] During that decade the U.S. Supreme Court, as a counter-balance to this arousal of Christian religious fervor, began to put more legal flesh on the religion clauses in the Constitution. These changes in the legal climate began to shape how public universities balanced their obligations to students and to the public with respect to religious issues.

Two clauses in the First Amendment directly pertain to religion. The first prohibits government from "establishing" religion (known as the establishment clause or the nonestablishment clause). The second protects individuals' free exercise of religion from government interference (the exercise clause). The other clauses apply more broadly to the freedom of speech and assembly. The Supreme Court has been reticent to articulate definitive standards for adjudicating establishment clause issues, instead emphasizing a need for government neutrality in religious affairs. However, the tests used to delimit or measure "neutrality" have depended largely on the circumstances of the particular case before the Court.

Several early cases involving elementary or secondary schools were significant in the Court's developing these legal tests. In the case of *Everson v. Board of Education, 330 U.S. (1947)*, the Court ruled that "neither a state nor the federal government can set up a church. Neither can pass laws which aid one religion, aid all religions, or prefer one religion over another." In *Abington School District v. Schempp, 347 U.S. (1963)*, in which the Court prohibited the official reading of Bible verses at the opening of school each day, the justices articulated a two-pronged test that any sanctioned religious activity must have a "secular legislative purpose and a primary effect that neither advances nor inhibits religion."

Further, the Court wrote:

> The wholesome "neutrality" of which this Court's cases speak thus stems from a recognition of the teaching of history that powerful sects or groups might bring about a fusion of governmental and religious functions or a concert or dependency of one upon the other to the end that official support of the state or federal government would be placed behind the tenets of one or of all orthodoxies. This the establishment clause prohibits. And a further reason for neutrality is found in the free exercise clause, which recognizes the value of religious training, teaching, and observance and, more particularly the right of every person to freely choose his own course with reference thereto, free of any compulsion from the state. This the free exercise clause guarantees.

Nearly ten years later, in *Lemon v. Kurtzman 403, U.S. (1971)* and in Justice O'Connor's concurrence in *Lynch v. Donnelly 465 U.S. (1984)*, the Court added a third prong to the test of "wholesome neutrality" and said that the state must not "foster an excessive government entanglement with religion." Furthermore, the Court must ask where state action amounts to government endorsement or disapproval of religion.

Justice Kennedy, in *County of Allegheny v. ACLU 492 U.S. (1989)*, developed an additional test of neutrality, the "coercion test." He wrote that the government may not coerce anyone to support or participate in any religion or its exercise and may not, in the guise of avoiding hostility or "callous indifference," give direct benefits to religion "in such a degree that it, in fact, establishes a state religion or religious faith or tends to do so." The state court accepted this coercion test in *Lee v. Weisman 112 S. Ct. (1992)* when it ruled that public schools violate the establishment clause by having clergy deliver invocation and benediction prayers at graduation ceremonies.

While the government's institutions may not coerce anyone to practice or participate in religion, neither may they treat religious organizations less favorably than secular ones. In *Keegan v. University of Delaware, 349 A.2d 14 (1975),* the university had banned all religious worship services from campus facilities. The plaintiffs contended that this policy was unconstitutional as it applied to students' religious services in common areas of the residence halls. The Court not only found that the university could permit religious worship in the common areas without violating the establishment clause, but that the university was constitutionally required by the free exercise clause to make the common area available for students' religious services.[26] In *Rosenberger v. Rectors and Visitors of the University of Virginia 515 U.S. (1995)*, a student-run publication (*Wide Awake: A Christian Perspective at the University of Virginia)* was denied funding when the university declared that the publication was ineligible because it promoted a "particular belief in or about a deity or ultimate reality."[27] The Court, finding for the plaintiff, wrote: "we must in each case inquire first into the purpose and object of the governmental action in question and then into the practical details of the program's operation." The university's argument that it denied funding so it would not violate the First Amendment's establishment clause was rejected by the Court, which ruled that the student fee allocation program at Virginia *was* neutral toward religion. Therefore, the student publication was eligible to receive funds.

A very recent case, *Board of Regents of the University of Wisconsin System v. Southworth 529 U.S. 217 (2000)*, involved a conflict over the definition of free speech and what members of organizations can be compelled to do to support it. Scott Southworth, with several other self-described "conservative Christian" students, sued the Board of Regents of the University of Wisconsin system seeking to stop them from requiring students to pay an activity fee to be used for student organizations—some of which were involved in political activity with which the students disagreed. The students claimed that the fee violated their free speech rights, coercing them to subsidize the objectionable speech of others.

The University of Wisconsin argued that providing funding for as many diverse positions as possible within the university community promoted its educational mission. The university argued that the fee process was fair since it was student-initiated, and neutral since all organizations could seek funding, regardless of political ideology. While the lower courts found in favor of Southworth, the U.S. Supreme Court concluded that the University was not subsidizing political speech as much as it was providing a viewpoint-neutral forum for as many viewpoints as possible. Wrote Justice Kennedy:

> The University may determine that its mission is well served if students have the means to engage in dynamic discussions of philosophical, religious, scientific, social, and political subjects in their extracurricular life outside the lecture hall.

A public university may not favor or support one religion over another, and cannot favor or support religion over nonreligion.[28] A public university is entrusted with the task of creating a learning environment which is neutral toward religion while exercising its secular academic mission to encourage the exploration of religion as one among many scholarly disciplines or social identities. Student affairs appropriately supports the academic mission of the public university by nurturing a learning environment (a "secular" purpose) in which religious faith and practice is legitimated as one form of expression (among many) and by supporting students' affective and cognitive development by providing the means of dynamic engagement with multiple viewpoints.

These legal decisions are imperfect and incomplete articulations of principles that characterize (in part) what is generally known as "the separation of church and state." However, members of university communities sometimes interpret this separation to mean that religious experience, beliefs, or commitments may not be explored or expressed within the setting of a public university. This misunderstanding has resulted, at times, in humiliation, fear, and social invisibility for some students.

During the task team's inquiry, student affairs staff at Michigan reported (to their dismay) that some students from religious organizations often seem to expect poor treatment from university offices. A few students have said that they do not feel that the institution values their contributions because their group is religious. Sometimes, faculty or staff acting in good faith, but lacking a deep knowledge of the complexity of these issues, may play a role in creating a climate in which religious expression is suppressed. One student told one of our task team members that a scripture verse serves as part of her "signature-file" on her personal e-mail. (It is fairly common among university e-mail users to include a quotation of some kind with their "signature.") When this student communicated with a professor about a course she was taking, he scolded her about her signature-file saying that using scripture in university correspondence is illegal and unprofessional. This anecdote was echoed in some students' stories of interactions with members of the university community.

Given the evolving nature of constitutional law, it is not difficult to see why public universities would be reticent to support a more robust program of spiritual and religious exploration by their students. If the kinds of programs that are sufficiently neutral from a constitutional standpoint are not clear to university adminstrators and faculty, then it is safest to do nothing. However, if a college or university can foster appropriate partnerships with religious organizations and provide equal access to all student organizations, it is well on the way to cultivating a climate that nurtures spiritual development without coercing or establishing religious practice.

CURRENT EFFORTS IN STUDENT AFFAIRS

Students expect that a public university campus—because it is a public institution—will foster an atmosphere of tolerance of differences, fair treatment, and free expression. The majority of students we interviewed experience a general respect for diversity and some acknowledgment of their groups' contribution to the university community. As is the case for all institutions in which student affairs staff attempt to provide seamless services, some student affairs efforts were evident to students and others were not. Efforts most often cited by students were those that facilitate the groups' functioning, such as the Student Organization Account Service, Student Activities and Leadership staff, and individual staff members who have made themselves available to students as advisors. The most commonly mentioned programs were the student organization information festivals at the beginning of fall and winter terms, which groups used to inform students and recruit new members. Students appreciated the opportunity to have free office space provided to them by the university. Students and members of the Association of Religious Counselors (ARC) said that they felt the personal interest and support of some prominent and highly placed university administrators was important in sustaining their work. The religious professionals said they preferred forms of support that did not inhere in individual people, but rather in the policies and procedures of the institution.

Curiously (or perhaps not so curiously), groups affiliated with a religion or denomination which has its own off-campus meeting space and paid staff reported a higher level of satisfaction with the *university's* support than those without external resources. This response most likely reflects their own sense of security and the fact that they need less from the university overall. Smaller groups with less independent financial or staff support said that they spend a significant amount of their time trying to survive as a group (recruiting new members, raising money, finding space to meet). Those groups were less likely to know what resources were available to them. Students whose organizations have established good relationships with university staff or faculty reported a higher level of satisfaction with student affairs efforts than those who had no regular contact person.

Some of students' most treasured relationships are with the faculty, though at a large public research institution, those relationships, for undergraduates, are more difficult to develop due to the pressures on faculty who already work sixty to eighty hours a week. One junior faculty member with deep connections to a church community described her dilemma this way: "I feel like I'm becoming the kind of faculty member I always hated. As soon as I became a parent, I could no longer do everything I needed to do at work and at home. Now when I see a student coming down the hall, I shut my door. I feel terrible but I don't know what else to do." Students are sensitive to these pressures and yet expressed a desire to establish more meaningful relationships with supportive faculty members. They would like to have academic mentors but also mature adults to assist and advise them in other areas of their lives. However, students are reticent to initiate conversation about religious matters for fear of being "marked" as a religious person and, therefore, not intellectually serious. Students asked for help in making meaningful connections with faculty and staff outside the classroom.

We found that most of the student religious organizations without an independent religious professional simply do not know where to turn for guidance within the university. Some had found one staff person on whom they could rely, while others said they were reluctant to seek help for a religious organization. Student organizations with a joint focus (e.g., ethnic and religious) were more institutionally savvy and more likely to reach out to university offices for funding, space, or troubleshooting. Members of organizations with a sole focus on religious concerns were likely to believe that they were only eligible to sign-out meeting space and a student organization financial account—a small percentage of the advice, guidance, and funding available to them. These students also described feelings of exclusion and the concern that there were biases against them in room assignments and funding decisions.

Students and religious professionals alike said that having a visible staff person is vital in linking students with religious organizations and the organizations with the university. In collaboration with the Office of New Student Programs, the University of Michigan's liaison for ethics and religion had facilitated a yearly survey of incoming undergraduates that permits students to request information from student groups about religious opportunities at the university. This has served as a primary tool for linking students with organizations of their choice while giving students some control over who may contact them about religious matters.

The liaison also helped to create a system of accountability by orienting religious professionals to the University of Michigan's policies, procedures, and community norms. This has served students' interests in two ways. First, having knowledgeable religious professionals serving as advisors to student religious organizations means that these groups have fewer problems in administering their programs and interacting with the university. (Hence, they reported a higher level of satisfaction with current university efforts.) Second, this process affords students a measure of protection from exploitation and intrusion by unscrupulous representatives of religious groups.

IMPROVING POLICIES AND PRACTICES TO SUPPORT STUDENT ORGANIZATIONS

There are a number of steps that campuses can take to improve the clarity of their policies and the quality of their services to student organizations with a religious or spiritual focus. The prospect of a paid liaison for religious activities in a division of student affairs at a public university is a locus of tension at the University of Michigan and other campuses. Students and professionals alike said that it is very helpful (even necessary) to have a staff person available to them to interpret university policies and guidelines, and to assist with problems. However, since public universities are obligated to avoid "entanglement with religion," there is an appropriate reticence to initiate full-scale spirituality programming. However, recent court decisions suggest that such a liaison, provided the position was structured such that the liaison was uniformly available to all groups ("viewpoint neutral"), would be appropriate.

In recent years, the Supreme Court has reaffirmed First Amendment protections of student religious organizations and their activities on public campuses. Public universities must have "equal access" policies permitting student use of campus facilities for both religious and nonreligious purposes. Universities should review their policies to assure that a student religious organization is permitted access to space and university resources equal to that of other student organizations. Since the practice of university units (including student government) may not cohere with the written policies, universities may want to undertake an educational program to alert staff and students of their responsibilities.

Students said that while all student groups on campus need meeting space, student religious organizations have unique needs for more frequent gatherings and very quiet places to pray or meditate. Interviews and focus groups with students during the task team's inquiry took place in the same facilities students use for their religious gatherings. In some cases the ambient noise was so loud that the participants had to repeat themselves several times to be heard; hardly adequate for quiet study, meditation, or prayer. Some student groups reported that it has grown more difficult to procure appropriate meeting space. Building policies differ across the university depending on the unit that manages the facilities, and if a group needs a large space, it gets very expensive. This is particularly true of very large groups (200–400) and those needing to meet more than once a week. The task team recommended that student affairs and university facilities managers attempt to create comprehensive and consistent principles or guidelines to govern the use of university facilities by student groups. Student affairs units should provide training for administrators in charge of campus buildings to facilitate student groups' access to meeting space and prevent intentional and inadvertent disparate treatment of student religious organizations.

The dignity of every religious perspective is honored if the college or university ensures equal access to student religious organizations in the allocation of student organization funds and meeting space. We learned that well-meaning people often misinterpret otherwise fair policies because they do not know what religious groups are entitled to under the law or even under university policies. Every unit of the institution should be informed of the policies governing the availability of funding to student organizations and access to gathering space and how these policies apply to religious groups. Because of people's confusion about what "separation of church and state" means at a public institution, it would be useful for the policies or guidelines to be explicit about access by groups advocating religious or political beliefs.

One way to increase students' sense of legitimacy on campus is to launch a concerted outreach program to student religious organizations. This will probably be most effective throughout the institution if accompanied by purposeful and substantive dialogue within student affairs units and beyond regarding the role of religion and religious student organizations in a public university. This conversation could be especially helpful in the on-campus housing units where religious differences can erupt into full-scale conflicts or disputes about morality or truth. Resident advisors, hall directors, and other housing staff can play key roles in creating a campus-wide environment that not only tolerates religious pluralism but honors the journey of the spirit, the relationship with significance and ultimate concern of our students.

We found that many student groups and even the officers of the student governmental body were confused about funding guidelines and processes. Most students thought that special rules guided the allocation of funds to religious groups, when this was not the case. It is important for student affairs staff to assist student government budget and finance officers to improve the quality and timing of information available to students about funding priorities, processes, and application guidelines.

Students expressed a desire to establish a relationship with faith communities soon after arriving on campus and most students expect to find what they need on the Web. However, information about religious groups on or near campus is often not readily available to incoming students. Many universities' Web "gateways" or homepages do not include religious groups or opportunities, so it is impossible to assess the full range of opportunities for religious participation. Even among some institutions where spirituality in higher education is a visible concern, the quality of the Web-based resources was poor. In some cases none were listed; in others, there was a phone-directory style listing with no additional information to guide the student, e.g., contact names, descriptions of the group, meeting times or places. The Maize Pages at the University of Michigan is a wonderful resource but it is difficult to find from the university's homepage, so it is underused. This is an excellent area for collaboration between student religious organizations and student affairs units so that timely, accurate, comprehensive information about student religious groups and opportunities is available to students through a variety of media. This information should be publicized to prospective and newly admitted students, since associating with the religious or spiritual community early on helps a student adjust to college life.

Most, if not all, colleges and universities have policies about religious holidays. The University of Michigan does not, as an institution, observe religious holidays. However, at the beginning of each academic year, the provost sends a copy of the university's policy on religious holidays to all faculty, deans, department directors, and selected other administrators. This policy places responsibility on students to alert their instructors if they have a conflict between a religious observance and course requirements. The student may not be penalized for missing class due to a religious observance; however, he or she is fully responsible for the coursework conducted during that time. Faculty are encouraged to be aware of major religious holidays and to avoid, if possible, scheduling examinations on those days. This policy was developed with the input of students when it became evident that students and faculty needed information about their rights and responsibilities when conflicts occur. Policies of this kind help to clarify community norms in this regard; however, it is also important to have an educational component. Furthermore, the policy should explicitly state which university office is responsible for educating the university community with respect to the policy or to whom they should go if they feel it is not being administered properly.

CREATING A CAMPUS CLIMATE WHICH HONORS THE SPIRIT(S)

It's frustrating and offensive when an instructor makes a judgment about whether having a faith or religious commitment is okay. — *Muslim student*

I almost dropped a class when the instructor caricatured Christian faith implying that you're stupid if you believe in God. — *Christian student*

Public universities have unique legal responsibilities in fostering a neutral campus environment for the free expression of different religious viewpoints. However, every campus community—public or private—has an interest in fostering the spiritual and moral development of its members and providing opportunities for students to explore pluralistic tensions. An agent of the state may not support or encourage the establishment of a particular religion, but how might spiritual exploration and awareness in all of its biopsychosocial complexity be fostered at a public university in a way that honors many spirits, privileging none? I believe that there are at least five key activities anyone who desires to foster such a climate would be advised to undertake.

First, as in any work that requires us to cross boundaries of difference, it is critical to engage in self-reflection about one's social location: one's history of religious training or experiences, the main sources of authority for our life decisions, what guides the making of our priorities, and our own relationship to the institution which we are trying to influence. I have had many opportunities to talk with undergraduate students and graduate professionals in medicine, social work, education, and public health about spirituality and religion. I have witnessed in each and every classroom the ambivalence that many people—young and old—have about their own religious traditions and how they quietly go about trying to find a spiritual practice that "works" for them. Many have experienced religious institutions as hypocritical, oppressive, and even violent, so the prospect of engaging in conversation about spirituality or religion is not always welcome. If in nearly every classroom, many (or most) students are in the process of questioning their religious beliefs, we have a responsibility as educators to take that mostly unspoken reality seriously. When we fail to acknowledge—even to ourselves—the complexity of our own feelings (e.g., disappointment, frustration, longing, rage) about, and relationship to, religion and spirituality, we lapse into disassociative or defensive positions and fail to use what we know to move our institutions toward a healthier response to our students, faculty, and staff.

Second, it is important to identify stakeholders and allies within the institution. Who benefits from the status quo? How do they perceive their interest in spirituality or religion? Who has the administrative or social power or moral standing to enact the kinds of changes you'd like to see in the university? Who already acknowledges the legitimacy and importance of spirituality in higher education? Are they willing to talk about their views? Can they lead you to others or give you insight about what resources and obstacles you may encounter? It is important to begin a constructive conversation that acknowledges the challenges to creating change without dwelling on them.

Third, begin on multiple levels to engage students, faculty, staff, and administrators at all levels in a conversation about religion and spirituality at your university or college. The task team at Michigan was formed because the dean of students and the vice-president of student affairs were hearing multiple voices within the institution about these concerns. This committee is only one of a number of conversations throughout the division of student affairs, and throughout the university. Because so often perception is reality, especially in very political institutions, low-profile conversations can sometimes get things moving more effectively than high-profile protests or programs. These conversations can assist you in discerning goals, objectives, and methods for creating change.

Fourth, engage student religious organizations and campus ministers in dialogue about their needs and perceptions of the university. Students and campus ministers are essentially outsiders to the making of university policies and decisions and, therefore, don't understand how decisions get made or implemented. They may experience themselves as cut off from the institution in significant ways and, therefore, not see where the world of the university and theirs may overlap. Precisely because of their "outsider" status, these groups, through their critique, can stimulate a clearer expression of your goals and objectives. Likewise, because these groups are potential allies in the movement toward change, dialogue with them can assist in discerning common interests and concerns that will generate opportunities for collaboration and mutual support in activities that serve the interests of all students.

Fifth, in the movement from dialogue to action for change, the creation of partnerships within student affairs, across the university and beyond, is critical. As you cultivate partners for action, it will be helpful to ask: What kinds of partnerships will achieve your goals? What kinds of relationships do you currently have with those individuals or groups? What kinds do you wish to have? What shape does the partnership need to have at this particular time to effect the kind of change you envision? Is there room for growth and change?

CONCLUSION

The composition of student bodies at many public universities around the country reveals a twenty-first-century America in which the religious affiliations are increasingly varied and in which the university is a crucible for religious pluralism. With the proliferation of student religious organizations reflecting the cultural diversity and spiritual interests of the student body, student affairs professionals and their allies and partners are challenged to nurture the development of students through the responsible exploration of this significant aspect of students' social identity. The creation of educationally purposeful programs to address religious diversity as one component of a rich and culturally diverse campus community would be a tremendous step toward improving the climate for free expression. To do less may unintentionally create the conditions for increased marginalization of students for whom spirituality is a guiding principle in their lives and education.

ENDNOTES

1. The author would like to acknowledge the contributions of the members of the task team on student religious organizations at the University of Michigan: Janie Bowens, Zain Bengali, Diane Christopherson, Dana Fair, Carrie Hatcher, Smriti Isaac, Neeru Khanna, Krishna Kishore, Matthew Lawrence, Kevin Richardson, Stephen Rush, Kalindi Trietley, Donna Wessel Walker.
2. Clarence P. Shedd, *The Church Follows Its Students* (New Haven: Yale University Press, 1938), 69.
3. Howard Henry Peckham, *The Making of the University of Michigan, 1817–1992* (Ann Arbor: The University of Michigan, 1994), 48.
4. Ibid., 95.
5. Leonard E. Scott, "An Historical View of the Office of Ethics and Religion and Its Predecessors at the University of Michigan." Unpublished manuscript. (Ann Arbor: University of Michigan, 1999).
6. Seymour E. Smith, *Religious Cooperation in State Universities: An Historical Sketch* (Ann Arbor: The University of Michigan, 1957), 46–48.
7. The Board of Regents, *Proceedings* (Ann Arbor: The University of Michigan, December, 1936), 118.
8. Seymour E. Smith, *Religious Cooperation*, 76.
9. Ibid., 57.
10. The Board of Regents, *Proceedings,* 1956, 1037.
11. Ibid., 1037–1038.
12. For a fascinating account of this turbulent era of religious activity on college and university campuses, see Sam Portaro and Gary Peluso's history of contemporary campus ministry, *Inquiring and Discerning Hearts* (Scholars Press, 1993), especially chapter four, "A Profound Dis-Appointment."
13. *Maize Pages*, Michigan Student Assembly, University of Michigan, November 2000 (www.umich.edu/~maizepgs).
14. Representatives from Hillel and Chabad House, two prominent Jewish organizations on campus, were also invited to join the task team. These groups elected instead to participate in focus groups.
15. Sharon D. Parks, *The Critical Years: Young Adults and the Search for Meaning, Faith, and Commitment* (San Francisco: Harper Collins, 1986).

16. Laurent A. Daloz, Cheryl H. Keen, James P. Keen, Sharon Daloz Parks, *Common Fire: Leading Lives of Commitment in a Complex World* (Boston: Beacon Press, 1996).

17. Ernest T. Pascarella and Patrick T. Terenzini, *How College Affects Students* (San Francisco: Jossey-Bass, 1991), 59.

18. Ibid.

19. Brenda M. Rodriguez, "Creating Inclusive and Multicultural Communities: Working Through Assumptions of Culture, Power, Diversity, and Equity," in *Cultural Diversity: Curriculum, Classroom and Climate,* eds. J. Q. Adams and Janice R. Welsch (Illinois Staff and Curriculum Developers Association), 33–40.

20. Kenneth Pargament, *The Psychology of Religion and Coping: Theory, Research, and Practice* (New York: The Guilford Press, 1997).

21. Jeffrey Rosen, "Is Nothing Secular?" *The New York Times Magazine,* 20 January 2000, 40–45.

22. Jeffrey S. Levin, Linda M. Chatters, Christopher G. Ellison, and Robert J. Taylor, "Religious Involvement, Health Outcomes, and Public Health Practice," *Current Issues in Public Health,* 2 (1996): 220–225.

23. John M. Wallace and Tyrone A. Forman, "Religion's Role in Promoting Health and Reducing Risk Among American Youth," *Health Education and Behavior,* 25 (1998): 721–741.

24. Cherry Danielson, *University of Michigan Entering Student Survey 1993–1999* (Ann Arbor, The University of Michigan, Division of Student Affairs, 2000).

25. Stephen M. Feldman, *Please Don't Wish Me a Merry Christmas: A Critical History of the Separation of Church and State* (New York: New York University Press, 1997), 219.

26. William A. Kaplin and Barbara A. Lee, *The Law of Higher Education, 3d Edition* (San Francisco: Jossey-Bass, 1995).

27. Thomas Hughson and Eric Michael Mazur, "The Public Interest: The Supreme Court Rules on University Student Fee Program Free Speech, Religious Freedom Issues Clash," *Religious Studies News,* 15:3–4, 17.

28. William Kaplin, *Law of Higher Education,* 57.

3. The Education as Transformation Project

Peter Laurence and Victor H. Kazanjian, Jr.

This essay will review the work of the Education as Transformation Project as it has explored the role of religious pluralism and spirituality in American higher education over the past several years. The project arose in response to a rapid increase in religious diversity among college students and the difficulty most institutions of higher learning faced adequately addressing this issue. Not only were those institutions unsure of how to deal with this growing diversity, but most religious facilities on campuses reflected an earlier time when a single religious tradition (most often Protestant Christianity) prevailed.

As the exploration deepened, the project discovered that many students and some faculty and administrative staff identified an interest in spirituality as part of the educational process, a spirituality that was not confined to religious identity. This sense of spirituality manifests itself as a desire for integration and a search for the deeper meaning and purpose of education. Institutional fragmentation on today's campuses is reportedly eroding the sense of integration that educational institutions seek to provide. It became clear to us that many in higher education believe that a process of teaching and learning which focuses on knowledge without connection, meaning, or purpose is insufficient to prepare students for life and work in a complex and diverse world.

This essay will provide an overview and reflections on some of the new visions, concepts, and models for dealing with these phenomena, as institutions of higher learning look for richer ways to bring religious pluralism and spirituality to the center of the learning/living environment.

BACKGROUND

The Education as Transformation Project was initiated in 1996. It began with the hypothesis that religious diversity among students at America's colleges and universities was increasing, and that those institutions were not adequately equipped for serving the needs of this religiously diverse student population.

To test that hypothesis a survey on issues of religious diversity was sent to approximately 650 religious life professionals throughout the United States. The names of those who received the survey were taken from the membership lists of three professional organizations serving religious life staff at colleges and universities—the Association for Coordination of University Religious Affairs (ACURA), the National Association of College and University Chaplains (NACUC), and the National Campus Ministry Association (NCMA). From the start it was clear that these existing networks did not by and large include representatives from rapidly growing religious groups on campus such as Buddhist, Hindu, and Muslim. However, in the 155 surveys which were returned (from institutions in all but nine of the contiguous United States), 74 percent of the respondents reported an increase in religious diversity on their campus. Almost all indicated an interest in having additional resources to help them address this diversity.

In response, a small planning committee was formed to consider ways of assisting religious life staff with this challenge. The committee included participation from Brown University, Dartmouth College, Harvard University, Princeton University, Wellesley College, and Yale University. One of the first insights that came from the committee was that the fact of religious diversity provided only a starting point for our concerns. The challenge was how to celebrate and engage that diversity. The movement toward religious pluralism was identified as the next step, and the first goal for the project emerged: to explore the impact of religious diversity on higher education, and the potential of religious pluralism as a strategy to address the dramatic growth of religious diversity in American colleges and universities.

Another area of interest for the committee became the existence of what seemed to be a growing number of students who call themselves spiritual but not religious, and a growing number of faculty and administrators interested in the relationship between spirituality and learning and teaching. The concept of spirituality as a separate and broader issue was identified as a significant element for the project, and the second goal became the consideration of the role of spirituality in the educational process, particularly its relationship to teaching and learning pedagogy; the cultivation of values; moral and ethical development; and the fostering of global learning communities and responsible global citizens.

It was quickly determined that these goals were not just a matter for religious life professionals but affected all of the constituencies within educational institutions. The committee developed a model for encouraging schools to create multiconstituency teams that would include administrators, alumni/trustees, faculty, students, and religious life staff. Resource kits were created to assist in the formation of these teams, including guidelines for team formation, questions for discussion, and educational materials. After presenting these concepts at various national conferences and finding initial support, it was felt that a national gathering on the topic of religious pluralism and spirituality in higher education should be held. Wellesley College offered to host the event in the fall of 1998.

The planning committee realized that the success of such an event would rest on broadening participation in the planning process, so in October of 1997, seventy-eight representatives from twenty-seven colleges, universities, and related organizations were convened at Brown University to help shape the national gathering. This meeting was not widely advertised, and the institutions invited had been contacted through a limited networking process. They did, however, encompass a broad range of categories, from small independent colleges and denominationally based schools to large public universities. Each school was asked to attempt to create a multiconstituency team. They were further requested to include as much ethnic, racial, and religious diversity as possible within each team, and to bring as many members of the team as was feasible to the October program.

The diverse representation was an intentional effort to bring perspectives from a range of educational institutions to the planning process. The object was to investigate areas of focus that were of critical importance in a variety of educational settings related to the project's goals. An open space process was used to identify these areas, and from the outcomes of this meeting, the planning committee designed the national gathering.

It is significant to note that the process for preparing for the national gathering included a grassroots organizing effort in which the emphasis was placed on the development of multiconstituency teams on campuses across the country.

THE NATIONAL GATHERING

On September 27–28, 1998, the national gathering on Education as Transformation: Religious Pluralism, Spirituality and Higher Education was held at Wellesley College. While the planners had hoped for at least 300 people to attend, in the months before the gathering the registrations kept coming in. The design for this event included the use of a tent on the green in front of the chapel in the middle of the Wellesley campus as a central meeting place. As enrollment grew, participation finally had to be cut off at 800 people because this was the limit for the largest tent that the area could hold.

Reactions to entering this tent for the first plenary were similar. People had come thinking that they were among the few who would publicly state an interest in such a topic, and were all amazed to see so many gathered for the same purpose! It was particularly striking that the largest single constituency group at the gathering was faculty, although there was also strong representation from college and university presidents, deans, trustees, students, and administrators.

Shannon Hodges, director of student counseling at the University of Minnesota, Morris, described it this way:

> I learned that a large portion of the college landscape is interested in spirituality, spiritual and religious practice, and values and interests as an important part of higher education. That part was very affirming, especially in light of the large, diverse attendance.[1]

Some who had been tracking the development of this process were less surprised. "I came here," said Cheryl Keen of Antioch College, "because I knew that a movement was starting."[2]

Featured participants at the gathering included some of the top educators in the country on these issues. Leading off the event, Diana Chapman Walsh, president of Wellesley College, challenged those gathered with these words:

> Our task is to envision a whole new place, a whole new space and role for spirituality in higher education as an essential element of the larger task of reorienting our institutions to respond more adequately to the challenges which the world presents us. As we look to the new millennium, we know that we are going to need people committed to living in ways that will insure a sustainable future, people committed to bringing diverse communities together.[3]

Parker Palmer, the well-known author and teacher, spoke to the creation of a new epistemology that could move past the limitations of objectivism and return a relational dimension to our knowing:

The orthodoxy of objectivism insists that we can know the world only by distancing ourselves from it, separating our inner lives from the external objects we want to know. Such objectivism is morally deforming because its distancing us from knowledge prevents a moral engagement with the world we study and [prevents us from] taking responsibility for it. One of the most important contributions our religious and spiritual traditions can make through dialogue on our campuses is in the alternative epistemologies they offer which are more capacious, more relational, and more responsive than classic objectivism.[4]

Diana Eck, one of the foremost writers on religious pluralism, explained her understanding of pluralism, an issue at the heart of the gathering:

Pluralism is an encounter of all of our differences. It is a reconstruction and renegotiation of our common life in light of that encounter. Pluralism requires something of us; it is not a given—it is an achievement.[5]

And Vincent Harding, coming out of long experience with the civil rights movement, summed up the importance of relationship:

Before we celebrate diversity we need to be sure and encounter it, to engage it, to look it right in the eye. I'm going back and invite you to go back seeing this diversity...not being afraid to see it and recognize that seeing it is going to be difficult for us sometimes. I'm going back trying to seek out all my sisters and brothers because they will take me home...they will take me to the deepest levels of God. Because God is diversity, is truth, is love, is my sister, is my brother. I am going back pondering these things and I am so glad that I could be here to be inspired again to take them very, very seriously.[6]

Participants in the gathering affirmed Harding's reflection that it was now time to take the issues of religious pluralism and spirituality to the heart of the discussions about higher education in America.

RELIGIOUS LIFE PROGRAMS

One outgrowth of this inspiration has been a rethinking of the structure of religious life programs at American colleges and universities. New multifaith models have emerged in several settings, and they hold great promise. They not only provide religious advisors for students from previously unrepresented religious backgrounds, but they also create environments in which students have an opportunity to interact with each other across religious lines and thus discover the possibilities that arise from pluralism. One example of such a model is the Multi-faith Religious and Spiritual Life Program at Wellesley College.

In 1993, Wellesley College introduced a new approach to nurturing the religious and spiritual life of the college community. Seeking to respond to the rich diversity of religious traditions and spiritual beliefs represented among community members, the college instituted a multifaith program based on the principles of religious pluralism and the belief that spirituality plays an important role in the educational experience.

This process was not without struggle. The Protestant Christian ethos that was an element in the founding of the college was still embedded in the structures of this now secular institution. It was necessary to dismantle these structures (which included community rituals and the use of Christian prayer at public events, in addition to the Protestant Christian dominated chaplaincy itself) in order to build a new model based on the principles of pluralism. The leadership of the college president, Diana Chapman Walsh, was a critical factor in informing the community that this new model was consistent with Wellesley's commitment to a global education in which an understanding of the diversity of culture and religion is essential.

The Religious and Spiritual Life Program at Wellesley now explores the possibility that religious diversity can be a resource rather than a barrier to the creation of community, and examines how a secular academic institution can articulate a spiritual dimension to its educational program. By articulating these issues, the Religious and Spiritual Life Program seeks to contribute to a global discourse about diversity, multiculturalism, pluralism, and the critical moral and ethical issues which face the human community. Support and celebration for people of Bahá'í, Buddhist, Christian (Orthodox, Protestant, Roman Catholic), Hindu, Jain, Jewish, Muslim, Native African, Native American, Sikh, Taoist, Unitarian Universalist, Zoroastrian and other religious traditions is offered through the work of the Office of Religious and Spiritual Life, which is led by the Dean of Religious and Spiritual Life, and is comprised of the Religious Life Team of chaplains and advisors, and the Multi-faith Student Council.

The Dean of Religious and Spiritual Life coordinates religious and spiritual life at Wellesley College. In this work the dean does not represent any one religious tradition. The dean coordinates educational programs on moral, ethical, religious, and spiritual issues and leads multifaith community worship opportunities throughout the year. The dean offers weekly opportunities for reflection/prayer/meditation. The dean also acts as liaison to religious groups on campus, in the town of Wellesley, and beyond.

The Religious Life Team is comprised of chaplains and advisors currently representing the Buddhist, Hindu, Jewish, Muslim, Protestant Christian, Roman Catholic Christian, and Unitarian Universalist religious traditions. Together with the dean this team meets weekly for discussion, prayer/meditation, study, and program planning. Through this collective work the Religious Life Team models a new way of working toward common goals while respecting and celebrating difference and diversity. Members of the Religious Life Team are available to all members of the college community for spiritual guidance and pastoral counseling.

The Multi-faith Student Council is comprised of two student representatives from each religious tradition and spiritual practice represented at Wellesley. The council meets regularly to discuss religious and spiritual issues affecting Wellesley students, plan joint worship and program activities, and advise the dean on policy matters for religious life at Wellesley.

Support for the spiritual journeys of alumnae, faculty members, staff members, and students outside of an institutional religious context is also offered by the dean. In addition, all college community members are invited to discover the common spiritual threads which bind them together as one people through a series of educational programs and community celebrations exploring the movement from diversity to pluralism.

Since the national gathering in 1998 a growing number of colleges around the country have explored the Wellesley religious life model, and implementation of similar programs has begun.

THE CORE PROGRAMS

The Religious and Spiritual Life Program at Wellesley College is rooted in the work of the Multi-faith Religious Life Team of chaplains and advisors and the Multi-faith Student Council. In addition to celebrating the religious life of their own communities, these teams work together in a unique collaborative, modeling new possibilities for interreligious and intercultural cooperation and conflict transformation by leading communitywide celebrations and educational programs on religious pluralism and the role of spirituality in the educational experience.

Beyond Tolerance

Beyond Tolerance is an educational program of interreligious and intercultural dialogue aimed at developing an appreciation of the particularity of religious experience while seeking a greater understanding of common life-sustaining principles. The Beyond Tolerance program involves the leadership of the Multi-faith Religious Life Team and the Multi-faith Student Council in developing programs for the Wellesley College community and communities outside Wellesley. Central to this program are its many educational events (speakers, workshops, and presentations). In addition, the members of the Multi-faith Student Council created the Beyond Tolerance Workshop program, an educational training program on religious diversity. The group is currently developing this piece as an educational video on religious pluralism for use in communities, colleges, and universities.

Multi-faith Community Celebration

Multi-faith Community Celebration is a series of communitywide events that offer community members the opportunity to gather together and explore the spiritual dimensions to their lives and learning in a ritual which draws on the world's religious traditions and spiritual practices. These celebrations also offer community members the opportunity to experience the unique perspectives that different religious and spiritual groups have on common themes. Current annual celebrations include the following: Flower Sunday, Alumnae Council Weekend, Parent/Family Weekend, Baccalaureate, and Reunion.

Flower Sunday, which annually involves more than 1,400 Wellesley students, is a particularly poignant example of the new possibilities for community ritual in a pluralistic setting. Formerly a Christian service held on the first Sunday of the year, this event has been transformed into a multireligious celebration of spirituality and learning. The Flower Sunday program is created and led by the advisors and students from all religious and spiritual traditions on campus, and includes religion-specific elements such as African drumming, classical Indian dance, Christian gospel singing, and the chanting and reading of sacred texts. In addition, there are moments in which those gathered are invited to share in rituals that emphasize common spiritual principles.

Exploring Spirituality

Exploring Spirituality is a series of programs offered by the Office of Religious and Spiritual Life for students, faculty, and staff on the role of spirituality in their lives and learning. Programs which have been offered through the Exploring Spirituality program include the following:

1) The Exploring Spirituality workshop is a six-week series in which students, faculty, and staff explore their own understanding of spirituality through conversation, guided meditation, and interactive programs.

2) In the Moments of Meaning series, faculty members and students are invited to explore the moments of meaning, connection, wonder, and awe that they have experienced through teaching and learning and how this constitutes a spiritual dimension to the educational process.

Leading from Within

Leading from Within is a collaborative project of the Office of Religious and Spiritual Life at Wellesley College and the Wellesley Centers for Women. It offers workshops and presentations for alumnae and student leaders on the spiritual dimensions of leadership. Based on the belief that there is an essential relationship between our inner spiritual lives and the outer expression of our lives in leadership, this program engages student and alumnae leaders in a series of workshops designed to make the connection between the inner and outer dimensions of our lives.

MULTIFAITH SPACES

As noted earlier, today's students come from a variety of religious backgrounds. How can campuses make these students feel welcome? Certainly not by continuing to represent religion in the form of a dominant mono-religious chapel. Most colleges and universities have religious facilities left over from their original affiliation with a single tradition. In some cases these institutions have long ago shed their religious affiliation, and yet they have maintained the ethos of that particular tradition. The most visible symbols of this ethos are religious buildings. Many of these facilities are quite impressive and hold considerable sentimental value in the minds of the community and the alumni/ae. This obviously presents a challenge when the institution attempts to address the religious needs of a diverse student body.

However, some schools have already begun the process of renovating their existing sacred spaces or of building new facilities for multireligious use. Such spaces may be set aside for religious/spiritual practices but unadorned by religious symbolism, or they may contain separate facilities for particular forms of prayer, worship, or meditation. Here are some examples of such spaces from institutions around the country.

Babson College, an independent business college in Massachusetts, completed the Glavin Family Chapel in 1997. Its roots can be traced to the college's founder, Roger Babson, who spoke of the need for meditation and spiritual reflection. The college had always provided space for students to practice their respective faiths, but there had never been a structure on campus solely for that purpose. The new multifaith chapel is dedicated to "Following one's faith, learning about other faiths, and respecting all faiths."[7]

The College of St. Rose in Albany, New York, a private, independent college with a Roman Catholic heritage, dedicated its Hubbard Interfaith Sanctuary in 1997. The college is "proud of its Roman Catholic heritage and committed to providing for the spiritual growth of all its students." It had to address this question, however: "In a diverse world, with a diverse student body, how does a college committed to spiritual life as well as intellectual, emotional, psychological and physical growth, provide for those needs?" The resulting multifaith sanctuary occupies a new building on the campus and is "a spiritual center where people of all faiths can come for prayer, worship, celebration, reflection, dialogue, and quiet peace."[8]

Johns Hopkins University, an independent university in Baltimore, Maryland, with a strong emphasis on graduate education and research, opened its Bunting-Meyerhoff Interfaith and Community Service Center in 1999. Located across from the main campus, the former United Methodist church, whose congregation had dwindled in size, was purchased by the university using funds specially donated for the purpose. The center

> now serves as a vibrant focal point for a new way of understanding who we are as one human family representing multiple religious traditions. It is where the religions of the world become part of the neighborhood, part of the campus community. Students, faculty and staff who come to this place, come as seekers of truth, many as people of faith, most from differing creeds. This center embodies a collective coming together, an intentional, deliberate embrace of difference and a commitment to understand, to protect and to celebrate religious diversity.[9]

The Massachusetts Institute of Technology (M.I.T.) had built a striking new nondenominational chapel in 1956.

> The original plans for the chapel had called for attached offices and a small library. Financial constraints left these intentions unmet but the changing nature of M.I.T. meant that eventually the idea would be revisited. Events near the end of the 1980s made the time right. There was a renewed concern for the quality of student life on campus, which generated questions about the nature of community itself and about the education of the whole person. Many discussions centered on the spiritual dimensions of the student experience.[10]

The outcome was the renovation of a visual arts facility right next to the chapel as a multifaith religious activities center, containing worship and study spaces, meeting spaces, dining areas, and chaplains' offices.

Pennsylvania State University is a large public university with over 33,000 undergraduates and more than 6,000 graduate students. The university is currently planning for a $9 million expansion of the current Helen Eakin Eisenhower Chapel. The expansion will be referred to as the "Spiritual Center." According to Penn State President Graham Spanier,

> The most fundamental challenge facing colleges and universities today is developing conscience, character, citizenship and social responsibility in their students. Our chapel and related programs form a central part of our attempt to meet this challenge. The men and women who work in the interfaith activities that take place there help to put a "human face" on the University—they are an essential part of students' co-curricular activities.[11]

The United World College of the American West, located near Santa Fe, New Mexico, is a unique two-year international school with 200 students from seventy-five to eighty countries. The college's dedication to bringing together students from all over the world to share and confront cultural ideas and beliefs led to the construction of the Dwan Light Sanctuary, a nondenominational spiritual space that provides a quiet place for reflection. In addition, the college's Cross-Cultural Values Program is centered in the Dwan Light Sanctuary. Being a small school, the United World College is unable to have a multiplicity of chaplains and separate spaces for each religion. Because of this, according to a faculty member,

> We are pursuing a different model from Wellesley, and one of the main benefits we derived from the Education as Transformation conference was a clarification of these differences, for which we are grateful. We have made use of a student advisory committee, perhaps somewhat comparable to Wellesley's Multi-faith Council, which has been very helpful in setting up our program, and have also been assisted by a faculty advisory committee.[12]

The University of San Diego is a Catholic university with just over 6,000 students, and is

> committed to its mission and goals which express this identity and founding spirit. At the same time, there is recognition of the many faiths that are represented in the university community. With this is a desire to provide a place of prayer for not only the Catholics, but for those of other faiths as well. This has led to thoughtful discussion about how to make a prayer space which is welcoming and appropriate for many different religious and spiritual traditions.

The resulting space will be housed in the Joan B. Kroc Institute for Peace and Justice, which will open its doors in 2001 with a meditation area that "has been planned as an all-faith venue for reflection and prayer."[13]

Finally, Westfield State College, in western Massachusetts, is a rapidly growing state-supported school with over 5,000 undergraduate, graduate, and continuing education students. "In the early 1980s, the president of the college, who was searching for ways to introduce a religious dimension at a state college, conceived the idea of setting up a non-profit private foundation that might serve to help finance a religious center."[14] The result has been the Albert and Amelia Ferst Interfaith Center, located on land in the heart of the campus that was sold to the Foundation by the Commonwealth of Massachusetts for $1. Private donations completed the funding for construction and maintenance of the center.

ACADEMIC ISSUES

The fragmented and utilitarian nature of many academic programs has come under close scrutiny lately, as educators search for ways in which the college campus can provide a sense of connectedness, and in which the teaching/learning process can provide a sense of meaning and purpose beyond being satisfied simply with the transmission of knowledge. But these concepts—connectedness, meaning, and purpose—fall into a realm that might be considered more subjective than objective, and academia has worked very hard to provide an education that can be considered "objective."

Reconsidering the concept of objectivity as the basis for higher education has become central to academic discourse about spirituality and education. Examining objectivism, Parker Palmer observes that

> Objectivism insists that we can know the world only by distancing ourselves from it, by separating our inner lives from the external objects we want to know. According to objectivist doctrine, we must safeguard those so-called objects from what this epistemology perceives as the extreme danger of subjectivity—a subjectivity that, if unleashed, will slop over onto the objects in question and render our knowledge of them inaccurate, impure.

> The central doctrine of this orthodoxy is that inside the subjective self are dangerous things—like bias, ignorance, prejudice, error, blinders, limitation—things that would distort our knowledge of the objects of the world if we allow the self into the knowing equation. So objectivism, with its distrust of the human self, insists that we can know the world truly and well only by holding the knower at arm's length from the known.[15]

In hopes of providing a resource for educators who see the value in combining the objective and subjective natures of teaching and learning, the Education as Transformation Project has developed a program called "Scholarship and Spirituality." Searching for a way to present a more inclusive vision of education as an integrative process encompassing all dimensions of life and learning, this program has emerged as a response to the gulf between mind and spirit, head and heart which is deeply embedded in Western education. Specifically the program arose from an experience at Wellesley College in which a group of students was asked to explore stories of transformational moments they had experienced in their classes.

In Wellesley's program, the students told of moments of inspiration, connection, wonder, and awe in the classroom. The classes in which these moments occurred cut across the curriculum from biology to history, sociology to theater, ethnic studies to mathematics—story after story of moments when students were awakened to a deeper understanding of themselves, of others around them, and of the world.

One student told of a moment in a molecular biology class when she suddenly made the connection between the smallest forms of life and the largest living ecosystems of the planet. Another related an experience of working on a psychology project with her mentor when the faculty member's encouragement of her research resulted in their coauthoring a paper. Still another student explained how her political science studies came alive during a winter trip to Mexico with her class. Students spoke of moments of meaning experienced through service, through learning opportunities, and through literature. In each case, the students talked of these moments as representing a spiritual dimension to their education.

Within the stories was a vocabulary that seemed to bridge the chasm between the language of spirituality and the language of scholarship. Students repeatedly used words such as *meaning, inspiration, connection, relevancy, purpose, understanding, wonder, awe, joy*, and *love* in describing the transformational dimension of their educational experience.

During discussions with students, a definition of spirituality was articulated. Spirituality in the context of education was defined as that which animates the mind and body, giving meaning, purpose, and context to thought, word, and action.

After these initial programs with students, faculty members from the classes in which the students reported transformational moments were approached through e-mail, telling them that a student in their class had described having experienced a transformational moment which they connected to a spiritual dimension of their education. Faculty members were invited to a discussion about such moments in the learning and teaching process. Sixty were invited and fifty-seven agreed to participate in the discussions.

Over the course of the next month, faculty members met for discussion and shared similar stories with one another about such transformational moments in their own learning and teaching. Eventually, the discussion centered on their original decision to become scholars and teachers. Some spoke of a passion for seeking truth, others of a desire to kindle a flame within their students. Many described having been affirmed by a faculty mentor in their own lives as someone whose ideas were of value. Many spoke of the joy of watching students come alive as connections between self and world began to be made.

Some faculty members—who had responded in the past with blank stares and occasionally overt expressions of anger at the presumption of speaking about spirituality and scholarship in the same breath—seemed now to see the connection. Indeed, it was becoming clear to students and teachers alike that the process of teaching and learning was more than the transmission of information, but what is still lacking is an educational language to speak about this process.

The stories told by the students and faculty awakened in them a vision of education as liberation for the human spirit from the bondage of ignorance and a process of making meaning out of their lives and learning. This vision challenges the notion that colleges and universities are simply dispensers of marketable skills that enable individuals to manipulate others in order to gain power, prestige, and material wealth.[16] A holistic model of education that includes spirituality better enables students to integrate their academic learning into the broader process of understanding self, other, and the world.

As educational institutions consider how best to prepare students for life and leadership in an increasingly interdependent world, including religious identity in their diversity initiatives and spirituality in their educational programs is crucial to their becoming effective global learning communities. Just as experiential education has become an essential aspect of the pedagogy of educational institutions across the country, aspects of spirituality and multicultural education that includes religious diversity are beginning to appear as elements of the educational programs of colleges and universities. In a letter to the alumnae of Wellesley College, President Diana Chapman Walsh described her college's religious and spiritual life program as affirming the understanding of a liberal arts education as a spiritual journey as well as an intellectual one—a journey in which we are reaching toward a future where managing the new global realities will require the ability to move from culture to culture, to collaborate and communicate with fluency across national, racial, religious, and socioeconomic lines, and to appreciate diversity as a vital resource for learning and growth.

CONCLUSION

The college or university campus is America's most promising experiment in religious pluralism. Students who have spent their early years in the context of their family, usually with a single religious practice, are suddenly thrust into close relationships with others who are vastly different. It's not uncommon to find several religious and cultural backgrounds in a single dormitory suite. These students are in the process of discovering what it means to be in community while developing their own respective worldviews. Students who develop a sense of pluralism during this critical time of their development can later play a key role in the building of a more stable and inclusive civil society. If spirituality creates openness, then rediscovering the spiritual dimension of education offers students, and consequently American society, the possibility of embracing diversity as a necessary step toward the actualization of a global community.

In the years to come, given the changing religious and cultural face of America, higher education in this country will look very different than it does today. Colleges and universities will see themselves as global learning communities in which all kinds of diversity—cultural, racial, ethnic, ideological, and religious—are essential elements in a vital and vibrant educational experience. Education of this kind will include an exploration of the moral, ethical, and spiritual issues that are facing individuals, communities, countries, and indeed the world. Education, of this kind, may therefore play a significant role in leading the world into a more just and peaceful future.

ENDNOTES

1. Shannon Hodges in Peter L. Laurence, "Can Religion and Spirituality Find a Place in Higher Education?" *About Campus* 4, no. 5 (November–December 1999).
2. Mary Gottmann, *Summary Report of the National Gathering* (Wellesley, MA: The Education as Transformation Project, 1998).

3. Ibid.
4. Ibid.
5. Ibid.
6. Ibid.
7. Peter L. Laurence, ed., "Chapel's Brochure" in *Creating Multi-faith Spaces on College and University Campuses* (Wellesley, MA: The Education as Transformation Project, 2000).
8. Reverend Christopher DeGloving in *Creating Multi-faith Spaces.*
9. Peter Laurence, ed., Chapel's Brochure in *Creating Multi-faith Spaces.*
10. Ibid. Interview with Dean Robert M. Randolph.
11. Ibid.
12. Ibid. Lawrence Tharp.
13. http://www.acusd.edu
14. From interviews with the members of the original planning group.
15. Parker J. Palmer, "A Vision of Education as Transformation," in *Education as Transformation: Religious Pluralism, Spirituality, and a New Vision for Higher Education in America,* eds. Victor H. Kazanjian, Jr., and Peter L. Laurence (New York: Peter Lang Publishing, 2000).
16. Victor H. Kazanjian, Jr., "Moments of Meaning," *Connection* (New England Board of Higher Education, Fall, 1998): 37–39.

Authors' Note: Further information about the Education as Transformation Project, including a bibliography of articles and other publications, is available at the Project's website at www.wellesley.edu/RelLife/transformation.

4. Making and Maintaining a Religious Pluralism and Spirituality Group: A Case Study from a Jewish-Sponsored, Nonsectarian University

ORA GLADSTONE

In the spring of 1998 a colleague informed me of an upcoming fall conference at Wellesley College called "Education as Transformation: Religious Pluralism, Spirituality and Higher Education." As a secular but strongly identified cultural Jew with an interest in spirituality in academia, I was greatly taken with the theme of the conference. I had worked for more than fifteen years as associate director of the Brandeis University Hillel Foundation on this predominantly Jewish campus, where I saw little in the way of spirituality.

Those of us from Brandeis University who attended the conference were not the only people intrigued by the topic. The conveners were delightedly overwhelmed by the number of people who attended. The desire to discuss spirituality, or the lack thereof, on college campuses was clearly a deeply felt need. For our group from Brandeis, attending the conference was an exceptional opportunity on which we continue to build.

In preparation for the conference, a team was formed. With the help of the office of the Dean of Arts and Sciences, students, faculty members, and administrators were identified who were known to have interests in this area. The Brandeis contingent followed Wellesley's suggestions in their preparatory materials, and we met during the spring prior to the fall conference in order to begin identifying goals for our campus. This beginning has proven crucial in what two and a half years later remains a vital and growing Religious Pluralism and Spirituality (RPS) group on the Brandeis University campus.

There is, I hope, much that can be learned from the experiences of our group. However, before proceeding with this case study, it is important to understand the unique setting in which the group has been established.

THE SETTING:
BRANDEIS UNIVERSITY AND WHAT MAKES IT UNIQUE

All universities articulate the ways in which they are special, different, and better than other universities, especially those that fit into similar "type of school" categories. Brandeis highlights our rating as the leading up-and-coming small research university.[1] Additionally, the administration has put forward four "clear and unambiguous pillars" that comprise the identity of Brandeis: dedication to academic excellence, nonsectarianism, a commitment to social action, and continuous sponsorship by the Jewish community.[2] In comparing this mission statement to those of the universities with which we are most competitive in terms of admissions (e.g., Tufts, NYU, Cornell),[3] the emphasis on academic excellence is unremarkable. Social action is also addressed by some of these universities. Although nonsectarianism is alluded to on some of the other university websites, none has a statement as direct as Brandeis'. The aspect of Jewish sponsorship in conjunction with being nonsectarian is unique to our university.

Why has the administration of Brandeis emphasized the coexistence of nonsectarianism and Jewish sponsorship? Though we may wish otherwise, our history as the only Jewish-sponsored, nonsectarian university has read more as JEWISH-SPONSORED than nonsectarian to the outside world. Approximately 60 percent of the undergraduate population is Jewish, making it the only secular institution of higher learning in the United States with a significant majority of Jewish students.[4]

Brandeis also feels culturally Jewish to many of its students (Jews and non-Jews alike). Each year, within the first month after arriving on campus, students are confronted by four major Jewish holidays (Rosh Hashanah, Yom Kippur, Sukkot, and Shemini Atzeret/Simchat Torah). The reaction of non-Jewish students is often befuddlement and a sense that they don't belong. Even some of the Jewish students are not familiar with all of these holidays. With hundreds of Jews attending Friday night services and Sabbath dinner together at the beginning of the school year, and even more students either leaving campus or going to on-campus services during these holidays, this sense of Brandeis as a "Jewish school" is reinforced. As the university has made efforts to serve the religious needs of very traditional Jewish students, an influx of Orthodox Jewish students (beginning approximately a decade ago) has brought a significant number of young women in modest dress and young men in *kippot* (skullcaps) to campus, adding to the sense that Brandeis is a very Jewish place.

Finally, because of the history of Jewish sponsorship and the predominance of Jewish students, Brandeis is closed on the first day of all major Jewish holidays and throughout the eight days of Passover (as are almost all Jewish schools [which, however, Brandeis is not!]).[5] Many students are grateful that their vacation coincides with Passover, which is the most observed holiday in the Jewish calendar. However, to accommodate Passover, the spring semester vacation schedule is often quite bizarre, with two breaks: a mid-semester "spring break" and a Passover break. Because the Hebrew calendar is a lunar calendar, the Passover break occurs at different times each spring.[6] The mid-semester spring break, therefore, also occurs at different times, dependent on the timing of the Passover break. In 1999–2000, for example, Passover vacation ended just three days before finals began. During such years, Brandeis students complain about the timing of Passover break and about their inability to vacation with friends from other universities during the more traditional university spring breaks.

Clearly, the dominant Christian culture has, on many campuses, conveniently shaped the academic calendar to accommodate its major holidays. In shaping the Brandeis calendar around the Jewish culture, the Jewish nature of the university comes into conflict with its self-definition as a nonsectarian institution.[7]

Though the university administration tries its best to ameliorate this cultural conflict, it is hard to avoid repercussions. Many members of religiously, culturally, or racially identified student groups who are not Jewish tend to feel displaced. At the same time, the organized American Jewish community puts pressure on Brandeis to be Jewish in ways that other universities are not. It is not unusual for the following conversation to take place with observant Jewish parents of incoming first-year students.

> Hillel professional: "It's important for you to realize that Brandeis isn't only not Jewish, it's secular."

> Parents: "Oh, that's only for 'PR' to the outside world; everyone knows it's really Jewish."[8]

Brandeis is deeply committed to diversity. From its founding in 1948, Brandeis was not intended to be a parochial school built by Jews for Jews, but a gift to the world of secular higher education by the American Jewish community.

The tensions and conflicts created by these dynamics are some of the most challenging for the institution and can be seen within the administration and among students. Our most recent first-year student orientation core group included two students who wanted to present an optional session on religious diversity and spirituality. Their fellow core committee members were extraordinarily concerned that the university be represented as open and welcoming. They did not want any program to hint at the fact that there is a predominance of Jews on campus and that the campus culture is affected by that Jewish presence. The conflict between those seeking to "protect" Brandeis' reputation as nonsectarian and those advocating for open discussion about the ways in which Brandeis is Jewish is increasingly prominent.

There are both ongoing and evolving programs and initiatives to "create a welcoming community" on campus (often with the focus on the "minority" populations such as students of color, students from non-Jewish religious groups, students with disabilities, and even athletes, who are a small minority here). There is actually a monthly meeting, hosted by the office of the Dean of Arts and Sciences, entitled "Creating a Welcoming Community," which is open to all.

These attempts are seen in a very positive light by many students, administrators, and faculty members, but they have a long way to go to dramatically change the way the university is viewed and experienced both internally and externally. Jewish students who come to Brandeis because of its Jewish nature (especially many of the more traditional students) are generally quite happy with the status quo, and they are not necessarily interested in promoting diversity and pluralism. They seem to be the most contented group on campus. Many non-Jewish students, especially those who are nonwhite and recruited to Brandeis from outside the Northeast, come with little knowledge of the predominance of "Jewishness" and are often confused by, and feel alienated from, the culture they encounter. Maintaining a strong minority culture, when there are relatively few members from that same group, can be daunting to young adults who have only recently left their parents' home. Anger and resentment at what is perceived as misrepresentation by the university have at times tainted the four years of undergraduate life for some students.

Brandeis succeeds in providing a first-rate education. Few students leave Brandeis feeling that they did not have an exceptional academic experience. Many students, from all backgrounds, find a niche for themselves that provides them with a fulfilling social life as well. However, this nonsectarian, Jewish-sponsored dichotomy is an essential tension for Brandeis.

RELIGIOUS PRACTICE AT BRANDEIS

When Brandeis was first established in 1948, its approach to incorporating religion into campus life was seen as a model. At a time when most universities had one all-purpose chapel staffed by one all-purpose chaplain, Brandeis wanted to position itself as unique and visionary: three modern, beautiful chapels were built around a heart-shaped pond. Though the Jewish chapel was much larger than either the Protestant or Catholic chapels, the architecture intentionally minimized the appearance of that size differential. The university also funded three chaplains from those three faiths. In doing so, Brandeis was firmly establishing itself as a place for Jews and Christians to feel comfortable.

Fifty years later, this model no longer works well for a modern university seeking to demonstrate that it is a place where people from all faiths and cultures will feel welcome. Nationally, the domination of traditional religious groups on campuses is in decline. The number of Jewish students attending university, and moreover the percentage of Jews who make up the national college population, is shrinking yearly. The number of Moslems, Buddhists, Jains, Hindus, and others is growing. At Brandeis, the students who do not attend a Christian or Jewish chapel can feel disenfranchised. Recognizing this problem, sensitive chaplains and administrators who work with students began advocating for other faith communities. It is no accident that the Wellesley conference and the creation of the Brandeis Religious Pluralism and Spirituality group has come at this critical time of cultural and religious change in the United States.

GEARING UP FOR THE CONFERENCE

Arising from the unique context of Brandeis, our fledgling group of those interested in spirituality on campus met twice in the spring of 1998. Our plan was to attend the Education as Transformation conference as a group, having already engaged in preliminary discussions about what we hoped to learn. Utilizing materials provided by Wellesley in preparation for the conference, we began the process of formulating a consensus regarding the needs and interests specific to our campus. Key questions generated by our conversations included the following:

- On the broadest level, how might we expand academic or campuswide opportunities to explore spiritual and, perhaps, religious issues?

- Are there ways that a campus community as small as Brandeis (3,000 undergraduates) can support the religious needs of small minority groups?

- How can we bring spirituality into campus and classroom life?

- How can we introduce diverse religious programming which deals with controversial social issues (such as homosexuality and the death penalty) when diverse religions view these issues very differently?

The general consensus was that issues of spirituality and transformation were more relevant to campus life, but we did not want to ignore issues related to religion. Other topics that came from those earliest meetings were program oriented, i.e., could we have a spiritual emphasis added to first-year student orientation? How could we help the chaplaincy enhance its newly established annual Interfaith Thanksgiving program?

Prepared with these questions, Brandeis was well represented at the conference, with ten people attending. All who participated in the conference came back with great interest in, and energy for, creating change on campus. Of course, not all of our visions were the same. Faculty members came back from the conference with a focus on the classroom. Some students returned with an acute desire to recreate the Wellesley Multi-faith Student Council, which had presented an extraordinary program. Many sought a means for their personal expression of spirituality while others hoped to create programs for the campus. Forming a united set of goals and a common mission continues to be both challenging and enlivening for the RPS group.

BUILDING AND MAINTAINING OUR RPS GROUP

Having attended the Education as Transformation conference together, it was natural for us to establish a group that could approach some of these issues from a new, spiritual direction—adding to the other "welcoming" attempts that Brandeis advances. However, challenges quickly emerged related to both boundaries and objectives. A member of our chaplaincy, who had been with us since the spring 1998 meetings, was anxious for us to identify the ways in which we intended to engage the campus community. He hoped to clarify what the RPS would be doing so that its goals and those of the three university chaplains (Jewish, Catholic, and Protestant) would not conflict. He was also concerned that we were legitimizing all traditions equally, rather than making a distinction between what he called "revealed" faiths and other faiths.[9] We were unable to agree on the second issue, and we have subsequently presented ourselves as a group that is completely open to all faiths and traditions. As a result of these issues being raised, a productive dialogue ensued which yielded a mission statement that we continue to look to for clarification of our commitments. This mission statement clearly articulates a two-pronged agenda: religious pluralism and spirituality. It reads as follows:

> Our mission is to cultivate a welcoming environment and sense of connectedness for those of all religious traditions (or none) at Brandeis University. Our goal is to foster and facilitate opportunities, both in and out of the classroom, for moments of spiritual exploration and expression.

Although arriving at consensus on the wording of the statement was difficult, members of the RPS group were dedicated to being as inclusive as possible. We felt that the group was enriched by the inclusion of all voices representing any religious tradition while also embracing those who did not identify religiously (the "or none" group) but might be seeking things spiritual. This inclusivity has remained a constant. In developing our mission statement, there emerged a clear sense of what we are, and of equal importance, what we are not, i.e., an interfaith dialogue group, a religious programming group, a prayer group.

One of the more interesting dynamics in the formation of our RPS group had to do with the needs and goals of students and the points at which they were in harmony or tension with the needs and goals of staff members. There were common goals that the group was able to articulate on its return from the Wellesley conference, many of which were similar to those we had established as goals going into the conference. New goals that emerged included some initiatives and programs we hoped to accomplish that first year (1998–1999), including a multifaith colloquium as part of a larger university-wide, E Pluribus Unum celebration, the development of an academic program in religious studies, the development of a Multi-faith

Council, and assisting our health educator on her "Wellness of Campus" newsletter dedicated to the role of spirituality in promoting good health.

For almost all of the original and new goals it was easy to find consensus within the RPS group. One particularly enthusiastic and verbose student who had been involved with the group from the very beginning came away from the Wellesley conference with a deep interest in trying to model Wellesley's Multi-faith Student Council. There were others who also shared this goal. Two factors aborted that effort, however. The first had to do with representation on such a council. Given Brandeis' unique population, it was difficult to imagine how a group could be formed that would be representative of the different faiths on campus without having Jewish representation dominate. The second factor was that an interfaith "Theme House" (a special residential housing option for groups wanting to live together to bring their theme programming to campus) couldn't find enough students interested in a multifaith living situation to be able to continue that experiment for a second year. If this group of students, who had lived together successfully and brought multifaith programs to campus for a whole year, could not find a total of seven interested students to continue that experiment, what hope did we have of creating a vibrant multifaith council?

During our discussions about a multi-faith council, it became clear (and remains problematic) that it is very difficult to schedule meetings for a group consisting of students and staff/faculty members that are optimal for both constituencies. Students are nocturnal; faculty and staff members are not. The most active student in this process advocated for the RPS group to establish a separate, students-only group. That way, he argued, students could meet at times that faculty and staff members were unavailable and thereby make things happen that were not happening otherwise. Although the argument had merit, the lack of enthusiasm on the part of other RPS students prevented the establishment of this student-only arm of the RPS group. Although the RPS group has been and continues to be productive and successful, the lack of a stronger student presence and student voice at our meetings is something that continues to be of concern to some of us, and the ambiguity of whether we are a student group or a staff/faculty group is, at times, an issue.

As the first year progressed, we found ourselves with a small and committed group of students, staff members, and one or two academics, with fairly good representation religiously and ethnically. Indeed, it was quite a diverse group (especially for Brandeis) with the desire to "do" things. What we were not finding time for was a way to engage in things spiritual. Though our meeting agendas included time for spiritual sharing and discussion, we found ourselves planning and implementing events, while never having time to talk to each other about that which we found meaningful in our spiritual lives. To address this lack of "doing spiritual" and our feeling that we were only "doing programming," it was suggested that we add a spiritual reading at the beginning of each meeting. The tradition at RPS group meetings is to have someone volunteer to bring an appropriate reading to start the next meeting. The tone set by these readings has added greatly to our gatherings and many of us keep our eyes and ears open for appropriate poetry and prose that we can share with the group.

PROGRAMS

In the 1999–2000 academic year, to further address the need to "do spiritual," we began to organize programs with the titles "Stalking the Sacred" and "Seeking the Spiritual in Everyday Life" that were scheduled outside of our regular RPS meetings and advertised widely.

These programs provide space for members of the Brandeis faculty and staff, some of whom affiliate with the RPS group and others who do not, to offer initial thoughts on the role spirituality plays in their lives. The group takes it from there in the form of open discussion. During a discussion on spiritual transformation in secular lives, for example, a student shared a particularly meaningful moment. While driving on the New Jersey turnpike early in the morning, she pulled over to the side of the road. She got out of her car to watch an extraordinary sunrise. Other drivers also stopped for a moment to appreciate the magnificence of an emerging dawn. She said, "I found it spiritually uplifting to see strangers connecting about what was going on in the natural world. Even as a child, I found the image of sunlight streaming through the clouds a signifier of God."[10]

Although such events are still relatively new, participation has been good and the atmosphere at these gatherings has been warm, accepting, and supportive. The community's positive reaction to these programs has been gratifying for the RPS group and continues to help solidify our identity. The programs have added meaning to our work, and, most importantly, they allow us to explore together spiritual aspects of our lives.

Our newest venture is a two-part series being presented this year with the title "tuesdays with...." The name of this series is taken from the title of the book, *tuesdays with Morrie,* by Brandeis alum Mitch Albom, written with Morrie Schwartz, a Brandeis professor who went through the process of dying of Lou Gehrig's disease. The flyer reads, "Why wait until a professor is dying to hear what he's learned about life and how to live it?" Two popular professors, both known for their personal and academic interests in spirituality and religion, are this year's speakers. Our hope is to continue the series in the coming years.

Perhaps the most ambitious project we will be undertaking is the first pre-Passover communal seder at Brandeis.[11] The seder's themes of redemption and liberation resonate with people of all cultures. Although Brandeis is closed during Passover, in recent years a number of departments engaged with student life have suggested that non-Jewish students would welcome the opportunity to experience a seder and learn more about Judaism while at Brandeis, with the expectation that this may help to alleviate some of the feelings of alienation. We will begin working on this event, and we look forward to cosponsoring the seder with the Department of Student Life, the Dean of Arts and Sciences, and Academic Affairs.

Successes

There have been a number of initiatives that have helped to establish the success of the Religious Pluralism and Spirituality group. Chief among these has been the institution of the new program in religious studies that began in spring 2001.

Within a short time after the Wellesley conference, the RPS group began to discuss the need for an academic minor or concentration in religion. Although the university has a world-renowned Department of Near Eastern and Judaic Studies, we had no religion program of any kind. Among the chief advocates for this new program was an enormously effective and determined student who had joined the RPS group as a sophomore. In order to formulate a proposal, she found a faculty member who had long sought such a program. Within a year, they succeeded in getting the proposal accepted by the faculty senate, and the student graduated having seen a dream come true.

The newly established Brandeis Program in Religious Studies will involve sixteen departments offering over fifty courses that can be taken toward the requirements for the minor. Knowing that we provided encouragement and support for students and faculty members as they created a new and much needed program is enormously gratifying to the RPS group.

Another effort that we expect will come to a positive conclusion is encouraging the university to find or create a space dedicated to meditation, spiritual reflection, and quiet contemplation. For those who do not identify with any of the three chapels, such a space is especially important. A professor, not regularly involved with our group, came to us with the hope that we would help find students to join him in advocating for such a space. His connection to meditation was completely spiritual and specifically nonreligious in nature. (Interestingly enough, he incorporates meditation in his physics classes.) With the advent of a new campus center, which is currently under construction, the timing seemed right for such a request. It has been made explicit that this new building is not to be used for sectarian religious purposes. In their presentation to the university president, the group advocating for the space stressed that meditation and religion are not the same. Indeed, the faculty member maintained that a meditation space was as necessary to the students' emotional and spiritual health as the gym was to their physical health. This experience seems an excellent case in point as to the complexity of issues regarding spirituality and religion in higher education. It is clear that if the RPS group had not been in existence, there would have been no such consideration for a space of this sort. We are proud of our efforts, and we continue to hope that the final plans for the new center will include such a space.

A beautiful new event that the RPS group brought to Brandeis is the annual Winter Lights Celebration, which has now occurred twice. Brandeis is a place lacking in annual traditions. There are two major party weekends each year and a handful of cultural presentations by ethnic groups that have become anticipated annual events. Four years ago, a multifaith Thanksgiving celebration was introduced by the chaplain's office and, with assistance from the RPS group, that event has begun to be seen as an annual tradition, although attendance remains small. Focusing on the many positive aspects of the Thanksgiving event, the RPS group decided to find a way to do something broader and with more opportunities for spiritual expression near Christmas/Chanukah/Kwanzaa time. Not wanting to base this celebration on all or any of these holidays, the decision was made to base it on the role that lights play during this season.

Given that this darkest time of year always falls around the fall semester finals, we piggy-backed on a late night, finals week, study break, food-centered event that is very well attended. Setting the event by a pond immediately adjacent to the cafeteria, we recruit representatives from almost every ethnic and religious group on campus. These students, staff, and faculty members are asked to find a reading related to light or lights from their tradition, or which speaks to them in a spiritual way, to share with the community. Candles are held by all who attend and are placed around the pond. Guitarists play a few songs appropriate for the event, and students share their chosen readings and prayers. Both Winter Lights celebrations have been held on cold December nights. The community huddles together and quietly listens to what is offered. The feeling experienced by those in attendance is one of unity, companionship, community, and spirituality.

With the chaplaincy's multifaith Thanksgiving celebration and Winter Lights in place, and the current plans for the communal seder in the works, the RPS group will have helped to create three annual multifaith events that bring our diverse and disparate community together. Having begun by assisting with the Thanksgiving event in our first year, then moving on to create Winter Lights last year, and now hoping to bring a seder to fruition, we have made a slow and steady progression toward bringing more spirituality and, we hope, harmony to our campus. Had we attempted to do too much at first, I doubt that we would have experienced much success with any of these ventures.

Another smaller and almost completely student-centered project was the RPS group's contribution of an interfaith skit to a university-wide program called Culture X. Culture X is one of the largest and best supported new events at Brandeis and is greatly prized by the administration. It epitomizes what the university would like the campus to be all year round: integrated, open, with enthusiastic cultural exchange and no clear predominance of any one culture. Performances involve almost every ethnic/cultural group on campus. The goal is to bring the entire campus together and, indeed, almost a full third of all Brandeis students (and a good showing of the faculty and staff) have either attended or been part of the first two Culture X events. The RPS group wanted to bring a spiritual component to Culture X last year and chose to present a skit with expressions of peace from all religions represented on campus. The skit was one of two segments presented which were highlighted by the student newspaper. The newspaper described it this way:

> there was a poignant "Reflection on Peace" where students from various clubs around campus said prayers and recited poems on peace. The purpose of this was to show how people of all different religions ultimately have the common goal of peace and tranquility. After each speaker, everyone held hands and simultaneously prayed. Created by the Brandeis Religious Pluralism and Spirituality Committee, this act was inspirational and brought a tear to one's eye.[12]

THE RELIGIOUS PLURALISM AND SPIRITUALITY GROUP NOW

Aspects of one's life and involvement often appear very different depending on the angle from which they are viewed. The condition of the RPS group, like most things, can be viewed optimistically or pessimistically. On the one hand, we have an extremely committed group of students and staff members who meet regularly and who have moments of sharing that feel truly important. We are very proud of the programs we have brought, and continue to bring, to the community, and more people at Brandeis are becoming aware of our presence. Our success with the creation of the Religion Program and our work toward a meditation space feel truly significant. Our committee represents some of the diversity of the community and seeks to make our campus a better, more spiritual, and richer place for its student population. At the same time, we are relying on a very small group of students and staff members to keep ourselves moving ahead, and we can't seem to attract substantial numbers to our regular meetings (an experience not at all unique to the RPS group among campus groups). Our moments of spiritual expression and experience are too few and too far apart, and although some programs have been well attended, most of our events and meetings seem to have only a small impact on bringing our campus closer together.

Whereas the RPS group has strong connections with some departments and offices on campus, it has no specific ties to the administration outside of the office of the dean of arts and sciences. It is our sense that the administration is aware of our activities but we hear neither positive nor negative comments from them. Our relationship with the chaplaincy is more complicated. It is a very small department and each individual's perception is significant. It is fair to say that there are those who are very supportive of our work and feel that the RPS group is on target with its efforts. Others feel, quite strongly, that we are invading their territory and that, since they have heard no great demand from students for the things we are providing, we should not be filling a nonexistent void. Although some of the chaplains occasionally attend the "Creating a Welcoming Community" programs, I was sorry that none attended a recent program entitled "Observing Different Faiths," at which a Muslim student on the panel said: "The stereotypes and generalizations about Muslims make it difficult not to feel marginalized. The RPS group is the best thing on this campus."

Even when the feeling that the cup is half-empty is predominant, there is never an impulse to close shop. Our most active RPS students may be unable to take on more tasks because they're already overcommitted, but those same students, and occasionally some new ones, will still come to additional meetings to help ensure that a program takes place even if they can't take on the role of coordinator. When we're at a loss about how to find financial support for our initiatives, a student pops up to suggest that she get the RPS group chartered by the student senate or we find out about a grant that can help us with what we need. We seem to be able to maintain a core group with enough of a commitment to help bring an essential part of who we each are to our lives within the university. As one of our core members, also a panelist at the "Observing Different Faiths" program, said, "Being active in RPS and hearing other religious points of view has been a very important part of my growth. My Judaism has been enhanced by opening my mind to others."

If our goal as an RPS group is to truly transform higher education at Brandeis, we are far from reaching it. There is no doubt, however, that as we continue to bring new programs to campus and as we continue to offer opportunities for spiritual expression in this academic setting to those who attend meetings and other events, we are making some progress.

FUTURE

The RPS group continues to be more widely known at Brandeis. Students regularly comment that they are glad we exist and wish they could come to the meetings. Many staff and faculty members are extremely supportive of our efforts. We know that many see the initiatives and programs which we have created as "value added." The RPS group's e-mail list is used by many departments and individuals for publicity purposes. It continues to be our goal to expand our group.

But more importantly, wonderful, life-enhancing initiatives continue to be generated by the core committee. As long as a committed core of students, faculty, and staff members remains intact, it is clear that the RPS group will continue to have a positive impact on campus. Though our two-and-a-half-year history as a group is brief, it seems less brief on a college campus where things change very quickly. We have every reason to believe that we will be around for a long time to come and are enthusiastic about the future of the Religious Pluralism and Spirituality group and the future of Brandeis University.

Conclusion

Based on the number of people who attended and the level of enthusiasm generated at the Wellesley conference, as well as at subsequent initiatives at other institutions, it is fair to say that the question of incorporating increased opportunities for spiritual reflection on college campuses is an important one. The uniqueness of each campus (as is typified by Brandeis University) is also undeniable. However, there is much that can be learned from one campus' experience in creating a context for the exploration of spirituality that should be valuable to others.

Although this chapter addresses many such lessons, I want to end by highlighting just a few. What is most basic is the careful construction, as a grassroots initiative, of a multifaith (including secularists), multiethnic core of students, faculty, and staff members who are committed to meeting regularly to address the spiritual needs of their campus. An exploration into common values and goals and an ongoing willingness to work toward these goals should follow. The energy to then bring programs and opportunities to the wider campus can start the movement toward attaining those goals, and in that will come a sense of real accomplishment.

Endnotes

1. Nancy Diamond and Hugh Davis Graham, *The Rise of American Research Universities* (Baltimore: Johns Hopkins University Press, 1997).
2. See Brandeis University's website: www.brandeis.edu.
3. Office of Management Research and Analysis, *Market Position Analysis– 1999* (Waltham, Massachusetts: Brandeis University, 1999).
4. Ruth Fredman Cernea, ed., *Hillel Guide to Jewish Life on Campus* (New York: Random House, Princeton Review Publishing, 1999).
5. The reason for closing on Passover is the complexity of the kosher food requirements for the holiday.
6. An extra month is added every four years to realign the Hebrew calendar with the Roman calendar.
7. In general, what's striking in this age of ever-increasing diverse college populations is that no academic calendar is addressing the traditional holidays of other non-Christian religions.
8. Judaism as a culture which is both a nationality and a religion makes it possible for its members to identify with it in vastly different ways. Whereas some are tied to the religious practices, some identify completely as secular Jews (often relating to the cultural aspects).

9. By revealed faiths he primarily had in mind Judaism, Christianity, and Islam.
10. *The Justice* (Brandeis' student newspaper), Tuesday, April 11,1999, 7.
11. The seder is the retelling of the Jewish exodus from Egypt (our passage from enslavement to freedom and redemption), which is the seminal historic event of the Jewish people. An elaborate meal with symbolic foods is an important part of the ritual.
12. *The Justice* (Brandeis' student newspaper), Tuesday, March 21, 2000, 32.

Author's Note: Many thanks to Marci McPhee for her friendship, work, and support as co-coordinator of the Brandeis RPS group and in writing this chapter.

5. Religion, Spirituality, and Historically Black Colleges and Universities

MARIE V. MCDEMMOND, ARTHUR R. JACKSON, AND JACQUELINE A. CURTIS

"Amazing grace, how sweet the sound that saved a wretch like me. I once was lost but now I'm found, was blind but now I see."[1] The strains of this and other African American spirituals can be heard throughout the experience of the Historically Black Colleges and Universities (HBCUs).

It has been said that three of the most important institutions in the African American culture are the Black family, the Black church, and the Historically Black Colleges and Universities. Since many of the HBCUs have their origins in religious denominations, the abolitionist movement, and missionary efforts, spirituality is woven into the fabric of these institutions. While there is a clear separation of church and state at white public institutions, both public and private HBCUs are based on a set of cultural experiences that afford spirituality an important role in these institutions.

HISTORICAL ROOTS AND CONNECTIONS

The history of the HBCUs is also a history of how African Americans organized their society to meet the challenges and opportunities of life after slavery, disenfranchisement, and later, integration. Deeply rooted within the HBCUs is the belief that Black people can excel with quality teaching and motivation, coupled with their faith in God.

Community and service were often the guiding tenets of the early HBCUs, many of which began in the basements of churches or in private homes. The church has been the major and, in most cases, the only community focal point for many African Americans. The first lessons nearly all African American students learned were from the one book most families had in their homes—the Bible. Even though most HBCUs began as private, church-affiliated institutions, some later became public colleges or universities in order to receive better funding. However, religion and spirituality are still actively included in the lives of students and in institutional functions at both public and private HBCUs.

Since it was out of religious communities that most of the HBCUs were born and nurtured, these institutions inevitably remain connected to their religious foundations. Faculty and staff of the early HBCUs played important roles in community-sponsored meetings as consultants and group leaders because they were considered the elite of the community. They frequently acted as scribes and presenters at these community gatherings because they were able to eloquently articulate the thoughts, feelings, and ideas of the community. Some of the faculty members at HBCUs were ministers from the community who taught courses in biblical studies. These same ministers would allow time during worship services for members of the HBCU community to make presentations on behalf of their institutions. As a matter of reciprocity, students attending the HBCUs regularly helped the church community raise needed funds through voluntary work or concerts.

Although the HBCUs have a rich history embedded in the church, the issue for the public HBCUs of separation of church and state has not gone unnoticed. The public HBCUs have been required to comply with many state and federal regulations that their sister private HBCUs have not. However, the existence of religious overtones in the daily life of public institutions has not produced major problems. At most white public institutions that are heavily reliant on taxpayer dollars, religion is offered as an optional course to help "round out" students' electives, rather than help shape students' character, as is the case at the HBCUs.

CONFLICT AND COMMITMENT

In many ways, students attending HBCUs have experienced conflict with the society from which they came. While they are in residence at the HBCU, students are somewhat insulated from the hostile environment of the mainstream culture and can develop academically in a supportive and inclusive atmosphere. Conflict can still arise when students are stereotyped and discriminated against outside of the campus. Additionally, many of the emotions and experiences students bring with them can create conflict between their spiritual development and intellectual development.

Diana Chapman Walsh feels that conflict is essential to the art of learning. "Conflict is necessary—it is a creative force because differences and polarities are a critical part of this learning process. All learning, I would submit, involves first mastering new categories, learning them, and then integrating them into a larger more organic whole."[2] This is an excellent synopsis of the spiritual and academic growth of many students at HBCUs. Students first enter with preconceived constructs of their place both in the academic world and in society. Throughout their academic careers these ideals are refined and shaped with the acquisition of intellectual knowledge and the expansion of their spiritual selves.

These students walk a thin line, balancing their commitment to their own educational attainment with their commitment to the general African American population. It is important for them to comprehend that the progress of one member of the Black community is meaningless unless it is used to uplift others. They must also have a burning desire to act as mentors for the next generation of African American students in elementary and secondary schools. In many ways, they are servants of a higher calling and are used as vehicles to uplift the status of their community. Before this can happen, they must acquire the intellectual and spiritual knowledge that will carry them to success. For them, failure is not an option.

Further conflict can arise when African American college students start to see that HBCUs are as stereotyped in the local community as are African Americans in the society at large. It is not uncommon to have negative events that occur on an HBCU campus portrayed on page one of the local newspaper while notable achievements are relegated to the back pages. Also, for many HBCUs there is stiff competition for qualified students from predominantly white institutions in the same geographical area. Therefore, de facto discrimination may occur in the areas of funding, prestige, and even the reputation of the HBCU and its faculty members. This sometimes leads students from these institutions to adopt an activist mentality to protect their HBCU from external forces and to connect with those in the impoverished areas in which they may reside.

One of the purposes of the HBCUs has been to induct students into the growing numbers of the Black middle class. This is important because many of these students are first-generation college attendees. These students generally come from lower economic backgrounds than the average nationwide population of college students. However, the lack of financial means among these students does not diminish the richness of religious tradition and spirituality that are reinforced nationwide at HBCUs.

SPIRITUALITY AS SUBTLE POWER

Although 90 percent of all students who attend HBCUs belong to some type of church before their acceptance into college, some students tend to rebel against the spirituality practiced in the Black churches and the HBCUs that advocate progression to the Black middle class. However, they still remain very involved in political and spiritual activism, especially when working with the youth of their communities. St. Claire Drake, an African American political scientist, has asserted that the HBCUs will continue to provide "socially conscious and well informed political leaders."[3]

Further, some students attending HBCUs are opting to join nontraditional Black religions such as the Nation of Islam or other religious groups that espouse Eastern philosophies. Many of the doctrines of these religions are attuned to the self-esteem, pride, and awareness of the African American culture. This relates to the mental awakening that many first-generation Black college students have as they learn more about themselves and their communities.

Spirituality is the subtle power at the HBCUs. Because there is a sense at these institutions that God is "in charge," the HBCUs seem to give way to the presence of the Spirit at public functions, commencements, and convocations. These are times when all of the members of an HBCU community come together to celebrate and recognize a heightened awareness of the power of the Spirit. An unusual peace falls on these events when voices lift up together in singing familiar songs of faith.

A high level of spirituality is commonplace at many HBCUs that are directly or indirectly affiliated with religious denominations, usually the Baptist or the African Methodist Episcopal Church. Additionally, spiritual ideals are reinforced on a daily basis at public HBCUs. This is especially relevant when searching for truth and equality and striving for the greater good of the African American community, rather than the self. As explained by Parker Palmer, the HBCUs are spiritual communities where the success of the whole community is as important as the success of individuals.[4]

It is believed that the type of institution of higher education African American students choose to attend is often guided by their parents, who may themselves be religious. Another assertion is that the more religion is practiced at home, the more a family seeks an institution that offers overt religious options for their students. Many successful African American professionals want their children to study at an HBCU, hoping that it will introduce valuable insights into their children's developmental experiences. They want their children to work with African American faculty for the first time in their lives and want them to live in an environment where they are no longer in the minority population. This is particularly true of students who hail from an integrated or majority community where they attended elementary and secondary school with white students and were taught by white teachers. Parents also want religion and spirituality to be a part of their children's college education to provide balance to some of the vulgarism of the hip-hop philosophy and "gangsta" rap videos.

DEVELOPING THE HEART AND THE MIND

Some authors, such as Jenks and Reismann, have categorized Black colleges as "academic disaster areas."[5] Many of these institutions have been stereotyped in a fashion similar to African American culture in general. At the elementary and secondary school levels, academic achievement for many African American students has been lower than that of their white counterparts. Therefore, it has been an important function of the HBCUs to provide educational access for these students. This will insure that they can become academically, culturally, and spiritually enriched, eventually taking their place as productive citizens in their communities.

The Dalai Lama has indicated that the purpose of life is happiness and that ignorance causes pain and suffering.[6] Students from HBCUs have experienced these emotions in terms of the pain and suffering caused by the ignorance of racism and discrimination. The areas of religion and spirituality serve to uplift students so they no longer see themselves as "second class citizens" and can develop their hearts as well as their minds accordingly.

HBCUs often incorporate the principles of holistic education to address concerns that students may have during their academic careers. According to Ron Miller, some of these principles include:

- The development of the human being as a complex individual with a spiritual core;
- The development of students on the personal and transformational level;
- Holistic education including a cultural reality; and
- Cultivating meaningful relationships for students.[7]

While student affairs practitioners may not be actively involved in the spiritual development of students at predominantly white institutions, they are very committed to this ideal at Black institutions. Student affairs practitioners at HBCUs understand that college-age students need growth in the spiritual as well as academic domains. Although there is an implied moral obligation for students to attend chapel on Sunday at many private HBCUs, Christianity is not the only vehicle for spiritual expression and insight: all religious denominations, both Eastern and Western, are accepted on these campuses.

TEACHING FREEDOM

The spiritual and intellectual mission of students at HBCUs is both simple and complex. It has been said that what does not kill us makes us stronger. The discrimination that these students have experienced makes them stronger and more productive members of the American culture.

A leading cultural critic and educator, bell hooks, indicates that the teaching of academic knowledge becomes more meaningful when it is used to address social inequalities. She indicates that one of the goals of education should be "teaching students to transgress against the harmful boundaries in the stereotypes; teaching them to practice freedom."[8] This describes one of the greatest purposes of HBCUs. They not only teach students that they are equal members of the American culture, but they also teach them to be free in spirit, body, and intellectual thought.

The Historically Black Colleges and Universities have been, and will continue to be, an integral part of the postsecondary educational landscape in this country. Religion and spirituality will remain a strong force at these institutions. It is the quality of an academic education infused with the spirit that will allow the HBCUs to continue to be a lighthouse of hope for this nation.

ENDNOTES

1. John Newton, *Amazing Grace*, traditional Christian hymn in *Olney Hymns* (London, 1779).
2. Diana Chapman Walsh, "Spirituality and Leadership," in *The Heart of Learning*, ed. Steven Glazer (New York: Penguin Putnam, 1999), 203–216.
3. St. Clair Drake, "The Black College in America," *Daedalus* 100 (Summer, 1971): 80-103.

4. Parker J. Palmer, "Community and Commitment in Higher Education," *American Association of Higher Education Bulletin* (September 1992 1993): 37–48.

5. Christopher Jenks, and David Reismann, *The Academic Revolution* (Chicago: University of Chicago Press, 1968).

6. Dalai Lama, "Education and the Human Heart" in *The Heart of Learning,* ed. Steven Glazer (New York: Penguin Putnam, 1999), 85–96.

7. Ron Miller, "Holistic Education for an Emerging Culture" in *The Heart of Learning,* ed. Steven Glazer (New York: Penguin Putnam, 1999), 189–202.

8. bell hooks, *Teaching to Transgress* (New York: Routledge, 1994).

6. *I Do and I Understand: The Self Knowledge Symposium Model for Spiritual Exploration on Campus*

MARY ALICE SCOTT, GEORG BUEHLER, AND KENNY FELDER

The Self Knowledge Symposium (SKS) is a student organization in North Carolina that integrates "real-life philosophy" and spiritual inquiry into students' college experience. Over the past eleven years, the SKS has developed a conceptual framework and practical methodology for helping students explore spiritual questions within the context of a religiously diverse campus setting.

Rather than try to rigorously define what we mean by "spiritual," let us consider the following excerpt from a letter a student at Duke University wrote to her instructor of an SKS "house course":[1]

> When the SKS classes first began, I must admit I did not take it seriously. I observed it, like a child examining a curious new toy. I did not expect to get caught up in the game. However, I am truly impressed with the heat that the class has produced, the pressure which it subjects upon itself. Perhaps I still seem to be an unattached observer, but it is no longer true. I have walked home from this class with tears streaming down my cheeks, touched.

> Last year, I tried to pop amaranth, an ancient Aztec grain, at my friend's house. I had suggested it in a manner of jest, but we tried it anyway. Amaranth are the tiniest little dark grains, and we poured them into the popcorn popper. It was so incredible to hear the first few kernels popping, and then to watch them bounce wildly all over the kitchen counter. We laughed so hard, it was so beautifully unexpected. Anyway, a couple of weeks ago the memory came to me, and I realized that it was the same feeling I had towards my SKS class. It is so incredible to watch people turn inside out, revealing their rippled white core, breaking out of shells. So the question I must ask myself is, have I popped? Or am I a lone kernel, left at the bottom, unsuccessful and unpopped?

This passage describes the experience of "spiritual exploration," as the SKS defines it, at its best. What at first looked like an academic class about spirituality suddenly becomes an intensely personal, active process of self-analysis, an adventure that demands commitment but also promises a change of being.

Almost all students go off to college with the unvoiced hope for transformative experiences that will give direction and meaning to their lives. They may not express it as a desire for the "spiritual," per se. More often they look for some kind of "Dead Poets' Society" experience: intense friendships and late-night conversations; a sense of intimacy, belonging, and community.

But along with the excitement and anticipation comes a growing, anxious sense that they are making major life decisions without nearly enough data. Who am I, really? What do I find fulfilling? Am I truly capable of greatness, or even of happiness? What if I choose the wrong path? Many of them also sense that college—a time when they are surrounded by mentors and peers, and yet primarily responsible to no one but themselves—is the time to focus on these questions. As Niño points out, they are at "a fundamental turning point in the life-cycle" and "their central task is to build life structures with a sense of internal coherence, meaning, and purpose."[2]

A growing number of educators are recognizing that students are open to exploring and experiencing the spiritual,[3] that addressing the "big questions" is an essential dimension of students' development,[4] and that academic institutions need to find models for fostering spiritual development.[5,6,7] In short, *the primary goal of a college education should not be the imparting of facts, but the transforming of people*—enabling students to address their fundamental questions, and in the process, to become (rather than learn about) the answers they seek. The Self Knowledge Symposium has been providing students with the tools and the community they need to pursue this kind of spiritual growth within a religiously diverse context.

CREATING A VENUE FOR SELF-TRANSFORMATION

The kinds of activities that are taught in Self Knowledge Symposium classes and meetings are not particularly unusual. On the surface, an observer would see all the same things one might expect in any university-sponsored organization: lectures, discussions, field trips, special projects, social parties, and occasionally even communal living arrangements.

But SKS activities are characterized by an unusual, almost fanatic intensity. When SKS sponsored the "Spiritual Bach" organ concert in the Duke University Chapel, Dean William Willimon warned that a free organ recital might attract an audience of 100 people at best. But for the SKS students, the concert was not merely an organizational event. It was a spiritual challenge. They handed out fliers, manned tables, contacted local merchants and media, and in the end, filled an 1,800-person chapel with a standing-room-only crowd. SKS teaches that rising to organizational challenges (such as a concert) builds the character required for larger spiritual challenges.

This concert, like all activities on the three campuses that host SKS student groups, was almost entirely run and managed by the students themselves, since SKS is a grassroots effort. The juniors and seniors continually recreate and run the same community that they joined as freshmen and sophomores.

The SKS offers a model for encouraging spiritual development that is highly accessible to today's college students across religious and socioeconomic boundaries. It is a model that focuses on students' daily lives—going to classes, relating to their friends and families, and building and running the organization itself—but ties all of these activities into the deeper spiritual quest that the students are embarking on as individuals and as a group. It is a process of transformation through action and reflection.

Origins

The Self Knowledge Symposium originated with a series of lectures given by businessman and Zen philosopher August Turak in 1989. Turak is, by all appearances, a prototypical American capitalist. A onetime executive in the cable TV industry, and one of the early executives of MTV: Music Television, Turak climbed up the corporate business ladder before becoming an entrepreneur and founding a multi-million-dollar software company.[8]

Turak's real calling, though, was living and teaching what he called "spiritual work." Turak's own intensive questioning in religion and philosophy led him to drop out of college in the 1970s to study under an American Zen master, Richard Rose. Rose taught a synthesis of Eastern and Western mysticism that emphasized a practical, personal, experiential quest for truth in all aspects of one's life. Like most traditional Zen teachers,[9] Rose's philosophy was intensely individualistic, demanding that students arrive at their own experience of the truth rather than relying on systems, dogmas, or other authorities.[10] Instead of teaching specific practices or rituals, Rose's philosophy focused on cultivating the core aspects of spirituality that he considered common to all genuine religious paths: self-knowledge, an uncompromising desire for the truth, and the cultivation of personal character.[11] What impressed Turak the most about Rose, though, was the intensity of his personal life and the way every aspect of his daily life reflected his spiritual intent. Someone once asked Rose what he thought of prayer. Rose replied, "Your whole life should be a prayer. If your whole life was a prayer, it would be answered instantly."[12]

Turak's five-year apprenticeship with Rose was the most profound and important experience of his life. Even after he left Rose to finish his college degree and move on to the world of business, he found that "philosophy of transformation" continued to be a dominant theme. Turak found a new mentor in Lou Mobley, founder of the IBM Executive School. Mobley had discovered that turning middle managers into executive leaders was a transformational experience focused on values and attitudes.

> We departed radically from much of the conventional wisdom about education of that era. We leaned toward offering people as much opportunity for development—rather than training—as they could handle. Executive development is a process of differentiation, not a process of acculturation. [At the IBM Executive School] development was experiential.[13]

Having seen that practical professional growth and personal spiritual transformation were not far apart, Turak took to lecturing at colleges and universities, hoping that his experience and insights could be of use to a new generation. Turak's philosophy and approach to spiritual questions freely mixed the mystical aspects of Zen with the ruthlessly practical action orientation of business.

Students responded enthusiastically to Turak's stories.[14] Some students at North Carolina State University were inspired enough to start a student discussion group around the ideas that Turak presented. This new "Self Knowledge Symposium" tapped into the growing need for students to explore their meaning and purpose in a way that was directly relevant to their lives. As students transferred or went to graduate school, they carried the SKS methodology with them, setting up their own groups at other schools. Eventually a growing body of "graduates" from the SKS groups organized the Self Knowledge Symposium Foundation, to provide support to the SKS student groups and help other campuses incorporate the same ideas and methods into their own campus communities.

Religion and the College Campus

The Self Knowledge Symposium was created as an attempt to provide a new methodology of spiritual seeking that was suitable for a diverse student body. The diversity of spiritual perspectives is immediately evident just by talking to the students. For instance, the following are quotes from three different students who are currently active in the Self Knowledge Symposium.

> I came to college grounded in my Catholic faith, but I wanted to go deeper into it. I wanted something with more substance than just the pizza-party socials I found in the church youth group.

> I'm a recovering Methodist. I don't much see the point in religion. What I am trying to do is figure out what my life is about. I want to live a real, genuine life.

> I believe in God and I have a sense that he's out there, but I didn't feel comfortable going to church. Sometimes I would find in art or music or poetry a sense of the transcendent, and I would know that I ought to be doing my 'God-homework.' But I didn't know where to begin.

How can colleges and universities serve all these different perspectives? When a campus community holds a mix of religious and non-religious beliefs and everything in between, how can the school support students in their search for meaning?

Responses to this spiritual diversity have evolved over time. Based on our own observations over the last eleven years, we categorize responses into *tolerance, interfaith,* or *integration*, depending on the degree to which the college or university directly involves itself with spiritual matters.

Tolerance

Almost all universities foster basic tolerance. They permit religious or philosophic organizations to be active on campus, but make no effort to actively direct students or incorporate spirituality into the rest of college life. Given the constitutional mandate for "separation of church and state," universities are understandably reluctant to directly address spirituality, a topic our culture generally regards as personal and private.[15] This approach works very well to serve those who are already grounded in a particular religious tradition, but may not help the growing numbers of students who don't affiliate themselves with a given faith but who do want to explore that realm.[16] By establishing "non-belief" as the norm and religious belief as the exception, a policy of passive tolerance also has a tendency to marginalize spirituality, to push it off into an extracurricular (i.e., unimportant) category.[17]

Interfaith

Colleges and universities often recognize that the religious diversity on campus cannot be ignored. Religious and spiritual aspects of personal development are very important, and the growing diversity of religious perspectives on campus draws attention to differences. As Victor Kazanjian explains, "Tolerance as the ultimate goal has not and will not lead us to the healthy, peaceful, just society we seek. Tolerance is conflict arrested."[18] The interfaith approach draws together representatives of religious perspectives to talk about their faiths, with the goal of diffusing tension and improving understanding, appreciation, and mutual respect. This active approach is better than passive tolerance, since it recognizes the importance of spirituality and gives an open forum for discussion that transcends religious boundaries.[19] Public discussion gives students opportunities for openminded exploration of spiritual and religious issues. Some students have expressed reluctance to act as representatives for their entire faith tradition, though, since it is becoming more evident that a single person cannot speak for an entire faith with its own internal diversity of viewpoints.

Integration

Most recently a third approach has emerged, which continues the trend toward more active encouragement of individual, personal involvement in spiritual topics. This integrative approach seeks to redefine the academy's traditional notions of knowledge and scholarship, and to synthesize various disciplines into a more coherent whole that includes religious, moral, and spiritual dimensions as well as the intellectual.[20] It actively looks for universal aspects of spiritual life and encourages students to engage that spiritual process, without getting into the particular differences of belief. As David K. Scott says, "The greatest challenge for universities and colleges is the definition of this common core [of the world's great religions], this general framework which would be acceptable to most religious traditions at least in the abstract."[21] The SKS is one of a number of organizations now promoting this approach. Students respond to this approach because it is both practical and open-ended. It gives them a way to engage spirituality with a minimum of starting assumptions. It is a "hands-on" approach—rather than talking *about* spirituality, it gives them a way they can *do* spirituality, even when they are not sure what they believe or how far they want to go with it.

The idea of "spiritual synthesis" is nothing new. Aldous Huxley dubbed it the "Perennial Philosophy,"[22] and a host of prestigious scholars such as Joseph Campbell, Huston Smith, and Ken Wilber have richly documented that many of the essential aspects of spiritual life are universal.[23,24,25] In the same way that many schools now have "character education" programs that promote universal standards of moral behavior without presuming a particular religious grounding, so the SKS can recognize and elucidate universal aspects of spiritual life without espousing any given dogma.

So what do these "essential aspects of spirituality" look like? A full treatment of the topic is beyond the scope of this chapter, but here are some of the core ideas that help define the SKS and its approach:[26]

1) *An emphasis on methodology rather than belief.* The SKS doesn't try to tell students what to believe—it only can show them how to seek. In general, it frames spirituality as a *process of becoming* rather than a static set of truths. In that sense it recognizes that spirituality is inherently personal. The notion of a universal process yielding open-ended results is analogous to the scientific method: science tells us *how* to experiment but not *what* we will find.

2) *A commitment to truth.* The goal of spiritual seeking is to find the truth: the truth about one's self, the truth about the world, the truth about God. That might seem obvious, but it brings up some important corollaries:

- Seeking the truth is not the same as seeking happiness. This process cannot guarantee that it will make one's life happier. In fact, it can almost universally promise to make life uncomfortable and scary.

- Seeking the truth is work. Truth is not just something recognized; it is something one must actively live.

- Truthfulness is required at an interpersonal level (keeping one's commitments), at a psychological level (not rationalizing or "lying to yourself"), and ultimately at a spiritual level. This is the core of the SKS philosophy: by working hard to be rigorously truthful in thought and action, one will naturally and inevitably be guided to a more significant truth.

3) *A continual process of action and reflection.* Almost any system, religious or otherwise, that intends to transform a person involves a conscious process of action and reflection. Some of the more recent evolutions in college programs, such as service learning and curriculum-based alternative spring break programs, also use this action/reflection process.

- Self-knowledge (reflection) is the beginning (and perhaps the end) of all spiritual seeking. Nearly all religious traditions make reference to it: Jesus' "the kingdom of heaven is within you," or the Oracle of Delphi's "Know thyself." The SKS approach is psychology in the original meaning of the word: "study of the psyche, or soul." That self-knowledge can come about in individual practices of meditation or writing, but it is also critical to work together with others who share the same goal.

- Living deliberately (action) is the natural result of reflection. If a person deeply knows himself, he begins to see the consequences of every aspect of his life. Reflection has a tendency to create cognitive dissonance by drawing attention to the ways a person's lifestyle or attitudes are inconsistent with his or her philosophy. By taking conscious, deliberate steps to manifest his personal philosophy in everyday life, a person begins to live the spiritual life.

The best feature of this framework is that it is acceptable and useable by anybody who participates, regardless of personal religious beliefs. Students who do not consider themselves religious, or who simply don't know where they stand, can still appreciate the value of finding the truth for the truth's sake, or critically examining themselves and their lives.

ACTION AND REFLECTION

The philosophy and organizational structure of the SKS lend themselves to an open, accessible venue for spiritual inquiry. However, even these aspects would be useless without the continual focus on making philosophy *personal* and *relevant* to real-life problems. Transformation through action and reflection requires that both the action and reflection be directed toward the daily vicissitudes of one's own life. The following story illustrates this "philosophy-in-action" approach.

Ken was a member of the Self Knowledge Symposium at North Carolina State University. He was intelligent and friendly, but through the course of many weekly discussion meetings it became clear that many of his problems were rooted in timidity. He hated the agricultural fieldwork he was doing, but he was too afraid to switch career paths. He admitted that he needed to be more assertive in relationships, but resolutions to improve left him unchanged. Officers in the group noticed that he shied away from tasks that required any interpersonal tension, that he would rather put up posters alone than pitch a story idea to the editor of the school newspaper.

Eventually, Ken asked the group for personal guidance: what, specifically, could he do to deepen his spiritual potential? Instead of recommending specific readings or meditation (activities most people would consider "spiritual"), the group provided him with a spiritual exercise that was more unexpected and direct: sell 10 tickets to the upcoming SKS "Spiritual Bach" concert.

Ken was clearly terrified of the task given to him, but he must have recognized the purpose of the assignment. He announced that he would sell twenty tickets to the concert, to the cheers and encouragement of his peers.

Over the next month, Ken sold tickets as if his life depended on it. (In a way, it did.) After selling tickets to his parents and friends, his quest for buyers drove him to do things he had never done before. He visited other SKS groups in the area so he could be the first to offer tickets to newcomers. He started going to local music events, selling tickets during intermission. By the end of the month, he was standing in grocery store parking lots, hawking tickets to complete strangers until the store management kicked him out. The day before the concert, Ken sold his twenty-first ticket. In less than a month, he had visibly transformed himself from a "shrinking violet" into a bold, confident salesman.

What makes this a typical SKS story?

Ken transformed himself through direct action: he didn't just learn, he became. He came to recognize his personal limitations through reflection prompted by SKS discussion groups, but it was by doing something that he actually changed. Even though the action was seemingly mundane—selling tickets—it was a spiritual exercise, because it allowed Ken to directly address the flaw in his character that prevented his growth. By engaging in a real-life project, Ken subjected himself to interdependence, accountability, peer pressure, explicit goals, and risk. The SKS provided a context for him to test his character and push the limits of what he thought was possible.

GETTING PERSONAL

In order for the SKS process of continual action and reflection to be successful, the instructors themselves need to participate. The hardest part of making this new educational model work in real-life settings is that it requires both students and instructors to cross the traditional boundaries of higher education. They are required to share more of themselves than they are accustomed to doing and to directly tackle real-life issues that are normally dealt with outside the classroom. Intimacy is a critical component of the SKS experience: in order to talk about what really matters, students must be able to talk about themselves with an unusually high degree of intimacy. Such intimacy cannot be established if either the student or instructor behaves like an impartial bystander.

An example of this process came up in the spring of 2000, when two SKS graduate instructors co-taught an elective humanities course at UNC-Chapel Hill on "Computers and Society." Among other requirements, students were asked to write about the personal significance of the readings. While students were more than capable of writing well-reasoned, critical essays about the reading material, they were completely at a loss when it came to relating the material to their own lives. "Is a computer actually thinking?" was a question that seemed to have no bearing on their lives. Weeks of urging the students to dig deeper into their own experience had no effect.

Finally, out of desperation, one of the instructors came to class with her own essay. She read a true story about a fight she had had with her parents. She discussed the causes of the argument, the uncertainty of going against her mother's wishes, the pain of watching her mother cry. And she talked about her current life. In front of twenty students, the instructor disclosed her plan to leave graduate school as soon as she finished teaching the course. She admitted the fear and the excitement she felt about abandoning years of work without completing her degree.

The instructors were terrified that the students would lose all respect for them. The result was the opposite: the students began writing powerful, personal, insightful essays about their own lives and struggles and doubts. The tenor of the course shifted, from an opportunity for intellectual discussion to a forum for intimacy and personal change. At the end of the course, students were given evaluation forms to review the class. Some of the comments included the following:

This class has challenged my own perceptions of what it means to be human and make conscious decisions. I'm also proud to say I'm going back to church, this time with a more firm conviction in my *very own* beliefs. [Note: the class made almost no explicit references to religion of any kind.]

This class is one of the reasons why I'm still here today. This class is one of the reasons why I'm not on anti-depressants. That's all that I can say.

For the first time a professor wanted to know who I was. Not just my experiences but my thoughts and opinions which in turn let me know who I really am.

When asked for the best thing the instructors had done in the course, almost all of them pointed to the personal reading. The reading gave them permission to open up to a higher level of honesty, but it did more than that. It showed them how to do something that many of them honestly did not know how to do, i.e., how to write a personal story about their own lives, and draw a general lesson from it.

Intimacy, it seems, is contagious—being really honest provokes others to open up. Achieving that degree of intimacy requires a special kind of leadership. Whoever is facilitating the event has to be willing to take initiative in being vulnerable. This is inherently scary, unpredictable, and fraught with peril! It also happens to be the only way we've found that works. Spiritual exploration cannot really be taught—it requires a guide, someone who is making the same journey himself, someone who is willing to take the same risks and is equally committed to the process.

THE SKS COMMUNITY

The SKS model for facilitating transformation has undergone a rigorous workout over the last eleven years. The basic methodology has been successfully used with thousands of students. The community of students, faculty, and volunteers that has grown around this educational philosophy testifies to the soundness of its methods. The development of a self-sustaining community that fosters transformation is an explicit and ongoing goal for the Self Knowledge Symposium.

What does this community look like? The SKS community consists of several student organizations on separate university campuses, a few non-student organizations that operate off-campus, and a nonprofit foundation that organizes and guides the activities of the groups.

A typical student organization consists of the following:

- One or two nonstudent facilitators, usually instructors in the university or recently graduated alumni of the university who volunteer their time and energy to teach;

- Three to five officers, highly involved undergraduate or graduate students who do organizational work for the groups;

- Twenty to thirty members, students who regularly participate in weekly meetings and the numerous events sponsored by the SKS on campus;

- Hundreds of participants—students, faculty, staff, and the general public who attend SKS-sponsored events.

The students who participate in the SKS student organizations tend to be representative of the university population as a whole, although there are often more freshmen and seniors in the groups. (Freshmen are usually excited about exploring the opportunities of college and see the SKS as a gateway to transformative experience; seniors feel the pressure of looming graduation and use the SKS to prepare themselves for life beyond their academic careers.) Male and female students participate in roughly equal numbers. The student groups display a significant degree of diversity, both in race and religious background. Students who identify themselves as coming from a variety of religious backgrounds, as well as those who profess no religious affiliation, all commonly participate. No demographic pattern can be discerned in participants' major area of study: liberal arts, science, engineering, and preprofessional training are all evenly represented. Social sectors are also varied: future farmers rub elbows with future MBAs regularly.

While the total number of student participants is modest, the intensity of participation is remarkable. Officers can spend as much as 15 to 20 hours per week working with the SKS; student participants often put in eight hours or more a week in SKS classes and activities. It is possible, but not typical, to participate in the SKS casually. Students who participate regularly tend to take it very seriously and feel a strong degree of commitment to the organization and its goals.

The student organizations collaborate extensively with each other. The groups at Duke University in Durham, the University of North Carolina at

Chapel Hill, and North Carolina State University in Raleigh all routinely mix, both organizationally and socially. The organizations coordinate event schedules and pool budgets to sponsor Triangle-wide event series. The schools have sports days, picnics, paintball tournaments, and parties that pull students from all three campuses. Some diehard students, not content with a single SKS meeting a week, attend regular meetings at other campuses as well as at their own. Sometimes the groups even share housing; it is quite common for SKS students to band together in their own informal "SKS Houses" both on- and off-campus, and occasionally students will even make the half-hour commute to another city in order to live with their SKS peers. The student groups also collaborate extensively in the production of *The Symposium*, an entirely student-run, student-edited spiritual journal with a subscription base of over 3,000.

The student groups are all officially recognized by their respective universities and apply to the schools for operating funds and the use of facilities, just like any other student organization. The majority of the student groups' funds are internally generated by the students themselves, through weekly donations at meetings and occasional fund-raising efforts. The student groups are expected to be completely self-sufficient and receive little or no outside funding from the SKS Foundation.

The SKS originally focused its efforts entirely on-campus, and it still considers the university community to be its primary constituency. However, over time it became apparent that many people outside the university community were equally interested in SKS-style spiritual exploration. Recent college graduates, especially those who participated in the SKS during their undergraduate years, were eager to have a context in which to continue their personal growth. Other adults who had contact through the SKS within the campus community—faculty, staff, and continuing education students—were eager to participate in the SKS model but preferred to work with peers rather than participate directly with the student groups.

The SKS eventually started a "graduate" group that let students continue participating in the SKS community after they finished school, and occasionally the SKS forms other nonstudent groups to pursue specific interests. The organization of these groups is similar to that of the student groups—facilitators and officers running regular meetings for a body of members—but the "graduates" tend to be even more intensely personal and involved in the community than their student peers. "Graduate" group members also act as mentors and guides for the student groups.

Some significant aspects of the community that are essential to its success should be pointed out. First, the SKS community achieves religious pluralism and demographic diversity organically, without making it an explicit goal of the organization. Because the SKS approach focuses on universal aspects of spiritual transformation, it naturally transcends boundaries between differing religious, ethnic, and socioeconomic groups.

This philosophy resonates well with students today who have grown up in a more integrated society and who want a way to talk about religious experience without having to drag along the divisions and boundaries of previous generations. More importantly, it gives diversity room to exist without drawing attention to itself. It is possible, at times, to be so overly focused on being respectful of diversity that we are distracted from the real message we had to give in the first place.

Second, the SKS provides a series of concentric layers in its organization that allows people of differing levels of commitment and intensity to participate at any level with which they are comfortable. This "onion-skin" model is important for any kind of organization that wishes to both attract and sustain the interest of students. If an organization focuses exclusively on "entry-level" topics and never provides deeper content, the membership quickly loses interest and moves on to other venues.

On the other hand, if an organization caters to its veterans with advanced content and does not make itself accessible to newcomers, it fails to bring new blood into the organization and eventually stagnates. The SKS maintains a lasting community by hosting events with engaging themes in accessible venues but also by providing semester-long classes, community living, intensive retreats, and other means of greater involvement.

Third, the SKS combines a transient community with a permanent community. Similar in structure to the mixture of faculty and students at a university, the SKS has a relatively permanent community of facilitators and volunteers who work with a transient community of undergraduate and graduate students. This structure is important for both students and teachers. It is important for new students to get a sense of permanence and continuity in the community. In this way, they are reassured that they are participating in a community with structure and depth. By working with "graduates" who have gone through the process themselves, they get a sense of what is in store for them in the coming years. Likewise, teachers are challenged to continue their own personal transformation by continually working with new students. Teaching, especially in the context of spiritual seeking, is one of the most humbling undertakings a human being can undertake. Most SKS facilitators report that running the SKS meetings is far more difficult than simply participating in meetings. In the SKS approach, mentoring and teaching are a natural "next step" in one's own spiritual development and transformation.

CONTINUING CHALLENGE

While fostering transformation in its participants, the Self Knowledge Symposium is itself undergoing a transformation over time. What started as a simple extracurricular discussion group has gradually evolved into a full experiential curriculum that manifests in all aspects of university life. The SKS is even tentatively stepping into the academic classroom itself. Most of the challenges that the Self Knowledge Symposium faces involve explicitly integrating spiritual development into established public institutions. The separation of church and state is a very real boundary that must be carefully respected. The boundary between character development and remedial psychotherapy is equally fraught with danger—anyone who wants to facilitate spiritual growth on campus has to understand the difference between compassionate mentoring and practicing psychology without a license. Still, we are heartened by the results of the last eleven years. It is increasingly apparent that it is possible to foster deep personal transformation in a college setting filled with religious diversity, that professors can be mentors as well as teachers, and that students and professors alike can recognize how Spirit infuses the college experience.

ENDNOTES

1. A "house course" is a for-credit class at Duke University that is designed and taught by the students themselves, with the syllabus approved by faculty members.
2. Andrés Niño, "Spiritual Quest Among Young Adults," in *Education as Transformation: Religious Pluralism, Spirituality, and a New Vision for Higher Education in America,* ed. Victor H. Kazanjian, Jr., and Peter L. Laurence (New York: Peter Lang, 2000).
3. William H. Willimon, "Religious Faith and the Development of Character on Campus." *Educational Record* (Summer/Fall 1997): 73–79.
4. Patrick Love and Donna Talbot, "Defining Spiritual Development: A Missing Consideration for Student Affairs." *NASPA Journal,* 37, no. 1 (Fall 1999): 361–375.

5. Niño, "Spiritual Quest."
6. Willimon, "Religious Faith."
7. Susan M. Awbrey and David K. Scott, "Knowledge into Wisdom: Constructing a Wise University." Unpublished manuscript. University of Massachusetts Amherst.
8. Turak's company, Raleigh Group International, merged with Israeli-based MuTek Solutions, Ltd. in April 2000 to form an international pre-IPO corporation valued at well over $100 million. Turak remains the CEO of MuTek Solutions, Inc., the U.S. subsidiary of the corporation.
9. Alan Watts, *The Way of Zen* (New York: Pantheon Press, 1957).
10. Richard Rose, *The Psychology of the Observer* (Columbus: The Pyramid Press, 1979).
11. John Kent, "Richard Rose's Psychology of the Observer: The Path to Reality Through the Self" (San Diego: Ph.D. dissertation, The University for Humanistic Studies, 1990).
12. August Turak, "Five Years with a Zen Master: A Businessman's Story of Life with an American Zen Master," RealAudio recording available at http://www.selfknowledge.org/ (Raleigh: The Self Knowledge Symposium Foundation, 1998).
13. Lou Mobley and Kate McKeown, *Beyond IBM* (New York: McGraw-Hill, 1989), 25–27.
14. Turak, "Five Years with a Zen Master."
15. Love and Talbot, "Defining Spiritual Development."
16. Niño, "Spiritual Quest."
17. Willimon, "Religious Faith."
18. Victor H. Kazanjian, Jr., and the students of the Multi-Faith Council, "From Mono-religious to Multi-religious Life at Wellesley College," *Education as Transformation: Religious Pluralism, Spirituality, and a New Vision for Higher Education in America,* ed. Victor H. Kazanjian, Jr., and Peter L. Laurence (New York: Peter Lang, 2000).
19. Diana Eck, "Challenge of Pluralism," *Nieman Reports* (Boston: The Nieman Foundation, 1993).
20. David K. Scott, "Spirituality in an Integrative Age," *Education as Transformation: Religious Pluralism, Spirituality, and a New Vision for Higher Education in America,* ed. Victor H. Kazanjian, Jr., and Peter L. Laurence (New York: Peter Lang, 2000).
21. Ibid.
22. Aldous Huxley, *The Perennial Philosophy* (New York: Harper & Brothers, 1945).
23. Joseph Campbell, *The Masks of God* (New York: Viking Press, 1959).
24. Huston Smith, *The World's Religions* (San Francisco: Harper, 1991).
25. Ken Wilber, *The Spectrum of Consciousness* (Wheaton, Illinois: Theosophical Publishing House, 1977).

26. Summarized from the Self Knowledge Symposium Frequently Asked Questions list, 1996. The philosophy guiding the SKS derives primarily from August Turak's description of the essential aspects of Richard Rose's Zen teaching.

7. Looking at Diversity through the Lens of Religion and Spirituality: The Manhattanville Experience

MARGARET L. CAUSEY, RSCJ, AND
RICHARD A. BERMAN

From *U.S. News and World Report* to the Templeton Foundation guide to "Colleges that Encourage Character Development,"[1] diversity among the faculty and student body has become an important criterion for ranking colleges and universities, and dealing effectively with diversity has become the subject of ongoing internal debates among college administration, faculty, and staff members. Some parents and prospective students are looking for colleges that cater to their individual, specific needs in a broad range of activities and academic programs, and for colleges that offer a community of students, faculty, and staff members from diverse cultural, economic, geographic, and educational backgrounds. But a closer look at the statistics from many colleges indicates that the "diversity" described in the brochures and around which programs are designed pertains to cultural, geographic, and ethnic diversity, and to a lesser extent, economic diversity. What is often ignored in the statistics, as well as in the programming, is the enormous impact of religious and spiritual diversity on the campus culture.

Most colleges invest money and staff in multicultural centers and programs, and offer minors, if not majors, in areas such as African American, Latino, and Asian Studies. Interdisciplinary courses allow students to compare and contrast various cultures, while lecture series and teach-ins provide exposure to and dialogue on many of the critical issues that face students across ethnic and cultural lines. At the same time most colleges—whether religious or secular—provide some type of campus ministry office to assist students in their religious practices and search for spiritual wholeness, and many colleges offer courses in religious studies, religious practices, and spirituality.

Few colleges are considering diversity as the intertwining of religious, spiritual, cultural, ethnic, geographical, and economic aspects of individual students and their communities. Most administrative divisions within colleges still operate somewhat autonomously, dealing with diversity issues that directly affect their areas. The integration of multicultural centers, campus ministry programs, and the academic courses that address diversity issues with campuswide discussions on diversity concerns is the exception rather than the norm.

The reasons for this are as numerous as they are complex. For colleges with a defined religious tradition, encouraging open dialogue on religious diversity is awkward at best. For secular institutions, there is an inevitable tension between "being secular" and "fostering religion" and designing programs and centers that directly address religious diversity beyond the traditional boundaries of offering denominational services. For others, such as Manhattanville College, which began as religious institutions and are now secular, the challenge is to recover, in a new context, the spiritual values of their own foundations while ensuring that all religions and spiritual traditions are equally respected and provided for on campus. And as one Manhattanville alumnus recently commented, "Everyone from the alumni to the faculty to the students to the local community has strong opinions on what it means to 'recover' a religious tradition in a 'new context'." If ethnic and cultural diversity bring out strong opinions, religious and spiritual diversity bring out even stronger, emotional opinions. When all of the possible components of diversity are thrown together in the discussion and planning around the issue, the possibilities for conflict are endless and the reasons for not doing it are obvious. However, the real opportunities for learning to live in an interconnected world are lost.

What cannot be ignored is that almost all cultural and ethnic diversity is laden with religious and spiritual overtones and underpinnings. For example, those who claim their Irish heritage are rarely just "Irish," but they identify themselves as "Irish Catholic" or "Protestant." Israelis often distinguish themselves as "ethnically Jewish" or "religiously Jewish." Many people of Arab descent align themselves with Islamic beliefs; some do not.

Many of these religious backgrounds can unite people across social and cultural divides. However, others may be divisive.[2] Only a brief look at history reveals the number of wars fought in the name of religion, and our contemporary world is rife with examples of ethnic conflicts with deep underlying religious roots. Today colleges host students from around the world as well as from the United States who bring with them not only the cultural, ethnic, and religious struggles embedded in their histories, but often a rebellion against organized religious institutions as institutions, as well as their own ideas about dealing with the past while moving on to the future. These same students indicate a real desire for deepening the spiritual side of their lives as part of their self-exploration.

Addressing religious and spiritual diversity is complicated by the fact that "religious pluralism," the rubric under which religious and spiritual diversity is usually discussed, is hard to define. "Religious" is too often used to refer to those within organized institutional religions, but probably more important for college students is the quest for meaning, purpose, and identity.[3] "Pluralism" is often used in this context to suggest some form of equal respect for all views, but often excludes open dialogue that "involves not only hearing 'the other' in the other's terms and interpretative framework, but also requires at least the openness to self-definition."[4]

Too often when religious pluralism is discussed, it is done with little or no reference to the cultural, national, and ethnic diversity that underpin and shape many of the religious issues.[5] For religious pluralism to be more than just a concept of mutual respect, a community must be challenged to enter into the world of the religious experiences of others with an openness to "feeling" the experiences and to learning with both the heart and the head. This learning can come both from formal lectures on the spirituality and beliefs of institutionalized religions and from hearing how the intertwining of religion, culture, and ethnicity are evident in the religious experiences of others. Thus, programs and discussions focused on religious pluralism can become the means of transformation and self-definition of one's own religious experience, rather than just an intellectual exercise in understanding and accepting the experience of others. As the civil rights and women's movements have taught us, changes made on the intellectual and legal levels do not guarantee changes in attitudes and acceptance, nor do they lead to the celebration of the differences that mark our equality. The emphasis on hearing with an openness to transformation is essential for helping people to reach the deeper levels of understanding where attitudes and behaviors are most affected.

Equally problematic is deciding who on campus should be responsible for addressing religious diversity beyond providing basic services and spirituality resources within denominational structures. There are few good models on how religious, cultural, ethnic, and economic diversity can be addressed as an integrated whole, let alone models for integrating academic components with student life components on the college campus.

While we do not claim that Manhattanville College is a model of "how to," we are confronting the issues and problems as well as the questions directly. We have taken a comprehensive approach to addressing religious and spiritual diversity in the context of the broader diversity that characterizes the college. Our successes, while modest, are notable, and, hopefully, our problems are instructive.

According to *U.S. News and World Report*, Manhattanville ranks sixth in campus diversity for East Coast liberal arts colleges and twenty-second nationally.[6] The Manhattanville community includes students from forty countries and over thirty-five states. We have some of the richest students in the world and some who are poor. We have students who are academically well prepared (SAT scores over 1,500) and students who are not as well prepared (SAT scores under 1,000). Twelve percent of our students are international. American students of color comprise 28 percent of our student community, with 15 percent Hispanic, 9 percent African American, and 4 percent Asian. Men comprise 66 percent of our population; women, 34 percent. Our undergraduates range in age from 17 to 50 years of age and indicate a variety of sexual preferences. Religiously, Manhattanville students identify themselves predominantly as Catholic, but there are growing numbers of Jewish, Muslim, and Protestant students who participate actively in religious and multicultural clubs and programming. The differences among the Catholic students in terms of their relationship to the institutional church and their personal spirituality is probably as great as the differences between the Jewish and Muslim students. Some students no longer claim a religious denomination, while professing to be strongly religious.[7] Some of our Jewish students are more cultural than religious; others consider themselves spiritual Jews with no attachment to a particular tradition within Judaism; others are active in the Conservative or Orthodox traditions. Some of our Palestinian students are Muslims; others are Christian but closely allied politically with the Palestinian cause and thus are active in the Muslim Student Association. In short, no set of statistics can accurately describe our diversity because the diversity crosses religious as well as ethnic and cultural lines.

What underlies our comprehensive approach to diversity is both the nature of our student body and the mission of the college to educate students to social and ethical responsibility in a global community. We are committed to doing this by ensuring three things: (a) the full intellectual, ethical, and social development of each student within a community of engaged scholars and teachers; (b) the application of students' development as independent leaders and creative thinkers to their career and professional goals; and (c) a diverse campus community whose members know, care about, and support each other and actively engage the world beyond. Our common understanding of religious pluralism flows from these values and reflects the values of the college from its beginning as a Catholic institution committed to social justice, to its present secular status and continued emphasis on justice and social responsibility. Religious pluralism at Manhattanville includes all students of all denominations and spiritual persuasions as well as those who are in search of meaning in life without specific denominational attachments. Pluralism does not just mean tolerance, acceptance, and respect, but it also means pursuing the open dialogues that involve faculty, staff members, and students in hearing the other in the other's terms and interpretative framework.

Dimensions of Pluralism: The "Six I's"

We design our programs and measure our success in terms of the "Six I's": Inclusive, Integrated, Interactional, Introspective, Intellectually Sound, and Instilled in the college's culture. These six criteria were developed to facilitate the integration of the intellectual and experiential dimensions in all of our programming on campus. They have proven effective in helping us provide comprehensive and multidimensional programs that reach beyond the walls of Manhattanville and create opportunities for personal as well as institutional transformation.

Inclusive
Inclusiveness is a popular buzzword that can have many meanings on many levels. At Manhattanville all programs, clubs, events, lectures, etc., must be open to *all* administrators, faculty, staff, and students. However, this is on the first level of inclusiveness and does not guarantee that a broad spectrum of the college community participates in most activities. The greater challenge is to attract diverse representation through involvement of a cross section of constituencies in the planning and implementation processes. On a deeper level, inclusiveness means providing opportunities for the dialogues that truly bring all the students, faculty, and staff members together in a way that each is challenged by the interpretative framework of the other. This means going beyond lectures, teach-ins, and information sessions to small group interactions that provide multiple opportunities for

students to explore their own views and be changed by the views of others. This is not just an issue or set of programs for students—it must include the entire community: students, administrators, staff and faculty members, etc.

There is no better example of the integration of religious and spiritual diversity with ethnic, cultural, and economic diversity than the present situation in the Middle East, with its range of conflicting opinions and feelings experienced by those with a stake in the peace process. There is no general agreement as to where religion and national politics should be separated or linked in this dispute, but there is agreement that the passions generated on the subject stem not just from political issues, but from deep underlying religious and cultural disputes that span the histories of the varying ethnic and religious groups who are fighting for homelands in the same area. If the complexity of the views as well as the depth of the passions involved are covered with facile attempts to avoid conflict among students and faculty, real inclusiveness is lost.

A teach-in on the Middle East crisis such as was recently held at Manhattanville can be labeled "inclusive" since everyone in the community was invited to participate, and opposing viewpoints were included in the presentations. However, this inclusiveness would have remained shallow had there not been time for all sides to respond, question, challenge, and explore their own underlying assumptions on the issues presented. This is the difficult as well as the risky part. Faculty members can be viewed as being pitted against other faculty members and students against students if discussions become heated. The key to avoiding open conflict that is destructive rather than constructive is in the planning and implementation process of managed conflict and conflict resolution.

Integrated

Programs, lectures, and other events that are intended to be inclusive on all levels must be planned and implemented through an integrated process involving a cross-section of student organizations and academic departments with full administrative support. This process must truly be integrated—not isolated to the academic departments, one club, or one office, and not a parallel series of efforts (e.g., one in the academic area and one in the student affairs area). Too often events and lectures on college campuses are planned by solitary groups who want to "educate" the community about their point of view. The result is usually attendance by those who agree with this point of view and the speakers end up "preaching to the choir." Subsequent discussions tend to reinforce rather than challenge the interpretative framework of those in attendance. The few dissenting voices who attend the event then become the "outsiders" or rebels to be silenced or changed.

If the Muslim Student Association (MSA) at Manhattanville, the group that proposed the teach-in on the Middle East crisis with an emphasis on the Palestinian perspective, had acted alone, it might have ended up with a few speakers addressing a like-minded audience. However, the MSA is part of the multicultural advisory board, which includes all religious and multicultural clubs. Events such as this are not planned in isolation, but in collaboration with Manhattanville's social justice centers and partners. In addition to the multicultural center, the college's Duchesne Center for Religion and Social Justice and its Connie Hogarth Center for Social Action work on projects such as the Middle East teach-in with community organizations such as the Westchester Holocaust Commission, which is housed on the Manhattanville campus.

In the MSA are four Palestinian students, all members of Seeds of Peace, all friends of one of the students killed on the West Bank in Israel in the week prior to the scheduled teach-in. From the beginning there was recognition that the issues were not simply Muslim or multicultural, but reached into political spheres, as well as national and religious conflicts that spanned Christianity, Judaism, and Islam and touched at the core of America's human rights policies.

The multicultural board, working with students and staff members from the Duchesne Center, Connie Hogarth Center, Holocaust Commission, and three academic departments, spent long hours, often late into the night, debating the issues and determining how to plan and implement a teach-in that was inclusive, but that also honored the passions and emotions of the Palestinian students who had lost a close friend in the conflict, and who felt the Palestinian side was not getting equal coverage in the American press. While the final teach-in could be considered a model of a well-balanced, integrated, and inclusive event with a broad spectrum of the administration, staff, faculty, and students participating on the panel and in attendance, the real inclusiveness and integration came in the planning process. It was the late night meetings of Muslim, Jewish, and Christian students with faculty and staff members where the real "hearing" took place with a subsequent change in attitudes and perspectives. The involvement of the administration in the planning process, from the president on down, signaled to students that the process, not just the product, was important. It was the cross-section of involvement by faculty members, administration, student clubs, and religious groups that drew a very diverse audience with divergent and conflicting views to an open and honest dialogue on the issues—a dialogue that continued in smaller groups and classes. At the end all embraced a consensus to stop the bloodshed and agreed on the importance of working together for peace.

Interactive

It goes without saying that any process through which students as well as faculty and staff members are challenged to examine their own perspectives and be touched and changed by the perspectives of others will inevitably involve the whole person—mind, heart, and soul. A teach-in that involved a review of the facts and issues would have touched the mind, but not the heart and soul. A teach-in exposing only the killing and destruction without the facts and issues would have touched the heart and emotions, but would have left the mind with its old prejudices and perspectives. A teach-in exposing the killing and the issues without examining the role of religion and religious sentiments as integral to the killing and issues would have distorted the reality of the situation.

Yet, it is much easier and safer to narrow our focus and isolate our efforts in hopes of avoiding conflict that we cannot control. Allowing open debate and dialogue that challenges all in the college community to examine their positions and views as well as their feelings and emotional commitments is risky. We are comfortable with academic debates and conflicts; we are much less comfortable when these debates become personal and involve people's emotional commitments to positions and perspectives.

The risks as well as the rewards become greater when we invite the community beyond the walls of our institutions to join us in our search for religious pluralism that is interactive, integrated, and inclusive. Beyond the walls of all of our institutions are those who have lived the issues and know better than we the deep meaning of the intertwining of religious with cultural and ethnic diversity. Their stories as well as their perspectives can provide a challenge and balance not found within the limited confines of our institutions.

At the same time, many in our local communities are hungry for the types of programs such as our teach-in on the Middle East that promote balanced presentations with open dialogue and debate without the media hype. The risk is that we will expose our internal conflicts and opinions held on campus that may not reflect the thinking of the campus as a whole, but are perceived externally as the college's position on an issue. In the case of our Middle East teach-in, this risk became a reality when the local press reported our teach-in as a "pro-Palestinian" response to the "pro-Israeli" march the day before in New York City. Nothing could have been further from the truth. But the rewards outweigh the risks when college events and programs are consistently offered to, and advertised in, the local community, and the college gains a reputation for tackling hard issues from multiple perspectives. To be truly effective, these programs must involve the mind, the hands, the heart, the soul, and the greater community.

Intellectually Sound

The best defense against a false or distorted interpretation of controversial programs, courses, and events, especially those that deal with religious, cultural, and ethnic issues, is to insure that the content is substantive and based on documented research. This involves having the faculty cross the line from academics into student affairs to spend time not just giving presentations to large groups, but being with students in the planning process and in small discussion groups. With faculty members feeling more and more burdened with increased class loads and publishing demands, securing this commitment is not always easy.

One way Manhattanville has bridged the gap between academic affairs and student affairs is through the club structure, which requires a faculty advisor for all clubs. In the case of the Middle East teach-in, a member of the African Studies Department, two members of the Department of World Religions, and the campus rabbi were all involved from the beginning because of their advisory positions to the clubs and individual students who initiated the teach-in. Their expertise was called on for the panel at the teach-in, but their presence and input at the planning sessions and behind-the-scenes dialogues provided an academic dimension to all of the discussions and planning, not just the final event. The content must be substantive, sound, idealistic but realistic, and built around mutual respect for every individual.

Introspective

What is often lost in our quest as academic institutions to maintain intellectual integrity is an emphasis on the introspective dimension of the learning process—the personal reflection that allows us to enter into another's interpretative framework in a way that may require a change in our own self-definition and interpretative framework. When an event such as the Middle East teach-in ends with all pleased that a balanced approach was presented and an honest and open dialogue ensued, it is easy, and often expedient, to move quickly on to the next controversial issue or pressing problem in front of us. But it is at the end of the event that our most important work really begins.

Ongoing discussions in classes and student affairs centers with individuals and groups are needed if students are to begin internalizing what they have learned and figuring out what their role should and can be in the crisis. One key to success is that these discussions not take place in single interest groups, but that the cross-cultural and religious dialogue modeled in the community event be the norm for ongoing campus dialogue. Another is the opportunity through journaling, e-mail, or one-to-one conferences for students, faculty, and staff members to explore their intellectual conclusions as well as their emotional reactions with others in the community. It is also important for people to take time alone to reflect on their journal or notes.

Instilled

It is somewhat easy to isolate an event such as the teach-in on the Middle East to show how a comprehensive approach can work. It is harder to show how a college can make such an approach a part of the college's culture, the norm for how all programming is designed and implemented. But if the mission of the college is to educate students for social and ethical responsibility, the commitment to cross-campus planning, processing, and education is essential. This commitment is complicated by four factors present at Manhattanville and, we believe, at most colleges.

The first is that academic freedom and individuality are considered by the faculty to be untouchable icons that cannot be treaded upon without dire consequences. Especially on controversial subjects, faculty members want the freedom to present their views and positions without undue restrictions; participating in time-consuming planning processes with students is often not a priority. When they do get involved in lively debates or dialogue, there is no guarantee that what will be modeled is a civil discussion with both sides open to the interpretative framework of the other.

The second is that, while the many divisions and departments within colleges generally agree that they all must work together on programming and planning, there is an unspoken pecking order that puts the faculty in a superior position to student affairs staff and administration. This subtle hierarchy often results in faculty members ignoring or slighting student affairs programming and digging in their heels when it comes to time away from the classroom for experiential learning and exposure to the "real" world.

Many faculty members view their jobs through an intellectual lens, leaving the education of the heart and soul to others.

The third is that the mention of religion and spirituality evokes red flags that are not present in even the most controversial of other diversity issues. The faculty, staff, and alumni, especially of colleges with a religious identity or those with a historical religious identity, tend to have strong opinions about the boundaries of religious freedom even if they fully believe in academic freedom. Respecting all religions and religious views, learning about the history and traditions of different religions, and exploring forms of spirituality are acceptable. Probing the depths of religious views, the interconnectedness of religion, culture, ethnic identity, and politics, and challenging each other to be changed by this in-depth exploration, is much more problematic.

The fourth is that to instill real religious pluralism and dialogue into the campus culture requires time, staff, and money. It does not just happen, but it needs a process to make it happen, with adequate staff to support the process. But to instill this value in the community, to make it part of the college's culture, requires leadership from the top. The president and board of trustees must constantly model, reinforce, and support this value. It must be part of the mission statement and it must ring true in everyday life on the campus if it is to work effectively during crises or when struggling with issues of great emotion and passion.

With the monetary crunch most colleges experience and the long list of competing priorities for limited resources, a commitment to religious pluralism that openly addresses all forms of diversity can easily remain an enticing advertisement on college brochures and a goal for the future. But for our students, the future is now.

In closing, we would like to rephrase what we have said thus far, this time in the form of questions, questions that we think need to be answered by each of us before we can truly say we are looking at diversity through the lens of religion and spirituality.

1) How are religion and spirituality addressed throughout our college community? This includes asking if our basic mission statements reflect the need for religion and spirituality to be addressed, not just what is being done at the concrete level.

2) What changes are needed to build a bridge between the academic, student life, and administrative areas of the college that will allow

for the integration of religious and spirituality issues throughout the entire community?

3) How can this change be guided so that a unified foundation can be built with minimal "digging in" by distinct factions, departments, or constituents?

4) How can this change be managed, encouraged, and prioritized with the inevitable competition for limited resources and no one department or group feeling sole ownership of this area?

5) How can we "educate" the entire college community, not just the students, on the need to integrate experiential and academic programs that touch all dimensions of students' lives—academic, social, and spiritual?

There is no better way to focus on helping individuals to reach their own potential and to recognize the beauty of their individuality than to look at diversity through the lens of religion and spirituality. For most students, the four years at college are a period of vital development for the body, mind, and heart. As educators and administrators, we have a responsibility and an opportunity to truly make a difference. To not help our students find themselves—their spirit, their heart, their passion—and enjoy a better world would be a real tragedy—an opportunity lost, a trust violated.

Any success we might have had or will have at Manhattanville is because:

*   together, we dare to dream;
*   together, we dare to pioneer;
*   together, we dare to push ourselves beyond our individual traditions; and
*   together, we dare to embrace our ever-changing and exhilarating new world!

ENDNOTES

1. John Templeton Foundation, *The Templeton Guide: Colleges that Encourage Character Development.* (n.p.: Templeton Foundation Press, 1999).
2. Darren E. Sherkat, "Tracking the 'Other': Dynamics and Composition of 'Other' Religions in the General Social Survey," *Journal for the Scientific Study of Religion* 38 (December 1999): 551–553.

3. Ronald Massanri, "The Pluralisms of American 'Religion Pluralism'," *Journal of Church and State* 40 (Summer 1998): 590. See also, Robert N. Bellah, "At Home and Not at Home: Religious Pluralism and Religious Truth," *Christian Century* 112 (April 19, 1995): 423–428.

4. John W. Healey, "From Diversity to Pluralism: The Roman Catholic Challenge and the Roman Catholic Opportunity," in *Education as Transformation: Religious Pluralism, Spirituality, and a New Vision for Higher Education in America*, ed. Victor H. Kazanjian, Jr., and Peter L. Laurence (New York: Peter Lang, 2000), 129.

5. For a rare example of an integrated discussion, see Sam Portaro, "Whence Pluralism, Whither Denominationalism?," *Cross Currents* 50 (Spring/Summer 2000): 203–211.

6. U.S. News and World Report Online, "2001 Campus Diversity Rankings—National Liberal Arts," usnews.com/usnews/edu/college/rankings/natl_div.htm.

7. For this phenomenon in the broader population see, Kosuke Koyama, "A Theological Reflection on Religious Pluralism," *Ecumenical Review* 51 (April 1999): 160–171, and Tom Beaudoin, "Irreverently Yours: A Message from Generation X," *U.S. Catholic* (April 1999): 10–15.

8. *Dancing on the Edge*

Leon Tilson Burrows

> *Religion is danced out before it is thought out.*
> —R.R. Marrett, anthropologist

Protestant worship at Smith College's Helen Hills Hills Chapel is experiencing a renewal of interest by students that has led to a significant increase in attendance at chapel. Protestant chapel life at the present time, however, is not a repetition of previous eras at Smith College. Students who attend and are actively involved in chapel desire a Protestant community that honors and is open to religious, ethnic, and cultural diversity and one that welcomes persons of different sexual orientations. This chapter will address how the spiritual consciousness and mission of the Smith College Protestant chapel, in the new millennium, has been influenced by, and is reflective of, the gains achieved through social activism among various minority groups in America over the last forty or more years.

The civil rights, feminist, and lesbian, gay, bisexual, and transgender movements have opened doors for a current generation of students to explore ways of being a religious community that were impossible for former generations. Reflecting on my role as chaplain to Smith College and Protestant religious advisor to students, I will also address how embracing spirituality has been integral to exploring ways of blending many styles of Protestant worship into a cohesive and distinct religious expression for the Smith College Protestant community. All of these factors contribute to a community that is experiencing a renewal, a community that is learning a new dance.

As a community, we are in the process of learning a new dance with the Divine, God, Spirit of the Universe, and with each other. The Protestant chapel community at Smith College was named "The Ecumenical Christian Church" in 1978 to acknowledge the many Protestant denominations that the chapel is challenged to serve. The Ecumenical Christian Church is the weekly Smith College Protestant chapel worship that takes place during the academic semesters in the Helen Hills Hills Chapel. Smith College, located in Northampton, Massachusetts, is one of the Seven Sisters Colleges and the largest women's liberal arts college in America. Religion has played a prominent role and held a significant place at Smith College since its founding in 1875. "Sophia Smith would direct in her will that the Bible should be read in the College and that the principles of Evangelical Christian Religion (her model for which was New England Congregationalism) should pervade its teaching and discipline."[1] Today, in addition to the Ecumenical Christian Church Protestant community, a vital and significant inter-religious presence is created by a multitude of religious organizations that are active on Smith's campus. Religious and spiritual life is not limited to or dominated by any one particular religious, sectarian, or denominational perspective.

Students attending Smith College are offered a wealth of religious traditions in which to affirm and/or discover a religious faith or spirituality. Religious and spiritual life at Smith has evolved to reflect the increasingly diverse student constituency. Organizations with an active student participation include Muslim, Jewish, Bahá'í, Buddhist, Hindu, Eastern Orthodox, Roman Catholic, Quaker, Unitarian-Universalist, and Society of Pagans (those embracing feminine goddess, nature, or earth-based spirituality). There is also wide representation from diverse Protestant religious communities such as an Episcopal/Lutheran fellowship and several conservative Christian fellowships. In that light, the thoughts and beliefs that are expressed here are not meant to delineate a norm for spirituality and college worship, but to share an approach to Protestant worship that is evolving at Smith College.

As a community our challenge has been to learn to lift up our arms to the Divine while also stretching outward to recognize, accept, and respect human diversity. Embracing a communal posture of respect and civility is a challenge to learn a new dance—a dance not only with God, the Sacred, the Spirit, the Numinous but also one that risks dancing with those who are not always compatible dance partners.[2] At an institution such as Smith College, with the presence of great religious diversity even among those who identify themselves as Protestant, the Protestant chapel has been challenged to think outside of traditional denominational models.

Much of what defines the new character of the Smith Protestant chapel community is due to students' initiative in planning and facilitating chapel worship. Another aspect that has contributed to the renewal of interest among students is the strong collaborative relationship between students and the chaplain. Students advocated for the Protestant chapel community to be open and welcoming to those of different sexual orientations, and so we have joyfully affirmed this commitment. Students requested that the chapel be more diverse in our music, so we now have music from the African American gospel genre each Sunday in our worship, as one means of embracing this diversity. The students' mission statement states:

> The Ecumenical Christian Church, or ECC, is an open and affirming community at Smith College that worships in the Protestant tradition and is open to all. We welcome and respect people of all races, sexual orientations, genders, and creeds. We seek to provide a safe atmosphere for studying, exploring, questioning, and sharing our faith through prayer, hugs, conversations, and chocolate chip cookies.

The Ecumenical Christian Church at Smith seeks to make worship at Helen Hills Hills Chapel a community gathered in a spirit of civility, reconciliation, and cross-cultural sensitivity. The challenge is to gather a community that affirms diversity and seeks ways of celebrating the richness of the Protestant faith. This mission is affirmed each Sunday as a part of the congregation's Confession of Sin. This prayer is used at the beginning of each service of worship to speak to and acknowledge the community's collective shortcomings.

> Creator God, we confess that we have sinned against you and against our sisters and brothers in thought, word and deed. We ask your forgiveness for the sin of judgement, which has hindered the recovery of unity and caused schism in the body of Christ. We ask forgiveness for intellectual pride and isolation, for prejudice and for the sin of thinking we are better than others of different religions, ethnicities, cultures, and those who are of different sexual orientations. Lord have mercy.

This prayer is an adaptation of the traditional prayers of confession used in Protestant denominations such as the Episcopal and Lutheran churches. The purpose of the prayer is to affirm the congregation's mission and focus our minds and hearts on the ideals of justice that are embraced and advocated as a community through empowerment by God's Spirit.

Since the students also come from various religious traditions, their different experiences contribute a breadth of religious perspectives to our worship services. This was exemplified when some of the students of the Ecumenical Christian Church asked to observe the Stations of the Cross on Good Friday. The Stations of the Cross is observed primarily within the Roman Catholic and Episcopal liturgical traditions during Lent, the forty days before Easter, and it traces the last journey of Jesus to the Cross through fourteen final scenes before the crucifixion. Leading this liturgy was a first for me, an ordained Baptist. It was also a revelation for me to witness how students from "non-liturgical" traditions, such as the Baptist Church and the United Church of Christ that historically would not observe this liturgy, were moved to tears.

In contrast, the Protestant chapel community, through student initiation and facilitation, occasionally has revival meeting services in the African American tradition that feature guest preachers and gospel choirs. The chapel has also featured gospel concerts that have turned our quintessential New England meeting style chapel into a rocking, body swaying, hands clapping house of Pentecostal-style praise. These experiences of encountering the Divine in many and varied ways are a movement of the Spirit that encourages unity without assimilation in a singular approach to worship.

Chapel worship takes on many forms, featuring sermons given by a student or a storyteller in the continental African tradition, in addition to those sermons given by the Protestant chaplain. Topical approaches to worship, designed and led by students, are also integral to services at the Ecumenical Christian Church. We have celebrated worship in the African American tradition led by students of the Black Student Alliance, as well as having a chapel service in affirmation of the lesbian, gay, bisexual, and transgender communities. Attempting to reach a diverse community has challenged the students who plan worship with the chaplain to explore ways of acknowledging diverse religious traditions within the Protestant faith.

Another critical aspect that is contributing to the renewal of interest in chapel is the blending of sacred music traditions from various Protestant perspectives. Each Sunday the college organist plays music voluntaries from the masterworks of organ literature and supports congregational singing from a repertoire of traditional European Protestant hymnody. However, hymns are also drawn from a variety of traditions, including African American gospel and contemporary praise chorus styles popular in the Pentecostal and Charismatic traditions.

Music has been provided by a great range of people: from a gospel jazz instrumental ensemble and gospel choirs to European classical music; from the Smith choirs to visiting high school and college concert and gospel choirs; from solo instrumentalists to instrumental ensembles performing with organ. The vocal music offerings have also been diverse, with a faculty member from the music department singing classical works, to a talented voice major singing the popular sacred ballads that are favorites of contemporary

Christian recording artists. While this musical eclecticism gives a breadth to our worship, there is a more significant aspect to our efforts. The diversity of sacred music we celebrate also seeks to address the position of dominance that European classical music has historically occupied within mainline Protestantism. A critical criterion in evaluating music for chapel is that it authentically represent each culture and genre from which it draws.

The Protestant community at Smith College also embraces the use of inclusive language for ritual, scripture, and prayers. Inclusive language is an outgrowth of the feminist movement. Elisabeth Moltmann-Wendel speaks of how the "contemporary women's movement, [and] feminism...seeks to analyze and change the psychological, social, economic and cultural situation of women."[3] She contrasts the contemporary women's movement to the women's movement at the turn of the twentieth century that was concerned mainly with equal rights and integrating women into a patriarchal society. Moltmann argues that the contemporary feminist movement is concerned about "the self-determination of women and changing of values in a patriarchal society." The feminist movement had a strong impact on theological education in the 1970s, and, with the genesis of inclusive language, continues to advocate for a reformation of ritual language within Judeo-Christian corporate worship. Hardesty poignantly describes the problem of traditional language:

> The water torture begins. Like an incessant dripping on the head, the words come: *man, men, he, his, him, father, son, brethren, brotherhood....* "Christ died for all men" and "God in Christ became man" [in contrast to human].[4]

Patriarchal language traditionally existed in the Hebrew and Christian scriptures and the traditional liturgical language used in corporate worship. The intent of inclusive language is for women to hear themselves included proactively in scripture, prayers, and the text of hymns. Women's fight to be directly addressed and acknowledged responds to the historic reality of women always being alluded to by male pronouns that were assumed to collectively speak to, and for, women. It has been of critical importance that chapel at Smith, a college for women, uses language that is sensitive and affirms the dignity and equality of women.

Another facet of inclusive spirituality for the Ecumenical Christian Church is that it is a community open to and affirming of lesbian, gay, bisexual, and transgender people. A service of affirmation is organized and led by students and allies of the lesbian, gay, bisexual, and transgender communities. A teach-in on homosexuality and Christianity follows, with dialogue among theologians and guest clergy. It is in our commitment to being an inclusive community, however, that the mission of the Ecumenical Christian Church can be deemed "exclusive."

Some students have expressed their view that homosexuality is a sin, and they state that they cannot feel comfortable worshipping within a community that affirms people of different sexual orientations. This polarization of views was illuminated when the Ecumenical Christian Church extended an invitation to the conservative Christian student organizations on campus to lead worship one Sunday. It was a noble effort, an attempt to be an inclusive Protestant chapel open to all people. We discovered, however, that for a conservative Christian group to be authentic in its beliefs compromised the authenticity of the beliefs and mission of the Ecumenical Christian Church. The effort did, however, bring about the opportunity for dialogue and a sense of acceptance that one religious community cannot be all things to all people.

Our efforts to create musical eclecticism have also been only partially successful. The introduction of diverse musical styles has energized the worship experience, especially for those who come from European mainline traditions that adhere to a more quiet, introspective, and reflective approach to worship. Our attempt at meeting the worship needs of some African American students remains compromised. Many African American students have expressed that the worship remains too dominated by a European aesthetic without incorporating more fully their cultural religious traditions.

As one who has experienced the emotionally charged energy of many African American worship traditions, I can empathize with this perspective. The addition of some music from African American traditions cannot substitute for the totality of an authentic experience. Thus, I have grown to accept that attempts at being inclusive cannot necessarily be comprehensively successful among the diverse ethnic and cultural Protestant student population at Smith. A critical aspect of diversity is the resolve to accept that sometimes there will be irreconcilable issues and differences in a community. As we continue to be reminded, within the mission of openness of the Ecumenical Christian Church, dealing with the issues and complexities of culture, religion, and human sexuality often bring us to a place where we must sometimes agree to disagree. This is another moment when we are challenged to respect difference in a spirit of civility.

We understand that some students do not feel comfortable being a part of a religious and spiritual community that is seeking to address the issues of diversity. The dynamics of stretching and pulling, so characteristic of the academy, can propel some students to seek grounding, stability, and comfort in a specific religious tradition that affirms their familial heritage or their religious upbringing. The goal of those who facilitate religious life at Smith is not to proselytize and convert students to any one particular religious ideology. Our mission, rather, is to offer opportunities that can nurture the religious and spiritual lives of students on campus. Thus, the chapel also makes available a listing of churches of various denominations within the local community to encourage students to seek out a religious community where they can be nurtured and feel comfortable.

Smith College's commitment to perpetuating an inter-religious presence on campus challenges all to embrace the highest ideals of learning, that of mutual respect and civility in the midst of a diversity of ideologies. Voices from various traditions are encouraged to sing not necessarily in unison but in harmony, improvisation, and even within the cacophony of atonality. The embrace of spirituality has been critical in broadening my understanding of Judeo-Christian ecumenical worship.

Having a religious foundation in the Judeo-Christian faith as well as a willingness to be open to learning about different religious faith perspectives and how others outside of the Christian faith perspective understand God, the Divine, the Spirit of the Universe, has been an asset to my work. This faith perspective has allowed me to have a nonconfrontational consciousness when interacting with others of various religious and secular worldviews, within the context of the diverse, pluralistic, and secularized environment of a private college. This openness to religious diversity is a contrast to my background and experience as a Baptist minister who had been a pastor before assuming the position of a college chaplain.

I came to embrace a "theology" of spirituality because adherence to a specific religious tradition or organized institutional religious dogma did not comprehensively address my beliefs about God, the Mothering One, Supreme Being, Spirit of the Universe. The richness of diversity within the Judeo-Christian catholic (universal) church, for me, defies the restriction of propagating one set of ritual or rite as definitively "right." My appreciation for religious and spiritual diversity evolved from having been exposed to many religious traditions through my career as a church musician. Before going to seminary to prepare for ordination, I was exposed to a diversity of Christian religious traditions such as Baptist, Lutheran, United Church of Christ, United Methodist, Episcopal, Seventh Day Adventist, Pentecostal as well as Roman Catholic.

As one illustration, I was the organist and music director for a historic affluent suburban mainline Protestant congregation in Connecticut. Each Sunday I would play classical organ works and accompany and direct a choir in choral anthems written by great European and American classical composers. Immediately after the service, I would drive to New Haven to play the organ for a Roman Catholic Mass celebrated by a predominantly African American parish. This service featured Black gospel music in which I would play a Hammond "jazz" organ, leading music accompanied by drums, bongos, guitars, tambourines and enthusiastic hand clapping. These experiences gave me an appreciation for the unique diversity and specificity of religious communities and their distinct subcultures.

Another critical factor related to my embracing spirituality as a vehicle for respecting the plurality of religious belief systems was my seminary training during the mid-1980s. It was an atmosphere of religious diversity, dialogue, and sometimes even contentious debate over issues such as gender-sensitive language and sexual orientation. Daily chapel featured an opportunity for students to experience a variety of religious traditions: the silence of a Quaker Meeting, worship with clown ministry, or worship in the African American tradition.

This background was the beginning of my developing not only a tolerance for, but also an appreciative respect of, the many and often unique ways that one can be ushered into the presence of God, the Sacred, the Spirit, the Numinous. This was the beginning of the challenge to my orthodoxy, a challenge to what I had been brought up to accept as right and appropriate religious belief. Embracing spirituality has allowed me to affirm the validity of Judeo-Christianity for my personal and communal faith perspective while acknowledging that there is more than one path to God. I have grown to recognize and celebrate the many ways in which humans not only seek to name the Divine but to also accept the impossibility of human language fully articulating in totality the reality of God, Mothering One, Supreme Being, Guiding Spirit of the Universe. Spirituality, with its increasing mass appeal in postmodern society, can be characterized as the "People's Religion."[5]

The increasing number of people who embrace and affirm spirituality reveals a gap within organized religion. Spirituality has opened doors for dialogue instead of debate and mutual respect instead of the hegemonic domination of any one religious ideology. Denominational and doctrinal dogmatism inherent within organized religions can be understood as anathema to our postmodern society. Organized religions, historically, have often been apathetic, slow, and even resistant to pursuing equal rights, justice, civility, and mutual respect with regard to issues such as racism and discrimination. Thus, organized religions increasingly find themselves paralyzed and unable to provide a paradigm or theological witness to address the reality of religious and spiritual diversity within the broader context of secular American society and the specific context of higher education.

> The loss of the West's political-military and economic-cultural hegemony has also been accompanied by a jolt to the hegemony of Christianity as the "one true," "beatific," or "absolute" religion: For the first time we are witnessing an encounter between Christianity and other religions on the level of roughly equal rights. This implies a loss of credibility among Christians and secular post Christians when Christianity is still looked upon as the a priori "higher civilization." Instead of this, on the Christian side nowadays people are genuinely prepared to listen and to learn from the other religions.[6]

Our society has reached the place where Christians are affirming the richness of other cultures and world religions. The rigidity and hegemony characteristic of modernity has been challenged by the revolution of deconstruction that is one of the ideals of postmodernity. The phenomenon of spirituality has given us a world that is increasingly populated by Zen-leaning Lutherans, Protestants embracing Buddhist principals, or Jews incorporating Quaker beliefs.[7] It has become commonplace to find people who blend various aspects of faith traditions to create a unique personal faith perspective.

After the two world wars, disillusionment was rampant concerning the ideology of modernity perpetuated by the Enlightenment. Hans Küng, postmodern theologian, observes that, "Modern ideals of the Enlightenment elevated rationalism, science, and technology to a modern secular substitute religion."[8] The sociocultural upheaval surrounding the two world wars ushered in the ideology of postmodernity. The ideology of the Enlightenment and modernity were not the only things to be challenged within postmodernity. The minority liberation movement also evolved from disillusionment with WASP sociocultural hegemony.[9]

The minority liberation movement encompasses people of color, women, the disabled, and members of the lesbian, gay, bisexual, and transgender communities. The movement began with the civil rights movement in the 1950s, spreading to the feminist movement of the 1960s and the Stonewall Revolt in New York City of 1968 that gave birth to the lesbian, gay, bisexual, and transgender liberation movements. The advancements brought about by these revolutions transformed not only American society in general but also the environment of higher education.

Transformations in education are evident through curricula such as Women's, Ethnic, and Lesbian, Gay, Bi-sexual, and Transgender studies (often defined by the community as "Queer Studies"). These revolutions are transforming campuses that were historically and often exclusively male-dominated bastions of sexism, racism, and homophobic discrimination. The minority liberation movement has fought to demand that American society be inclusive so that all might have equal acknowledgment and respect. The victories of the minority liberation movement have challenged institutions of higher education to acknowledge and affirm the diversity in today's students. Conversely, there has been an ideological shift with regard to the presence and role of religion on college campuses.

Many institutions of higher learning that were established to educate students within a Judeo-Christian environment have, in the spirit of modernity and the Enlightenment, separated the secular and sacred. This approach has often relegated religion to the periphery of campus life. Given this bifurcation of the secular and sacred, college chapels, if they still exist, are challenged to remain relevant. Some might even question the necessity or appropriateness of acknowledging the Divine, the Sacred, within the context of the academy. Many assert that the academy should uphold the ideals of modernity and the Enlightenment as sacrosanct. For some people intellectual enlightenment alone, however, has proven to be insufficient, and they seek spiritual enlightenment to obtain a holistic consciousness. I meet many students who tell me their lives feel empty, and students who attend chapel say that it helps them cope with the isolation of college life.

College is a time of exploration and finding oneself. During this time, many students choose to distance themselves from the faith tradition in which they were raised; others choose to reject religion altogether. For many students at Smith, however, involvement in religious communities on campus becomes an anchor to help survive in an academic environment that can make overwhelming demands and cause high levels of stress associated with academic achievement.

Many students acknowledge a desire to have a life that is connected with God. This relationship with the Divine can range from being solely committed to affirming a familial faith perspective to having a yearning for interfaith exploration. There is generally a sense of acceptance that God is acknowledged and defined by different individuals and groups in many ways such as the Higher Power, Buddha, Allah, the Force, or the Spirit of the Universe. Therefore, the model of inclusive spirituality, as affirmed by the Ecumenical Christian Church, is modeled after the witness of Jesus.

Jesus, as depicted in the Christian scriptures, is one who constantly challenged the prejudices perpetuated within organized religion and who embraced the disenfranchised. Jesus' relationship to God, the Spirit, is illustrated in many stories such as one found in John 4:1–42. It is an account that challenges us to enlarge our understanding of religion, spirituality, and human interconnectedness. When Jesus addresses worship, he speaks of relationship with God, Spirit of the Universe, as not being necessarily entrenched in religious traditions.

> The hour is coming when you will worship God neither on this mountain nor in Jerusalem.... The hour is coming and is now here, when the true worshiper will worship God in spirit and truth.... God is spirit, and those who worship God must worship in spirit and truth.[10]

The context of Jesus' assertion about relation with God, through worship, is in the setting of a dialogue with a woman. Her negation and anonymity seems to be emphasized all the more by her only being referred to as "the Samaritan woman."[11] She represents a divergent ethnic and cultural perspective with the prevailing societal norms of both cultures negating women as marginal. This story is profound because Jesus converses with the Samaritan woman from an egalitarian position that was antithetical to the cultural norms of his day, norms that negated women as little more than indentured servants or property. The fact that the woman is identified in the context as a social outcast because of her questionable morals also demonstrates the uniqueness of this encounter as one based in human compassion rather than judgment and condemnation.

The Samaritan woman's notorious social reputation distinguished her as a person who would normally be shunned by a religious man. The woman's choices in life and situation alienated and ostracized her from the broader society. Jesus converses with this woman as she subsequently attempts to turn conversation into a debate, through apologetics surrounding the different and confrontational religious ideologies of their divergent ethnicity and cultures. In Jesus' response the social and societal context surrounding his thoughts on worship, God, and the Spirit are significant.

The setting illuminates Jesus transcending and challenging, by his actions, the orthodoxy and conventions of the time period's historical frame of reference. He was speaking with a person of a different ethnic group against the existing system of religious separatism and battles for hegemony between ethnic groups. Jesus transcends these societal norms and boundaries to enter into dialogue about the issues of encounter with God in worship. Jesus acknowledges and affirms the specificity of his religious heritage and orthodoxy as it contrasts with that of the woman. Yet, he makes the assertion that in an encounter with God, the Spirit must ultimately transcend the strict, neat, human, cultural, societal, organized religious dogma perpetuated in theological dogmatism.

Jesus asserts that worship is an ephemeral encounter, an experience of spirit dancing with Spirit. The wisdom of this story for those who embrace spirituality and an invitation to dance with the Spirit individually and corporately is that "we are not human beings having a spiritual experience but spiritual beings having a human experience."[12] Spirituality affirms that there can be many styles of dance when we accept the invitation to dance with the Divine and that the search for truth and illumination is a lifelong journey. The Smith College Protestant community known as the Ecumenical Christian Church has committed itself to being a gathering of people that strives to give respect to all regardless of religious beliefs.

The Protestant chapel community at Smith has accepted the challenge to be open to dialogue and accepting of religious, ethnic, and cultural difference, especially within the diversity among those who identify themselves as Protestant. For all, including myself as the chaplain, we have witnessed how this spiritual enlightenment has brought about a renewal of life in the Protestant chapel at Smith College. The renaissance that the Ecumenical Christian Church is experiencing affirms the value of being open to exploring diverse ways of worship that celebrate the breadth of religious traditions represented among the members of the Protestant religious community at Smith. We are continually learning, as a community, that unity does not mean being unified. Through this journey of learning, we are continually brought to the realization that our evolution, as a community within a college setting, is a perpetual educational process.

"[We] are enrolled in a full-time informal school called life"[13]

Et Non Impedias Spiritum

ENDNOTES

1. Richard P. Unsworth, *A Century of Religion at Smith College* (Northampton, Massachusetts: Smith College, May 1975).

2. Marcus J. Borg, *The God We Never Knew* (San Francisco: HarperSanFrancisco, 1997). This work comprehensively addresses an understanding of God, the Sacred, the Spirit, the Numinous as a theological paradigm for moving "beyond dogmatic religion to a more authentic contemporary faith."

3. Elizabeth Moltmann-Wendel, *A Land Flowing with Mild and Honey: Perspectives on Feminist Theology* (New York: Crossroads Publishing, 1985), 14.

4. Nancy A. Hardesty, *Inclusive Language in the Church* (Atlanta: John Knox Press, 1987), 2.

5. Harvey Cox, *Religion in the Secular City: Toward a Postmodern Theology* (New York: Simon and Schuster, 1984), 240. Cox argues that "People's religion is not elite or clerical religion or the religion of cultivated intellectuals—what we have today is two separate universes, that of the academic theological enterprise and that of the world of ongoing, everyday religious beliefs and practices. They touch each other only by accident."

6. Hans Küng, *Theology for the Third Millenium: An Ecumenical View*, trans. Peter Heinegg (New York: Doubleday, 1988), 176.

7. Donna Schaper, "'Me-First Spirituality' Is a Sorry Substitute for Organized Religion on Campuses," *The Chronicle of Higher Education*, August 18, 2000, Volume XLVI, Number 50, A56.

8. Küng, *Theology*, 3.

9. Elisabeth Moltmann-Wendel, *Land Flowing,* 14. The author uses the term "minority liberation movement."

10. John 4:21–24.

11. John 4:7–9.

12. This is a quote I saw on a car bumper sticker that is attributed to Stephen Covey.

13. Cherie Carter Scott, *If Life Is a Game, Here Are All the Rules* (New York: Broadway Books, 1998).

Author's Note: Special thanks to Brenda Allen and Alan Scott for their invaluable comments and Hyatt Abuza not only for her comments but for the contribution of the title for the chapter.

PART TWO

Spirituality and Leadership:
Self and Organizational Transformation

9. *Private Conversations about Public Spirituality*

Sarah Stockton

This chapter explores two different aspects of spirituality and higher education. First, I will discuss the findings of my graduate thesis research, including observations and recommendations, which considered the place of spirituality and religious pluralism among academics and administrators at a public university. Although not my original intention, the data led me to pay particular attention to the issue of bias against Christianity, as acknowledged and alluded to by the participants in the study.

Secondly, this chapter details some of my own personal observations as a staff person working in student services at the university, which appeared to dovetail with my research. Issues of diversity, inclusion, tolerance, and meaning have imbued both my professional and academic university careers.

WHERE I BEGAN

My graduate coursework in education included readings on transformative education theory, critical learning theory, adult development, feminist learning development theory, and other aspects of how adults learn and integrate meaning. On my own I sought out authors and educators who addressed issues of spiritual development and meaning making in adult educational theory and practice. Yet even in a curriculum designed to address issues of inclusion and diversity, something was left out. For me, education in all of its aspects, from being a student to working in a university, was a form of vocation, and I wanted to hear and learn more about that. Trying to identify myself as a spiritual person in a secular academic and work environment led me into uncharted territory. Without a mentor or a model to guide me, I felt isolated and without voice. If our current educational theories and university policies are focused on inclusiveness and giving everyone "voice," who is to say that the spiritual voice is not valid, just as valid as those voices that speak from a powerful place of ethnicity, or gender, or class? And from there, who then is to say that I should discard or ignore my own spiritual "heritage" (European American, Protestant), manifested in a Christian-based educational system and culture? Not to promulgate that system, but to acknowledge, deconstruct, and find what value remains in it.

These are some of the questions that arose as I made my way through the thickets of learning and working. I quietly looked for signposts in my studies and in my work that might lead to a sense of the spiritual, looking for code words like *authenticity* and *meaning* or the more overt, *spirit*. For instance, Paulo Friere, a well-known Brazilian educator, also played a significant role within the Liberation Theology movement, yet his religious affiliation had never been mentioned in our class readings or discussion, and because of that, I had framed an image of the philosopher and his beliefs that was incomplete. I found it puzzling that the concepts of engaged teaching and the liberatory classroom would exclude the spiritual or religious dimension. I began to wonder how we could isolate this aspect of the classroom experience from the rest of our exploration into diversity in the areas of class, gender, race, ethnicity, and so on.

Yet on one occasion a professor stopped and lectured me in the hall about the inappropriateness of my research interest, claiming he went into academia to "get away" from all that. My graduate advisor was one of the most skeptical of all when I broached the subject of writing a thesis about spirituality in higher education. He warned me to be discreet and to keep things anonymous, so as not to "get in trouble." He was really only convinced it was a legitimate area of study when I showed him the Education as Transformation Project website, the starting point of my research.[1] Then he grudgingly allowed as to how it might be valid. It was up to me, however, to conduct my own literature review and find my own sources. The highest compliment I received after four years of study was his note on the last page of my completed thesis: "You've convinced me."

THE RESEARCH

The setting for the study was a large public urban university, with a predominantly commuter population and an approximate student enrollment of 26,000 with 3,000 faculty and staff members. I conducted a qualitative case study over the course of a semester in which I interviewed eight faculty members, five of whom were also administrators. Four of the participants were women. Two of the participants were African American and one was Native American; the remaining four were European American. Although two of the participants were relatively new to the university (one for one and a half years, one for six years), the average length of employment at the university was eighteen years. The thirteen questions centered on the area of personal knowledge and experience of spirituality as it pertained to the participants' academic lives. Some of the key questions were the following:

- What is the level of comfort in revealing one's spiritual or religious orientation or practice in a work or classroom setting?

- What is the relative importance of acknowledging a spiritual or religious viewpoint when in dialogue about ethics and values in the classroom or workplace?

- How important is one's spiritual or religious orientation or practice as compared to one's ethnicity, class, gender, or sexual orientation? If important, does that mean that we are obligated to consider it?

The interviews generated thick data that could have led off into many more directions, given more time. It was gratifying to receive such in-depth, thoughtful responses to the questions. All the participants appeared engaged in the process, as they sought to articulate their own experiences and observations about spirituality and university life. What follows are some observations based on the transcribed and coded data.

TALKING ABOUT SPIRITUALITY: A DESIRE FOR CONNECTION AND PARTICIPATION COINCIDES WITH FEAR

Cautious curiosity was expressed by the study participants as to how conversations about spirituality and religious pluralism with others on campus might proceed, with the caveat that there be no opportunity for proselytizing, and that involvement in such conversations be voluntary. The participants generally agreed that they would welcome the opportunity to engage in conversation about spirituality or religion, as long as someone else initiated it. It appears as though a strong sense of self-protective caution, mixed with the desire to play by the polite rules of established academic discourse, acts as a natural inhibitor toward venturing out into this previously uncharted territory. They also emphasized that if they thought that referring to spiritual or religious viewpoints might make someone else uncomfortable, then they would immediately stop. One participant referred to this as the university's version of: "Don't ask, don't tell." This same participant, in examining the demographics of his workplace, stated that:

> I think the cultural wars and fears that produced a covertly Christian and overtly neutral kind of culture are being challenged by who's actually sitting around the room now. It (also) may be that what being Christian means, varies more than it used to.

Here the participant grounded a sense of caution and fear historically, and also acknowledged changing demographics not only in terms of a more diverse group ethnically and culturally, but in terms of diverse faith traditions. He seemed to also recognize that Christianity, while no longer the dominant framework for university culture and academe in general, still maintains an influence (even if only a negative one against which people react).

One participant reflected on the silence about spirituality among his peers:

> Personal spirituality, they just don't seem to address that at all. You're sitting around a table and you're having a chat and you don't know if this person has it all worked out or they're still working on it...(yet) there are quite a few people on this campus who are very specific and strong in their (Christian) belief systems. The rest of us just don't really discuss it, because we have opposite or more liberal viewpoints, and don't really see the purpose of argument....It would be interesting to meet up with some people who are interested in discussing various spiritual ideas, but I don't know if this campus is open to that or not.

Thus the participant addressed how the status quo of what might be deemed a genteel politeness prevented open discussion, while also protecting against open conflict.

I could have introduced this participant to other members of the community who might have been interested, as he put it, in discussing spiritual ideas. But they did not seem to be people that he regularly interacted with (based on our discussion and my own personal observations), and he would not have had occasion to engage in conversation with them about these ideas. A university community functions like so many other communities in our society; there are many small groups operating in close proximity to each other, but rarely overlapping in any direct way.

Another participant had many insights into the dynamics that occur when colleagues gather together and issues of both race and religion are present but not openly acknowledged or included in the overt agenda.

> I think it's important that we respect a particular (view), such as a Christian point of view, but I can understand why some people don't trust it. But there are ways of having that discussion, because most of us in the room have had some experience of crossing. I think there's a fear though, that having conversations directly would imply that what you've done is confirmed a religious view in a state institution.

Does working for a state institution restrict one's identity within academe? Is an expression of spirituality included within the definition of academic freedom?

"Crossing," as I understood this participant to mean, is a form of communicating to others of the same background or experience, such as others of the same ethnicity or religious belief system, while still respecting the conventions of the dominant culture. One way to do this would be to use words that have varied meanings that can be construed differently, depending on the listener. For instance, if I say the word "detachment," this may mean one thing to a psychologist, and another thing to a Buddhist, depending on the context. I might deliberately choose to use such a word if I want to signal to a fellow Buddhist, for instance, a particular intention. We all may at times choose language that can convey particular messages to some, but not all, of our listeners.

He went on to reflect further on his experiences from the perspective of his race as well as spirituality:

> For African Americans, the notion of the split between spirituality and other parts of their life, is only accepted begrudgingly in the academic community. There was a cultural war, and a cultural truce made, and to mess with that, is to threaten (a) fundamental safety that some people feel in the academic culture. Others who didn't have that kind of cultural war—maybe they should have, but it didn't come from that, our history, it just doesn't seem like that big a deal.

The participant appeared to feel a sense of being on the sidelines in the "culture wars" (i.e., the process of moving from a religiously based to a more secular-humanist based academy), in the historical experience of being an African American in a secular educational system. The other African American participant I interviewed expressed a similar attitude toward her spirituality, in that she did not feel challenged or obligated by a historical precedent toward compartmentalization, and instead felt able to maintain a sense of unity in her academic and spiritual pursuits. I also received a similar impression from two other African American women at the university in administrative positions with whom I talked in the course of my study, although those conversations were not formally included in the data.

The participants were generally cautious about being seen as proselytizing; conversely, they feared allowing others to proselytize, and they expressed concern about respecting others and maintaining a neutral, noninvasive environment. This concern was particularly focused on anything that resembled Christianity. Other non-European practices and beliefs, such as meditation, "new age" spirituality, or Asian traditions, were perceived as less abrasive or intrusive, an observation that surfaced several times in the study and which I will expand on in more detail later in the chapter.

The participants also expressed ambivalence toward the concepts of spirituality and religious pluralism as addressed from the university role of an academician. There were also some ambivalent personal feelings about their own faith systems, further complicating the larger issue.

Yet only one participant dismissed the idea of having conversations about spirituality outright (or religion, which he equated with spirituality, no matter how I attempted to separately define the two in our discussion). The rest were curious but did not have any mechanisms for framing the possibilities. As one participant put it, when asked if there was a way to introduce spirituality and religious pluralism into the academic discourse: "I'd be reluctantly negative." He could not further speculate as to how such conversations might proceed.

The participants wanted some kind of safeguard that the tendency toward irrational emotionalism or personal attack, which may arise when talking about spirituality or religion, would be contained. They also wanted some way to guarantee that entering into this kind of discourse would not compromise either their place within the university community or the university community's expectations that conversation stay within the realm of scientifically based intellectualism. One participant pointed directly to the problem of framing the dialogue:

> I'd be interested in having discussion with colleagues, if there was a format, because otherwise, people think that you're immediately going to go into this convincing sort of thing, proselytizing.

My reading of the word "proselytizing," based on our conversation, is that this participant was referring to someone speaking from a Christian standpoint. The word "proselytize" or the more prosaic "preaching" was invoked throughout the research study by the participants as shorthand for the Christian (and by that one reads "evangelical") viewpoint.

Because one's spiritual or religious practice or heritage is not discernable through surface observation, unlike one's gender or often, one's race, it becomes more easily part of the hidden nature of who we are, more easily protected, and yet more easily overlooked. The need to include and validate expressions of various religious or spiritual belief systems in the academic community was not expressed with the same sense of urgency and moral imperative that characterizes the movement toward inclusion of the "other" as identified by race, class, or sexual orientation.

The participants placed spirituality and religious pluralism within a framework of academic discourse when envisioning an open discussion on campus. Yet they did not see how this could function, given the emotionally laden content of these topics, or even whether or not it should or could be attempted within the strictures of a public university. The thought of engaging with colleagues at what they considered an intimate level of interaction appeared to cause discomfort. One participant suggested the following approach:

> I would probably start very slowly. Because even those who want to (have conversations) also share the cultural fear, of what it means to do that. I share that fear. You are part of an institution that is supposed to protect your ability to have the ideas that you have, and there is also an experience that I have, of religious discussion becoming religious conversion.

When asked about working in a larger arena, he advised:

> I would do some sort of symposium. Let's do it the way we do it as educators, let's make it an educational training. I think it would be valuable. It will bring up stuff. When I do stuff on race, trust me, it brings up stuff. I go after something that is transformational work, which means that I ask people to speak from within. I would probably go after spirituality, rather than religiosity. It's safer and it's already so vague, that folks already know that you are signaling that you are not just offering a Baptist perspective, or something like that.

The concept of spirituality, for this participant, presented a more generic definition that, therefore, translates as more neutral, universal, and accommodating, yet does not reduce itself to pure secularism.

HIDDEN AND OPEN BIASES

As the study progressed I became interested in uncovering hidden biases toward particular religious views or practices. I wanted to explore the influences, both conscious and unconscious, which shape our level of understanding and tolerance toward differing expressions of religious or spiritual belief.

A certain bias against any overt Protestant Christian behavior or attitudes was prevalent. However, one outcome I found particularly interesting was an attitude of tolerance toward non-Western practices. Every participant I spoke with on this issue agreed that it would be more acceptable to mention the practice of meditation as opposed to prayer, and that the training we have received in academe (to be "politically correct") has instilled a certain practice of respect toward non-Judeo-Christian religious systems. One participant in particular noted this phenomenon:

> People would look less askance at someone saying they were going to mass then going to church—isn't it interesting that you brought that up. There really is a prejudice against talking about Protestant Christianity. I just realized that. I mean I knew it, but it's the first time I ever really said it. Well, it does have a history; (laughs) it's loaded.

Another participant expressed a view that was echoed in many of the conversations I had both formally and informally over the last two years at the university:

> It's so not often talked about that I don't really know, but I would guess that on this campus it would be cool to meditate and probably weird to pray. This is not a religious stronghold at all. (However) there is a Christian Right that is very intolerant, and I have very negative feelings about it, and I think that's what's given Christianity a bad name.

Meditation techniques are used in some courses on campus, most notably in the offerings by the Holistic Health program. I might speculate that since meditation has achieved some legitimacy as a health-based practice, with roots in a non-Christian religious tradition, and is especially in vogue in the local, off-campus community, it has achieved some legitimacy on campus—or at least doesn't engender any controversy.

This participant went on to describe her own religious background and experiences, which included active participation in a Unitarian Universalist church, but previously had included negative experiences of Christianity.

She explained that her feelings about the Christian Right are reinforced by the media. She did not indicate that she has made any examination of current Christian thought that might counterbalance the media portrait.

My educational experience tells me that each discipline perpetuates certain biases and assumptions that must be approached by the teacher and the learner critically and continually reevaluated in a reflective process. In academe, do we apply these same rigorous standards when examining our own deeply held religious stereotypes? If not, this may suggest an inability to deconstruct the topic of religion or spirituality in a neutral manner in an academic environment. Yet as a result, the areas of spirituality and religion are relegated to the shadowy regions outside the academy, like the deep and opaque waters beneath a boat at sea.

Sociologist Robert Bellah, in an interview on redefining institutional meaning, warns that whether or not religion is a factor in whom we are as people or as a society, including our cultural institutions, begs the question.[2] We must begin with the fact of religion's existence in people's lives, and then our educational institutions must find ways of engaging dialogue about religion in a preemptive and responsive, rather than reactive, form.

One participant felt that a religious view that allows for tolerance toward others and mutual respect showed a more mature and evolved form of spirituality, just as we equate tolerance toward others with emotional maturity. Yet the process of evolving means a necessary journey whereby we move from negating anything "other," to ambivalence about one's stance, before reaching the balance sought. This creates a place of tension and requires tools of learning and practice that are currently being developed in the field of higher education, through the work of the Education as Transformation Project and others. Ambivalence can be an uncomfortable place to be, especially if we arrive there from a historically painful place.

One participant, a Native American who talked about how Native American children have suffered in the dominant educational system, disagreed with my suggestion that religious pluralism might be similar to multiculturalism as a means of working toward tolerance. He equated religion with Christianity, Christianity with intolerance, and intolerance with racism:

> People have used biblical passages to support racism. On reservations, people would use those passages, to explain why the Navaho or the Apache were in the situation that they were in. And I never ever passed that up. I always took that on.

Interviewer: Let's leave Christianity aside for a moment. Say you were in a committee meeting, and someone is there who is a Navaho. And they're having a deep spiritual reaction to what's going on in the room, and they speak from that. Would you be comfortable with that? (Participant nods). Do you find that you are more uncomfortable with institutionalized religion?

Participant: Usually. (With) Someone speaking from an institutionalized religious perspective.

Interviewer: (What if) a Buddhist is in the room and he uses language that lets you know he is speaking from a spiritual perspective. Would that be less offensive to you, or less intrusive to you?

Participant: I would understand it. And if I thought that it made sense, then I would work with it.

This particular interview was the most difficult for me personally to conduct because I met with great resistance to the whole topic of spirituality in education. I spent a great deal of the interview attempting to find common ground for how we might discuss the topic, beyond "yes" and "no" answers. I felt traditional religious terminology to be a major stumbling block in my ability to invoke a neutral atmosphere of discourse, which is one reason I attempted to approach the topic through another "religious" venue, a technique which seemed to evoke a less negative reaction.

Although this participant's past experience with another religious tradition is not necessarily the norm for members of the dominant culture, it is important to acknowledge that there are deep wounds felt by many in academe, caused by what some have experienced as a form of spiritual violence in the name of institutionalized religion. Many purposely seek the nontoxic atmosphere of neutral discourse as a result. But the assumption that academic discourse is and must remain always scientifically neutral, and thus will be adequate to the task of educating and learning, is another form of belief that can generate its own toxicity.

RECOMMENDATIONS

The concern expressed by the participants about their roles or how they are perceived within the community is, for me, a valid one. The university operates within a very enclosed, hierarchical space. However, the participants also generally agreed that the institution has a role to play in respecting and considering *each* aspect of a person, just as we consider race, gender, ethnicity, and class, among other things. But as one participant pointed out:

> I think we still don't have the training on how to take that into account (a person's spiritual or religious beliefs/practices). But I think it's extremely important. I think it plays out, not only with the person dealing with it, but (with) any other kind of demographic, because it helps me figure out how they orient themselves, not only in the world but in relation to the stereotypes they do or do not identify with.

Concern about training is not surprising in an academic and is a valid approach to learning. However, training implies a clinical process in which outcomes can be predicted and controlled. Yet the condition of uncertainty, confrontation, and even chaos is part of the learning process, as is learning how to trust each other in community, something we might do well to model for our students as a means of disengaging from fear and encouraging participation. The academic community, as *community*, is an asset in and of itself, and should not be overlooked.

My research results culminated in the following recommendations for approaching the dialogue on spirituality and religious pluralism which I offer based on the themes of curiosity, fear, uncertainty, and isolation that arose over and over again in the participant interviews. Unexamined perceptions about what constitutes Christian language, customs, and worldviews need not prevail as the dominant mode of religious or spiritual discourse in the academic arena. Exposure to literature and discourse about the current evolutions in Christian doctrine, juxtaposed with personal, historical experiences and media representations of Christians, might lead to some interesting discussions. Further, an interdisciplinary approach in relation to other belief systems would necessarily be established, as a measure to prevent any attempts at hierarchical manuevering or even exclusion.

Programming

The university community can utilize the groundwork laid within the academic tradition in the areas of curriculum development, student services practices and principles, and forum presentations, to construct a means of learning about the varied forms of spiritual and religious beliefs that are being practiced in the community. Panel discussions, performing rituals or celebrations such as dances, or conferences that provide room for small group presentations and discussions are all proven methods for engaging others in participatory learning. These resources can promote and enhance understanding of the diversity represented within and throughout the university.

The framework of traditional academic discourse also provides an indigenous structure from which to begin to explore more nontraditional forms of expression. This kind of intellectual "home-base" would then serve to help alleviate some of the fear generated by the unknown territory of conversations about spirituality. Traditional frameworks of discourse such as papers or presentations could then be overlaid with media such as portfolios, collages, or even music, that allow for evolving metaphors and images and ultimately result in pedagogical and dialectical transformation.

The secular paradigm that currently dominates higher education, while originally seeking to rid itself of the rigidity of an exclusive Protestant worldview, threatens to engender the same rigidity and resistance toward any attempt to reinvigorate academic dialogues about alternative approaches to ethics, morality, and transformative processes. The evolving and more elastic definition of spirituality as it is currently developing within religious communities and the academic community may provide a way to steer a new course through uncharted waters. This definition includes a foundational belief in unity—not of doctrine, practice, or faith system—but of common and universal inter-relatedness, that seeks to build on our shared humanity and places us within the greater framework of all life. An example of this unity that transcends doctrine can be seen in the practice of meditation, a practice which, though differing in basic technique from tradition to tradition, inevitably encourages a state of openness and mindfulness. This same goal could be said to be at the heart of transformational learning.

Research Literature

There are many resources available for those who are interested in a current and comprehensive understanding of various spiritual and religious traditions, including those directly related to the history of our system of higher education. A discourse based on available literature could lead to more inclusive dialogue and could promote tolerance. A clearinghouse such as a website and/or a paper archive based in the religious studies program or student services area of the university could be made available for all to access and contribute to.

I found other sources in my research that have much to offer as well. For instance, *Tribal College: A Journal of American Indian Higher Edu-*

cation, contains much ongoing discussion about the effect of institutional religion on the American Indian learning experience. Yet there is also discussion about the role of spirituality in the process of learning, both within and outside of educational institutions.[3] The authors emphasize a need for unity both among Native Americans and between various religious faiths—even as the historical role of Christianity is documented as being divisive and destructive.[4] The writers seek a more simplified and holistic approach to incorporating spirituality within their educational settings. Fear of what the Christian religion has meant historically is acknowledged, but is not offered as a deterrent in the attempt to reestablish a spiritual component to learning.

Lessons from the Classroom

Some of the participants discussed teaching experiences in which they practice many of the interactive principles of transformative learning, including engaging students from the starting point of their own experiences, modeling an atmosphere of respectful inquiry, and acting as participatory learners within the classroom themselves. This approach promotes a "safe" classroom in that issues are identified and examined in the group, a process that cultivates the unmasking of hidden agendas. Classrooms where the students are not participants but are taught by rote create an illusion of safety at the sacrifice of open inquiry and engaged learning. This dynamic is extended into the work setting, and into other life situations, to the detriment of all concerned. The participant who spoke of a "cultural fear," in my interpretation, echoed this dynamic whereby we, as a culture, seek safety in a nonparticipatory, nonseeking stance in order to reinforce the status quo. True participation involves an approach that challenges the predetermined meaning of our lives and learning experiences. Of course, this approach requires that the educator, the learner, and the colleague as well, demonstrate a certain willingness to personally unmask, reevaluate, and learn from their own attitudes toward their religious and spiritual heritage and experiences.

Yet the fact that spirituality is less quantifiable or open to measurement and definition does not diminish its importance in the teaching and lifelong learning process. In the practice of "engaged pedagogy," teachers and students are encouraged to enter into the learning process with body, mind, and spirit, open to the resulting dynamics that can occur when everyone is fully engaged.[5] In *Teaching to Transgress,* bell hooks draws on the work of Paulo Friere to place the integration of mind, body, and spirit into a liberatory framework of learning and teaching. Yet the construct of participatory learning must be infused with the less structured and less delineated experience of engaging from a place of spiritual authenticity. While religious plurality is the intellectual journey to inclusivity and openness, the exploration of spirituality is the river that runs through it.

MY ROLE AS A STUDENT SERVICES COORDINATOR

In this section, I approach some of the same issues and questions raised in my research from my perspective as a member of the university community itself. My experience within the community allowed me to personally experience what might otherwise have been solely intellectual observations, thus enriched my understanding.

In my role as a student affairs coordinator for a college within the university, which serves approximately 3,000 students and over 200 faculty members, I had many opportunities to engage with people in academe on a personal basis. I found that talking to people about my research interest in spirituality and higher education either opened or shut down conversation. For example, one staff member confided in me that after her coworker committed suicide (off-campus) she was expected to move into the now vacant office. This upset her greatly, for religious reasons. She felt that she couldn't do so without first having someone from her church come and bless the office. She didn't know how to proceed or whom to talk to, but because she knew of my study, she asked me for my advice. (I suggested she bring in a priest on a Saturday so as not to ruffle any feathers.)

In my work as an academic advisor, I often saw students who were in some kind of pain, ostensibly because of poor academic performance, but more often the poor performance had to do with other, life-based concerns at the core. My role was not that of a therapist. I did, however, often feel myself being present with them in their pain as a way of trying to connect, in order to alleviate some of their stress and feelings of isolation. For me this was a spiritual process. I would have appreciated having a way to talk about this aspect of my work with other coworkers, or being able to refer students who expressed a desire for spiritual or religious comfort to someone on campus.

The same hidden bias that I observed as my research progressed, against overt acknowledgment of anything Christian, also played itself out among coworkers and supervisors (who were faculty members as well). In my day-to-day work life I personally observed that desktop "altars" were acceptable, as long as they contained no overt Christian symbols. Buddha statues, African or Native American symbols and artifacts, or anything "new age" were admired, while crosses and statues of Mary were ignored at best. One supervisor, a chair of a department, went so far as to ask the department secretary to remove such items from public display (i.e., her desk). Where did this general disdain or discomfort come from? Why are those from a historically Christian background, who work, learn, teach, and advise in this academic culture with its Christian heritage, so quick to discard their affiliations with a religious past? Commendably, many Christians are willing to learn from other communities in which religious or spiritual views are integral to the culture, and even more, may adopt those symbols and rituals for their own use. Yet others seem unwilling to explore the possibility of a spiritual life here in the present, based on Christian traditions.

As a student affairs advisor and student resource center coordinator in the college of a public university, I stocked the resource center with materials related to counseling support, substance abuse prevention, financial aid and housing information. If a student asked me for a referral for spiritual or religious guidance, I provided that information from one person to another, not as advisor to student, using my own knowledge of the various resources available. Regardless of whether that student wanted a Buddhist meditation group to attend, a Moslem community to meet with, or fellow Wiccans to talk to, if I knew of resources, I passed that information on. In retrospect, I could have personally visited the various student religious organizations on campus to gather more information, but to do so was outside of my frame of reference as to what constituted acceptable forms of "student resources."

CONCLUSION

Many of us in academe have effectively disengaged that part of our personal and public selves which contain our own knowledge and experiences of spirituality. As well, in our institutional efforts to eradicate perceived undue Christian influence from our centers of learning, we have locked the doors against what Parker Palmer refers to as our own desire to "know as we are known."[6]

We do ourselves a great injustice as educators, learners, advisors, and university employees by excluding our many religious heritages and our spiritual practices from the academic arena. The academic agenda has evolved to include perspectives on class, gender, sexual orientation, culture, and ethnicity, but there is no open forum at the public university where I worked and studied for discussing how our spiritual or religious views or even our religious backgrounds shape our decision making and growth. There is no sanctioned method for educating ourselves about the religious diversity of our students, professors, and colleagues, or the hidden and overt biases we carry toward various religious stances. Yet in every aspect of education today, the issues of ethics, inclusivity, and sensitivity to diversity, including religious and spiritual diversity, are more important than ever as we continue to grapple with the changing demographics of our time and place.

I believe we can educate ourselves about the diverse meanings of faith as people may experience faith, and divest ourselves of preconceived notions about the outcomes of religious and spiritual conversations, without engendering a permanent atmosphere of hostility and fear. In doing so, we must work to uncover the hidden assumptions and biases that cloud our view. Then we might begin to approach the topic of spirituality and religious pluralism in higher education settings with equanimity and open-mindedness.

ENDNOTES

1. Website available at www.wellesley.edu/RelLife/transformation
2. Benjamin Webb, ed., *Fugitive Faith* (Maryknoll, NY: Orbis Books, 1998).
3. Paul Boyer, "Living Spirituality," *Tribal College: Journal of American Indian Higher Education*, 6, no. 2 (1994): 4–5.
4. Carolyn Casey, "Crossing Cultures," *Tribal College: Journal of American Indian Higher Education*, 6, no. 2 (1994): 13–15.
5. bell hooks, *Teaching to Transgress* (New York, NY: Routledge, 1994).
6. Parker J. Palmer, *To Know as We Are Known: Education as a Spiritual Journey* (San Francisco: Harper & Row, 1983).

10. Learning to Connect: Spirituality and Leadership

KATHLEEN E. ALLEN AND GAR KELLOM

In this chapter we will take a look at ourselves as spiritual individuals and at our place in the institutions we serve. We will look at those for whom we have supervisory responsibility and at strategies to foster staff spiritual development. We will consider how we might create, within our colleges and universities, an environment more conducive to spiritual growth and how we might influence our institutions to take more leadership in our communities. We will also challenge higher education to play a larger role in the global community.

In the process we consider some Western ways of understanding spirituality and leadership as well as some Eastern ways. Our goal is to chart a course for individuals inside institutions of higher learning that will be fulfilling and meaningful for them. At the same time, we want to challenge ourselves to encourage our institutions to assume leadership roles on complex social issues.

WHERE TO BEGIN

The starting point for enhancing the spiritual development of ourselves, our staff, and our organizations is our own deep soul work, reflection on our own lives and what gives them meaning. What is it that matters? What are the values that guide our lives? Are there significant experiences that have made us into the people we have become? How have those experiences formed our relationships with others in our immediate family and in the workplace? How have we identified our talents and what we have to offer to the world of higher education? What are our reasons for choosing to work in colleges and universities and what are our own personal missions? We begin with examining our lives.

We suggest that getting in touch with our selves and what we believe in is the beginning point for working with staff on spiritual development and the beginning step on a journey toward effective leadership. The Bhagavad Gita says, "the mind is like the wind" and more difficult to control than wild horses. The Katha Upanisad describes the person who does not operate from a spiritual core as "scattered as the rain that falls in craggy places, loses itself and becomes dispersed throughout the mountains."[1] In today's fast-paced world, with the rate of change increasing exponentially, ancient wisdom cautions us that we need an anchor and a place to stand that will provide some stability and direction.

What are the elements of a spiritual life? Certainly one element is what we value. One way to help us identify what we value in a global community is being provided by the Institute for Global Ethics.[2] The Institute has undertaken a project to identify the values most commonly held in the world today across cultural boundaries. In a series of interviews with people from a variety of nations, traditions, and perspectives, the researchers asked about these individuals' essential beliefs and values. Here is what they identified as the most commonly held "values for humanity":

- Fairness
- Freedom
- Unity
- Tolerance
- Responsibility
- Respect for Life
- Love

One could ask, are these my values? What would I add to or subtract from this list? The purpose for asking these questions could be to get us in touch with who we are and what gives us our uniqueness. It allows us to find our voices and to speak about what we think matters most.

Speaking in the first person from our own experiences may be another element of a spiritual life because doing so can foster honesty, integrity, and authenticity in relationships. Michael Meade, author of *Men and the Water of Life*, has traveled the world in search of universal myths to use in drumming workshops with men.[3] He has recently focused his work on youth in gangs and attempting to invent new initiation rituals. "I would not last a minute in this work if I did not speak in the first person and from my heart," says Meade. "Authenticity is the litmus test with these young people and if you don't pass that test you don't stand a chance." The importance he places on integrity can be a model for work with staff and students.

We have found when working with staff that they are very willing to talk about their own spiritual journeys and what gives their lives meaning. We have yet to work with a group of student development professionals that was not on some level eager to share what was most important to them. We have found that one key is to speak of such matters in the first person and to be as autobiographical as possible. For example, staff members are welcome to participate in spirituality groups which offer opportunities for faith sharing through written first-person accounts of the key events in their lives.

Whether thinking of colleagues, students, or ourselves, the way we view student and staff development is that spiritual development is at the center. Physical, intellectual, emotional, social, and occupational development are intimately linked to one's spiritual development and are all connected to this spiritual dimension. We might go as far as to say that growth on a spiritual dimension is the key to the most significant development in these other areas of a person's life. Pursuing a passion, following your heart or doing what you love stimulates new ways of thinking, feeling, and acting. You can teach those you work with by appealing to their intellect, but you inspire those you work with by winning their hearts. Yet, the spiritual development of the people we work with often receives the least attention at our professional conferences and in our publications.

We might say that a staff or an organization is made up of many individuals with spiritual centers and the spiritual center of the organization is in large part the sum total of those individual cores. To develop a staff or an organization it is, therefore, wise to take into account the spiritual journeys of the individuals in that organization. Effective leaders have the ability to tap into the core values of the people in their institutions and can inspire those coworkers to pull an organization in the direction they themselves believe in going.

One further perspective from Hindu philosophy is that there are many spiritual paths. These paths have been categorized as the paths of knowledge, works, and devotion. Any institution of higher education will have an abundance of faculty or staff committed to a path of knowledge in which the intellectual pursuit of truth and the life of the mind are central to who they are. Likewise, many others are on a path of duty or works—getting done what needs to be done—and they find their meaning in that effort. Others (perhaps student development staff are abundant in this category) are on a more passionate path, one of emotion, feeling, faith and belief in the goodness of human nature.

The point is that the diverse sacred journeys of all those in our colleges and universities are necessary in order to create real community. However, this soul work is challenging in most of our institutions. Often the culture of our organizations and within student affairs works against these efforts. Naming these inhibitors is a necessary part of the process of developing the spirituality of our staff and our institutions.

THE CURRENT INHIBITORS TO SOUL WORK IN STUDENT AFFAIRS

Remember the hippodrome ride at amusement parks? When we enter, we cluster toward the center of a large cylinder. As the ride begins, the cylinder starts to spin. The spinning increases until one by one we are pulled away from the center to the outer edge of the walls. At its peak speed, the floor drops out from under us, and we stay plastered against the outer wall.

This image is an analogy of the kind of work-life that most of us experience in student affairs. We spin faster and faster and eventually we can no longer hold onto the center. Over time, we are pulled apart from one another as the speed of "to dos" increases. Eventually the floor drops out from beneath us. Needless to say, it is difficult to live an examined life if one is worried about the floor dropping out from underneath.

Spiritual principles flow from the belief that we are all connected and have an interdependent relationship with each other and all of nature. This idea stands in sharp contrast to the fragmentation we experience in our work lives. Despite efforts to "blur boundaries" in our organizations, separation is still prevalent.

Our language is one indicator of the boundaries we maintain. We use terms like departments and divisions to mark our territory. We have informal rules of behavior that tell us we should mind our own business; for example, "I won't interfere in your work, if you don't tell me what to do." There are also subtle forms of power that keep us in our own space and burden individuals who try to work across boundaries. How many of us have seen or created a job description that is impossible for one person to accomplish? Or how many of us have a job that is bigger than a 40-hour workweek?

The pressure to perform well, please superiors, and complete our jobs quickly keeps us from living in the present. We put our heads down and plow through our work, which often prevents us from being present to ourselves and to our students, or from developing the relationships necessary for facilitating collaboration and connection.

Finally, the pace of our work does not allow time for reflection. The action bias is strong in student affairs: we often define our worth by the speed with which we solve problems or by our ability to make problems disappear. This creates a treadmill effect that keeps the work coming while frustrating processes of internal reflection and the development of complex covenant relationships with others.

Another barrier to spiritual growth in student affairs is the need for approval. When we seek approval, we need to control those below us in order to create the conditions under which our boss will approve of us. These behaviors work to diminish others and can create fear in our organizations. When we are fearful, we cannot bring our authenticity to our organization. In this way, fear and control diminish the spiritual development of others and ourselves.

In student affairs we not only face organizational separation; we also have legal standards. The fear of being sued can cause us to be cautious and reduce our relationships to a transactional level. A transactional relationship is based in the principle of "you scratch my back and I will scratch yours." It shows up when we choose to act on the letter of the law but not the spirit of the law.

Spiritual relationships, on the other hand, are formed in a covenant between people. A covenant relationship extends beyond the legal minimum requirements. When we relate to each other only on the basis of legal standards, we can limit the quality of, and potential impact of, our relationships. We learn to protect our organizations and ourselves, which eventually diminishes our capacity to care for our students and ourselves.

How Does an Individual's Soul Work Affect the Community?

Our behavior has an impact on those around us—especially if we are in a position of leadership. When we hold a management position, we are metaphorically in the spotlight from the perspective of our employees. Others watch us more closely and use our actions as justification for their own behaviors. Here are some examples of how a leader's behavior elicits responses in others and affects the organization's environment. If people chose to do their soul work, their modeling would have this effect on others and their organization, as illustrated in the following chart:

Impact of the Soul Work of Leaders

Individual leader's behavior	Impact on others	Impact on the organization's culture
Integrity and authenticity in actions. Committed to the journey and living one's story.	Gives permission to others to be authentic. Allows others to be fallible human beings.	A leader's modeling creates a climate of authenticity within the organization.
Being trusting and trustworthy.	Invites others to trust them in return.	Allows people to talk frankly with each other, facilitating authenticity and integrity.
Being present.	Gives a feeling of appreciation to others.	Slows people down so they can live in the present, rather than past or future.
Humor and enjoyment—can see the humor in situations by changing their perspective.	Allows individuals to see humor in their own behaviors. Laughter opens up people to the positive and facilitates personal change.	Expresses joy and humor. It opens up people to work with each other in positive ways and diminishes judgment.
Not driven by self-interest—"their hearts are in the right place"	Gives permission to individuals to contribute to the larger community without need for self-protection and defense.	Contributes to the development of a culture that has integrative power. Integrative power exists when people are predisposed to trust, care, collaborate with one another and hold altruistic beliefs.[4]
Nature of relationships is based within a covenant framework.	People feel valued and safe.	The organization models care of employees and enables a community within a workplace to form.
Pursuit of knowledge and ideas related to spirituality.	Increases shared knowledge in others and staff.	Inspires the organization to create deeper meaning for their work.

CREATING AN ORGANIZATION THAT REFLECTS SPIRITUAL PRINCIPLES AND SUPPORTS SOUL WORK

Now that we have examined some obstacles to spiritual development in student affairs, we might ask, how can we create a different kind of organizational culture? If we were to create a living community that supported spiritual practice and development, we would need to shift our culture from one of a "fragmented, doing treadmill" to one that encourages reflection, caring, and integration. Here are some strategies that would help develop a culture in student affairs that would support such a living community.

1) *An environment of safety.* If people don't feel safe at work, they don't reveal themselves. Over time, this diminishes their spiritual development, authenticity, and integrity. Russ Moxley, in his book *Leadership and Spirit*, discusses the role of collusion and its negative impact on an individual's spiritual development.[5] He believes that control-based hierarchies actually arise from the unexamined emotional issues of positional managers. If managers are driven by approval, fear, insecurity, or anger, they are more controlling of the people who report to them. For example, if a senior student affairs officer (SSAO) were worried about gaining the approval of the insitution's president, she would need to control the outcomes and behaviors of her staff in order to deliver what the president wanted. The impact of this behavior would trigger another dynamic between the staff and the SSAO. If the staff members didn't feel it was safe to disagree, they would need to choose between collusion and commitment. If they collude, they would say "yes" when they really wanted to say "no," or remain silent when they want to speak their minds. When staff members choose collusion over commitment to their own authenticity and the institution's mission, their spirits are diminished. Therefore, it is important to create a culture of safety within student affairs and influence the larger institution to do the same.

2) *Spiritual norms.* The social norming strategy that recovery programs have discovered can apply to spiritual development as well. Often our perception of reality and the actual reality of staff members' behavior and values are different. For example, if we praise staff members who are at their desks seventy hours a week and dedicate their lives to busy-ness, new staff members will likely conclude that their value to the organization will be measured by their long hours and hard work. However, if the majority of staff actually take time to reflect and live balanced lives, the reality and the perception will not match. If an SSAO wanted to encourage a culture that supported spiritual development, she would highlight the efforts of staff members to engage in their own spiritual development.

3) *Shift the criteria for recognition.* Often we reward the very behavior that works against the spiritual development of our staff. For example, how many of our organizations applaud the overworked or the always-working individual? We may also subtly look down on the person who asks reflective questions or takes time to live a more balanced life. Sometimes the informal criteria we use to reward our staff is different from the formal criteria. Insuring congruence between the formal and informal criteria is important. If the organization's criteria for recognition supported spiritual development, it would reward people who were authentic, present

to others, treated colleagues with respect and care, were reflective, and balanced doing with being.

4) *Treat others as sacred.* What would happen if we treated each other as if we were worthy of reverence and respect? How would this change what we talk about, how we interact, and what we believe about each other? Today, the lean and mean paradigm of organizations leaves little room for treating each other as sacred. However, by regarding each other as sacred, we would be building an organizational culture that supports employees' spiritual development. Something wonderful happens when we recognize the strengths and unique gifts in each other. We begin to reveal ourselves instead of protecting ourselves. Our egos may then take a backseat, and we become more open to change, ideas, suggestions, and appreciation.

5) *Amplify meaning making.* Spirituality is a search for meaning. When we are busy doing things in our organizations, linking these task to something larger than ourselves can be ignored. When we don't create meaning, we also miss an opportunity to practice spirituality in the workplace. Amplifying the importance of meaning making is a way of enhancing our work. Using meaning as a form of cohesion in an organization builds on the spiritual need in all of us to work toward a higher purpose.

6) *Become aware of the power of symbolic presence.* People watch what we do as leaders and are influenced by our behavior. People in positions of leadership can use their visibility to heighten spiritual values that support an internal journey. For example, if we are authentic and have covenant relationships, the power of our position lends a symbolic importance to our actions. What we model can shape the nature of an organization's culture. Other symbols can also be used to reinforce and remind our staff of key values. A physical touchstone or an inspirational statement, for example, can help remind staff members of their commitment to each other and their ideals.

STRATEGIES FOR STAFF DEVELOPMENT

Efforts to reshape organizational culture can be enhanced through staff development. It is the leader's role to facilitate opportunities for staff development and to change ineffective paradigms of staff development. Below are some ways leaders can help facilitate the spiritual development of their staff.

1) *Centering before staff meetings*. Often we come into meetings with the thoughts and tasks we should have left behind. This preoccupation keeps us from focusing on the present, on each other, and on the deeper connections between us. Centering is a technique that helps people let go of their mental preoccupations and focus on the present moment. In some ways, it allows our various molecules to catch up with our rapid movement from our individual offices to the staff meeting. Centering can come in the form of quiet, a reading, a prayer, or storytelling.

2) *Reading groups*. Informal reading groups using spiritual books and articles can give staff members the opportunity to delve deeper into their own spiritual journeys. Reading groups bring people who are exploring together with a structured reading. They choose the amount of reading required for each session and leave time to discuss their individual insights, questions, or reactions. Groups often meet over a meal.

3) *Busy person's retreat*. This is an individually structured week in which a staff member agrees to take three 30-minute breaks each day for meditation, spiritual guidance, and quiet. The breaks in a week enable you to slow down, take time to reflect on your life, and be nurtured in your own spiritual journey. This can be life changing. For example one student affairs staff development program used the busy person's retreat each January. The campus ministry office, in cooperation with a local monastery, organized the program. Each person spent 30 minutes in meditation or prayer (their choice which). The next 30 minutes were spent sharing prayers with the monastics, and the third 30-minute time block was spent talking with a spiritual director. The staff members who experienced this program said that it gave them a new perspective on their jobs and their lives. They were also able to be more present to their students and colleagues.

4) *Telling your story*. One foundation for our spiritual development is our ability to be authentic. Often we withhold the fullness of ourselves in our work environment, and colleagues having only only fragmentary knowledge of each other. When we invite people to share their stories with each other, we come to know them better, which, in turn, gives us permission to be more authentic with each other. One staff member used storytelling at the beginning of each staff meeting. Individuals, on a rotating basis, were invited to share what was happening in their lives. This sharing helped staff to develop deeper understanding of each other. The following statement can be used to begin: "Share one thing with your colleagues that, if others knew about it, would help them understand you better."

5) *Celebrations.* Celebrations and rituals have a long history in religious traditions. As student affairs practitioners, we are often in the role of maintaining or initiating celebrations for students. However, we don't always see ourselves as one of the constituents for whom we should plan celebrations. Celebrations provide a breathing space to enjoy the present and focus on our strengths. They often give us hope and strength in the face of challenging times ahead.

INFLUENCING UPWARD AND OUTWARD

If the soul work that we began with becomes contagious, we can overcome the factors that inhibit spiritual growth and create an organization that supports spiritual growth. That organization might not only foster the spiritual journeys of its employees, but also be propelled toward its own greater institutional mission by the energy this process generates. Skilled leaders need to create the conditions for this growth to occur, like gardeners providing the right amounts of water and nutrients at the right times.

Where does that growth take us? What is the end result? Greater enrollments, greater endowments, notoriety, pay increases? We would argue that the outcome of this process on a local level might be to make our work in student affairs more value driven and influential and to help our institutions become better citizens. These outcomes would enhance the connection between us on an institutional and global level. Is there an American institution of higher education that does not have at its core the goal of graduating students as better citizens who will contribute to society? In the process of creating better communities internally, our institutions would become better connected to their communities and the world.

When student affairs practitioners have done their soul work it enables them to influence their institutions in powerful ways. The prevailing metaphor for student development is one of fragmentation and alienation from the heart of the institution. When we do our soul work we realize that we are connected to each other and to a common ground. Therefore, being a part or a fragment is no longer sufficient. This calls us to act in a different way. We no longer can accept fragmentation as sufficient or as an accurate reflection of reality. We call our institutions to the common good.

An example of the power of connection is the learning community movement. This learning methodology is founded on the values of connection, community, and the fundamental principles of student affairs. Using new and neutral language, faculty and student affairs staff are drawn to creating communities across traditional institutional boundaries. What attracts individuals from different departments to come together is a belief in, and commitment to, something larger. This enables individuals in the institution to see themselves in relationship to each other in a way that changes their identity from an isolated individual within a department to an integrated part of a meaningful community. This is an example of how spiritual development can positively affect how we work together. Spirituality is fundamentally about connecting to something larger than oneself, and any initiative that recognizes our interdependence would be an example of spiritual principles in practice.

Another example is occurring at Morehouse College in the heart of Atlanta, Georgia, in the midst of one of the fastest growing urban areas in the country. Its mission, while not overtly religious in nature, is guided by the values from a previous religious affiliation. Its challenge is to educate black males at a time in history when there are more college-age black men in jail than in college. Walter Massey, the president, was given a grant to dedicate to any issue he thought would be worthwhile. He chose to dedicate it not only toward addressing the declining college enrollments of African American men in the U.S. but also to the declining percentage of men of all races and classes graduating from college. This president is transcending an exclusive concern with issues that affect his institution and asking questions which can benefit the whole of society.

These are examples of what it looks like to bring soul work upward and outward through an organization. As we influence our institutions we create an opportunity for our institutions to transform themselves and in turn transform their relationships and connections to the world. Dr. David Martin of Oxford University is one educator now making a plea for colleges and universities to assume leadership on the local level and also in the global community. "We don't have global governmental institutions to take the lead on global issue," he says. "There is a crying need for higher education institutions to tackle the most difficult global issues."[6]

How then does an institution play a greater leadership role in the global community on complex global issues? We are back to the beginning. It will take individuals, departments, divisions, and institutions who have done their soul work and who are on a spiritual journey, finding within themselves the passion and the commitment to lead the way.

Theodore Hesburgh, the former president of Notre Dame, has written about the lack of presidential leadership on national issues today. He laments that college presidents today seem to be less involved in public debate than in the past.[7] In the 1960s and 1970s college presidents found themselves in the midst of "acrimonious and sometimes violent clashes not only on civil rights and the Vietnam War but other societal concerns," says Hesburgh. Issues he cites as needing attention today are affirmative action, developing educational programs that seek to improve the status of women, and harnessing technology for the common good. His charge to his colleagues is that, "We cannot urge students to have the courage to speak out unless we are willing to do so ourselves."

In Indian philosophy there is a metaphor of an isolated drop of water falling to the earth as a raindrop or snowflake. The journey of that drop is toward the whole, where it no longer exists as a separate entity but has flowed into the ocean through a river or a glacier. For student affairs professionals or entire divisions, our journey is to move from isolation and marginalization to becoming a part of the larger whole.

ENDNOTES

1. *Bhagavad Gita*, trans. R.C. Zaehner and Katha Upanisad: 4.14.
2. Rushworth M. Kidder, *Shared Values for a Troubled World: Conversations with Men and Women of Conscience* (San Francisco: Jossey Bass, 1994).
3. Michael Meade, *Men and the Water of Life: Initiation and the Tempering of Men* (San Francisco: Harper San Francisco, 1993).
4. Bela H. Banathy, "The Cognitive Mapping of Societal Systems: Implications for Education," in *The Evolution of Cognitive Maps: New Paradigms for the Twenty-First Century*, ed. Ervin Laszlo, Ignazio Masulli, Robert Artigiani, and Vilmos Csanyi (Switzerland: Gordon and Breach, 1993). This was published in conjunction with The World Futures General Evolution Studies. Banathy introduces Integrative Power, a new kind of power that is defined as power that brings people together and creates a predisposition toward collaboration and altruistic beliefs and values. Traditional forms of power usually divide people, integrative power reinforces the covenant relationships between people and allows organizations to work in vastly different ways.
5. Russ Moxley, *Leadership and Spirit: Breathing New Vitality and Energy into Individuals and Institutions* (San Francisco: Jossey Bass, 2000).
6. David Martin, in *Religion, Modernity and Postmodernity*, ed. Paul Heelas, David Martin, and Paul Morris (Oxford, UK: Blackwell Publishers, 1998).
7. Theodore M. Hesburgh, "Where are College Presidents' Voices on Important Public Issues?," *The Chronicle of Higher Education*, 2 February, 2001, sec. B, 20.

11. The College Campus as a Web of Sociality

Gil Stafford

Human beings, as spirit, are necessarily created in a community—that human spirit in general is woven into the web of sociality.

—Dietrich Bonhoeffer[1]

On September 13, 1999, Grand Canyon University celebrated its fiftieth anniversary. We invited sixty third graders from the neighborhood elementary school to take part in the festivities by singing "Happy Birthday." It was a wonderful event and the children significantly added to the joy of the day.

Tragically, on Wednesday of that week, Sydney Browning, a Grand Canyon alumnae, was murdered at Wedgwood Baptist Church in Fort Worth, Texas. Even though Sydney had graduated ten years earlier, her violent death had a dramatic impact on our campus and community at large.

Making sense of the bizarre event was very difficult for us. A man had walked into the Wedgwood Baptist Church during an ecumenical youth prayer meeting. As was her habit, Sydney greeted the man. She was his first victim.

Sydney lived in Fort Worth and taught school for the disadvantaged. She had committed her life's work to those in need. Passionately she gave all of herself to her students. With great compassion she embodied what Grand Canyon University sees as its mission: to educate people in a Christian environment to make a difference in their world.

Sydney Browning's death caused our community to do a lot of soul searching. Out of a great deal of prayer arose the sense of our need to honor Sydney. To this end, Grand Canyon University "adopted" the sixty children who came to our campus to sing. We have committed to tutor these children through their high school days, and upon their graduation, we will provide them with full tuition scholarships. These sixty children are known as *Sydney's Kids*.

Not only is our university dedicated to educating people for service, but we are now actively involved in serving the community around us. The essence of "education as transformation" is that the university will model its mission to its students.

The goal of this chapter is to explore how this environment of modeling can be created. I will outline a possible style of leadership for a college campus and how this style, *vulnerable leadership*, will be effective in creating a web of sociality.

As president of Grand Canyon University I struggle daily with the challenges that confront me as leader of a small private Christian liberal arts college. I am constantly asking myself, what is the best way to lead? And with over 2,000 books available on the topic of leadership, there seems to be no shortage of options. But the foundational question remains: how can I provide authentic and genuine leadership that is effective? For me, this is through vulnerable leadership.

Leading through vulnerability has meant that, in order to energize the organization, I must be honestly transparent and create an atmosphere of open dialogue. It is as if I must open my very soul to the souls of others, opening an intimacy of relationship between myself and those I lead. This intimate relationship tends to create a system of dependent networking: a web of sociality.

The web of sociality is a theological and sociological construct used by theologian Dietrich Bonhoeffer. I have adapted Bonhoeffer's construct in its reference to the structure of human sociology and expanded it to be inclusive of the relational framework of organizations. The web of sociality is a community that results from relationships built out of mutual transparency and openness.

It is my contention that leadership on the college campus must foster a web of sociality, and that this can be done effectively only through vulnerable leadership. In this chapter ideas about (1) vulnerable leadership, (2) the web of sociality, (3) the role of leadership on the college campus, and (4) the web of sociality on the college campus will be explored.

VULNERABLE LEADERSHIP

Effective leadership for higher education in this new century requires a radical approach. Might I be so bold as to suggest that for leadership to achieve a sense of effectiveness and success, it demands vulnerability?

Henri Nouwen, a former professor at Yale and Harvard, who spent the last ten years of his life as a priest to the physically and mentally handicapped men of the L'Arche community, challenges his readers to be vulnerable in leadership: "I am deeply convinced that the Christian leader of the future is called to be completely irrelevant and to stand in this world with nothing to offer but his or her own vulnerable self."[2] Being vulnerable as a leader suggests being open in such a way as to elicit a mutual openness and willing vulnerability in others.

Vulnerable leadership, whether specifically Christian or not, must exhibit at least four specific characteristics in order for this environment of mutual openness to exist. The leader will: (1) be spiritually sensitive, (2) develop a dynamic theology, (3) be a visionary risk taker, and (4) be willing to empty himself. These characteristics of a vulnerable leader will then be concretely manifest in specific behaviors in the leader's life.

A spiritually sensitive leader will be one who takes time to reflect on his life in spiritual terms. This reflection can best be done by actively participating in a community that fosters spirituality. Personal reflection is powerful in itself, yet, without a community context, the leader can become one dimensional and thereby lose the mutual openness needed in vulnerable leadership. Quite often a spiritually sensitive leader will have a mentor who provides the necessary guidance and accountability to ensure that she is in perpetual growth in the area of spiritual sensitivity.

A vulnerable leader will be open to developing a dynamic theology. Simply stated, theology is how we talk about God, and a dynamic theology is one that is not static or trapped in tradition. A dynamic theology will allow both the believer and God to be open to the mystery of the unknown. This mutual openness must exist in a relationship that is actively involved in a dialogue. Walter Brueggemann insists we can find this God in "elusive texts, which require polyphonic interpretations."[3] As the leader contextualizes himself and God in this kind of relationship, a model for the relationship between the leader and the led will emerge. This is a model that fosters an openness that yields a healthy vulnerability in our relationships with one another and with God. A dynamic theology is important because it can protect the leader from becoming trapped by "doing things the same old ways." It allows him to be constantly looking for the mystery and wonder of leadership, and it will often lead him to have an enthusiastic openness to uncertainty and an anticipation of creative change.

A vulnerable leader will also be a visionary and a risk taker. A visionary risk taker will provide radical leadership so that others can feed off the energy and are motivated to follow the risk being taken. The risk will benefit the greater good of the organization, even if it costs the leader something of value. This is the greatest risk of leadership: the leader being willing to empty himself into the organization for the gain of the organization at the risk of his own loss.

For me, being willing to empty myself for the good of the organization is difficult and has required a hero for me to emulate. My mother has emptied her own life out for the sake of my sister from the moment of her birth. Dinah was born mentally and physically handicapped, and my mother has willingly and without question sacrificed her own being for the survival of my sister. I have watched my mother take up my sister's cause at the risk of my mother's own physical and mental health. My mother's love is powerful and sacrificial toward her children.

However, as a leader, I have rarely had the privilege of being surrounded by people whom I could love like children or even a total group of people I could love in any measure. What is the model for emptying oneself for those who are not loveable? I find that example given by the writer of the New Testament letter of Philippians, speaking about Jesus, where it is written, "he emptied himself," even for those who never followed him or even believed in him. As a vulnerable leader, I may be called on to empty myself for those who do not believe in me or are not willing to follow me. That truly is a difficult model to emulate.

What then is vulnerable leadership? It is about love, relationships, living and dying. It is about giving oneself to something bigger than one's self. Leadership is commitment, sacrifice, and dependency. It will consume the leader's life, expose her life and open her soul to a world of others, for others. Leadership for the twenty-first century must be one of vulnerability. Being vulnerable for the sake of others demands such risks that one must be moored in a deep sense of spirituality and lead a life in which one sees leadership as a spiritual experience.

This spiritual experience of vulnerable leadership could be equated to a spiritual discipline. A spiritual discipline is a practice that enables one to make the transference of the mystery to the actuality of the concrete. The leader will practice leadership with the same care as praying the ancient prayers of her tradition. She will perform her leadership duties with the same endurance as she would perform a ritualistic fast. The leader will handle problems with the same calm as achieved in meditation. And she will carry out her duties with the same vibrancy as she would in singing a great hymn of faith.

Vulnerable leadership as a spiritual discipline calls us into daily practice with a requirement of diligent faithfulness. When the challenges of the job push us beyond our limits of tolerance, we can reach to the comfort of spiritual practice for confidence and stability. When the dark nights of leadership come, and they will, we must be moored in a discipline that continually and faithfully allows us to rely on the strength found within relationships. If we as leaders are willing to rely on the web of sociality for strength, our actions will consistently reflect the priority of the ethos of intimate human interaction.

A vulnerable leader will probably not be fully developed in all of these areas. I have found in my own situation that the complexity of integrating these traits into my life is a struggle. Hopefully, though, this struggle will lead to building a web of sociality on my campus as a means of conducting business and building the organization into a better community.

WEB OF SOCIALITY

Dietrich Bonhoeffer, a German theologian from the World War II era, constructed his understanding of the reality of God within the concept of the web of sociality. He contended that we know God through knowing others. This "knowing" is an intimate embrace extending beyond intellectual acknowledgment and into the realm of spiritual perception through experience. In other words, we can know of God only through the reality of experiencing others. When I encounter you, I am, in the truest sense, in contact with God. Bonhoeffer insists that relationships are dependent on a mutual openness to others and to God, which binds and weaves us into a web: a theology of a web of sociality.[4]

For Bonhoeffer, the manifestation of God, the revelation of God, is Jesus Christ: "Jesus Christ, God himself, addresses us through every human being; the other person, that puzzling, inscrutable Thou, is God's demand upon us, it is God himself who encounters us."[5] This encounter by God is an intentional act of openness, a deliberate action of vulnerability. In the encounter, God is revealing the very foundation and structure of God's substance. It is God's foundational nature to be open, thereby creating a structural openness. As God is in a relationship of structural openness with us, so we are to be structurally open to one another. Bonhoeffer's construct of the "structural openness"[6] of the individual to the "other" creates a definite imposition on the ideals of human and spiritual interaction.

When we view our concrete contact with God through those around us, we become intensely more responsible for our actions toward one another.

Bonhoeffer insisted that God is free to bind Godself to the limitations and constraints of this world. God is making Godself vulnerable to the reality of this world. God is emptying Godself of God's godness. As stated earlier, the New Testament writer of Philippians wrote, "he empties himself"[7] as his description of the goodness of God through Jesus Christ. For me, this is the model of being a vulnerable leader. As God makes Godself willingly vulnerable to the reality of the world through Jesus Christ, who emptied himself, so we too as leaders should be willing to make ourselves vulnerable to the reality of the organization and empty ourselves for its sake.

For Bonhoeffer, our relationships are the whole of our sense of being. Who we are and whom we perceive ourselves to be comes out of our relationships with one another. And our very understanding of God is derived through the experiences realized in relationships. In a sense, the relationships we have with one another may define our relationships with God.

Following this, we understand that relationships are rarely clean and are typically messy. Relationships require that we often be many things to many people, so too in leadership. As a leader of a university, my job often takes on a priestly, pastoral, or counselor role. As people walk through the door, I have to decide quickly if they are looking for specific directions about some task or if this discussion requires more listening than answers. It has not taken me long, as president, to discern that even the simplest decisions first require listening to the suggestion of the person I am dealing with. People want to be heard and to feel that they are significant in the decision-making process. The more I listen, the stronger the relationships. Then when it comes time to make decisions, people feel confident that their own perspectives have been considered.

At a recent student life retreat I was asked to conduct two breakout sessions on leadership. To illustrate how a web of sociality works, I handed them each an eight-foot piece of string. The instructions were that they had to simulate an organization in any fashion they wished. The only rule was that everyone had to be connected to someone else. I had a big plastic ball that represented problems the organization would encounter. Once they formed their organization I would throw the ball in the air, and they would have to catch the ball with whatever structure they had formed.

In the first session one young man tried to take a dominant leadership role. The group formed a loose organization that resembled an amoeba with tentacles. As the ball was thrown into the air, the group struggled to catch it. They could not move as a unit and the ball often eluded them. The few times they succeeded, it was because the group was dependent on a single person to break away from the group and make a valiant effort. They failed more than they succeeded.

The second group of students formed a circle and created what looked like a spider web. Almost every time I threw the ball in the air, they caught it. When I began to challenge the group by forcing them to move as a unit, they quickly made an adaptation. They assigned spotters who would give the group directions, and they would move in concert to catch the ball.

The second group worked as a team to create a system by which they could catch the ball even under difficult scenarios. They were creative in developing a model to handle challenges. The students were able to self-organize a web of sociality and put it into successful operation.

The first group of students reflected a top-down organization. Rarely are the majority of the people in this type of organization motivated to feel a total commitment to the well-being of the company because they are reliant on the success of a few. The group does not move as a team, and it struggles to self-organize to handle crisis situations.

The second group formed a web out of their perceived understanding that this was the best way to deal with problems. When the problems became difficult, they used a consensus method of doing what was best to solve the problem. They selected leaders who were strategically placed within the organization to look out for the best interests of the whole group.

The second group of students used the web to catch their problems, and they worked at the solution together. Each individual in the group was integral to the entire group's success. In a mysterious way the individuals were able to maintain their own identity, yet, at the same time, they yielded to the best interests of the whole group.

While this simplistic activity has little scientific significance, it does reflect recent synthesis of scientific and organizational insights. The concept of the web as a model for organizational structure is emerging from new applications of scientific discoveries. Chaos theory and the notion that patterns arise from seemingly random occurrences has inspired new ideas about organizational development. Highlighting the importance of the web of relationships, Helgesen believes that our identities are inseparable from our relationships with others.[8] This idea is in concert with Wheatley's assertion that "None of us exists independently of our relationships with others."[9]

The theory of holons is also a scientific model that is relevant to the area of organizational development. Wessels explains:

> The theory of holons (is) a description of the relationships that are fundamental to the universe. A holon is not a kind of matter or a particle or a wave or a process; a holon is a whole/part. The theory, as integrated and presented by Ken Wilber, is that whatever exists in the universe is a whole/part. Every whole is also a part and every part is a whole.[10]

This model reflects Bonhoeffer's web of sociality in that humans are no longer seen as isolated parts but as strands in the web, as integral participants in a larger whole.

Whenever I have discussed the concept of vulnerable leadership and the web of sociality with other leaders, the question inevitably arises as to how I can lead if I am constantly listening to and eventually "giving in" to the wishes of anyone who has a difference of opinion. From my perspective, it is not a matter of giving in; it is more about responding to a mutuality that arises from an understanding of wholeness. As in the theory of holons, we make decisions with respect to the fact that the decision maker and those affected are whole/parts, interwoven, and interdependent—much like the students in the second group at the retreat who were woven in a web they were able to move together for the good of all.

When decisions are made within a framework of teamwork and mutual dependence, or whole/part responsiveness, an atmosphere of acceptance and safety is created. Being a vulnerable leader is synonymous with being a leader who can create an atmosphere where those involved feel that their input in valued, appreciated, and respected. The leader creates an atmosphere in which people are encouraged to contribute to mutual dialogue and consensus decision making.

As the students at the retreat successfully formed a web to handle the ball, so too can the individuals in the community create a web of sociality. As leaders, we make decisions toward others as we would make them toward God, ever building an ethic and action toward the community as a whole. Our actions become responsive to the needs of others; as leaders we become willingly vulnerable.

A vulnerable leader willingly exposes the very essence of her own being, opening her soul to the soul of the other. The opening of one's soul is like the emptying of a container, making room for the needs of another. This soul exposure in relationships takes the leader beyond serving the other. As leaders we are more than being simply empathetic. As leaders we are exposing our souls to the soul of another, an intertwining of souls into one-ness, making the many individuals dependent upon one another.

This dependence becomes a web of sociality that is built upon an inter-active reliance. In other words, the leader and those in the organization create a covenant of inseperableness. A covenant is like a waltz.[11] It is a relationship established upon the mutually recognized agreement that one must lead and the other must follow in order for both dancers to enjoy the experience. The beauty and joy of the relationship is that it is mutually dependent upon the successful response and action of the other. The danc-ers, by their agreement to enter into the covenant, create a web of interde-pendence.

As I mentioned earlier, my sister Dinah is mentally and physically handicapped. She has Prader-Willi Syndrome. One of the frustrations that afflicts my sister is her inability to speak clearly. At birth she survived a very high fever, which affected her communication skills. She has an un-derstandable vocabulary of about forty words and another twenty or so signals and sounds that can communicate to those who spend the time to figure out what she means.

Having a conversation with my sister requires a tremendous amount of effort for both parties. My mother calls it "forty questions" and just simply "knowing" Dinah. When something happens to Dinah and she is trying to tell the story, the conversation is like dancing. To enjoy the beauty of the experience, she must lead and I must follow. Usually, I am not sure where we are going, but more than anything I want to go there with her.

I usually see my relationship with God in my sister. A conversation with God requires lots of questions and just simply knowing God. It is a dance and God is leading. The destination is undetermined but the beauty and the thrill of the journey energizes my life.

Wheatley invites us to imagine the dance of "chaos and order, of change and stability" and appreciate that these paradoxical forces are complemen-tary aspects in the process of growth.[12] This dialectical play and the meta-phors of webs and dances can be creatively stimulating and open a new way of envisioning corporate structures. The goal is to create a corporate structure within which decisions arise from relationships, a structure built on the notion that these relations connect us to God.

The web of sociality is a construct for community. On the university campus, as individuals and groups relate ethically and responsibly toward one another, as they are vulnerable to the needs of one another, they will develop a functionally interdependent community that makes decisions out of a web of sociality. This process must begin with a leader who is willing to be vulnerable.

When a leader opens her soul, the essence of who she is, to the known and the unknown, to the soul of another and to God, her actions in leadership begin to take on another dimension of responsibility. This dimension moves the leader from making decisions based on her own intellect, the information available to her, to making decisions out of the context of a responsibility to God carried out through relationships with others. For Bonhoeffer, this is responsibility ethics. Ontological reality is influencing the axiological action of ethics; in other words, how we view the nature of our being affects our actions. If people contextualize their own reality and their connectedness to God through their relationship with others, then their ethical actions, their behavior, will reflect that understanding.

To create an environment that promotes the evolution of a growing and expanding web of sociality, there must be a consistent emphasis on the model itself. The genesis must come directly from the leadership and it must evoke a sense of ownership from the majority of key groups on the campus. In order for the web of sociality to develop as the method of organization, key groups must find their empowerment in the actualization of a leadership committed to vulnerability. Only within this conviction can the web emerge as the dominant pattern.

THE ROLE OF LEADERSHIP ON THE COLLEGE CAMPUS

Being the president of a small Christian liberal arts university requires that I change hats at a minute's notice. The job description requires that I be a fundraiser, administrator, and mouthpiece for the campus. The underlying assumptions are that I can also perform the functions of priest and prophet. The bottom line is that I am a facilitator of relationships. I must be the person who works at creating an environment that supports a web of sociality. This, I believe, is the role of any leader, and especially a college president, in the twenty-first century.

A typical morning on my schedule can look something like the following scenario. A weekly standing meeting is followed by one of the attendees asking if I have five extra minutes to discuss a personal matter. Five minutes turn into an hour as I try to console the person who is suffering through a severe personal problem. The members of a faculty committee who had to wait an additional thirty minutes are now in an irritated hurry to plead their case about a pressing issue. Lunch consists of a high cholesterol meal of fried president, prepared by the hand of an unhappy constituent. The afternoon schedule does not get any better.

Being a vulnerable leader means being willing to expose my soul to the soul of God through others. The process is often painful and it will affect the actions and ethical decisions of the leader. We treat others in an appropriate manner because in reality, when we act toward others within Bonhoeffer's construct, we are in essence treating God in an appropriate manner. It takes our personal well-being out of the equation and replaces it with the well-being of the other. The leader responds and acts because of his concept of the person to whom the action is directed.

As a vulnerable leader in the web of sociality, the leader will depend upon the open-ended process of forgiveness. Forgiveness must be available to the follower as well as the leader as a matter of everyday practice. Jesus taught his followers a unique forgiveness. This is a kind of forgiveness which is always in process, never reaching a sense of conclusion. Jesus teaches this kind of forgiveness through his axiom of forgiving seven times seven.[13] Of course the vulnerable leader asks himself, how many times do I keep forgiving the same wanton mistakes that are costing my organization its lifeblood through this individual's actions?

Whenever I have been in a group and offered the idea of vulnerable leadership, the question of how far I go with a failing situation may be the one most often asked. As the person who is ultimately responsible for the welfare of the university, I ask myself that question every time I have to deal with an employee termination decision.

Several years ago, as athletic director, I had hired a friend to coach one of our teams. This person did not have any coaching experience, but I felt that the person was coaching material and would do a good job of providing a quality experience for our athletes. The team struggled, and it was not long before the players started coming to my office to complain. I started watching the team's practices to see what I could learn. It became quickly apparent that the coach had trouble communicating with the team. I started to work with the coach, and over the course of two years, I invested hundreds of hours trying to mentor the coach. Unfortunately, my efforts and those of many others had little of the desired effect. My only option was to terminate the coach. To say the least, that particular day was long and painful.

The decision to release the coach rested on the question of whether we could invest any more time in the coach, in the face of the students' negative experiences. The answer that emerged was "no." The students' experience on the team was not reflective of the mission of the university, and a change had to be made. Where is the forgiveness in this situation? Forgiveness and justice have to be balanced in an organization.

Walter Breuggemann may have some resolution for the leader through his concept of justice:

> The claim made is that power—political, economic, military—cannot survive or give prosperity or security, unless public power is administered according to the requirement of justice, justice being understood as attention to the well-being of all members of the community.[14]

This concept creates a balance within which the leader can operate. The good of the whole is most important. Again, like the theory of holons, the part and the whole are affected at the same time. Forgiveness and justice become intermingled.

Termination of employees, especially those with whom we may have close association, often demands a difficult decision-making process. It also means taking risks: a vulnerable leader will expose himself and take risks for the sake of the institution.

Dietrich Bonhoeffer may offer one of the most profound examples of taking a self-sacrificing action for the sake of the members of the entire community. Prior to World War II, Bonhoeffer, a college professor and pastor, had been an outspoken critic of Adolf Hitler and had openly opposed his rise to power.

Hitler's genocidal plan was contrary to everything Bonhoeffer understood about God and human responsibility for others. Bonhoeffer's life work was ecumenical in nature and his theology was universal in nature. He believed in the revelation of God through the other. His convictions were so compelling that he and members of his family made a failed assassination attempt against Hitler. These actions eventually led to the execution of Bonhoeffer and two of his family members.

Being a vulnerable leader demands that one must take sacrificial actions. While rarely in the American educational system are we called upon to take such dramatic actions as did Bonhoeffer, we may risk our careers for the sake of something in which we truly believe.

On a public campus the discussion of one's personal religious views may be risky business. Yet, on a Christian campus, the discussion of differing religious and denominational dogmas is no less challenging. The risk is even greater from the position of leadership.

As president, my role is to protect the integrity of an environment that fosters and encourages critical thinking. Instead of indoctrinating the students, I am responsible for promoting teaching and scholarship that challenges the students to be rigorous and analytical in their studies. At the same time, it is also my charge to ensure that an opportunity for exposure to, and engagement with, a Christian worldview is an integral part of the fabric of the university. At our Christian university, I must protect an environment that expects individuals to read and study the Bible, and by engaging God in prayer, come to an individual and a personal conclusion about what they believe. In the Christian religious world, filled with fundamentalists on one side demanding exact dogma and liberals on the other expecting dubious suspicion, providing a safe bastion for the exploration of the mystery of God is no small task. There must be a place in the world of Christian universities where students, faculty, and staff members are encouraged to remain in a dialectical journey filled with more questions than answers.

With this challenge in mind it is imperative to give great care to maintain a focus on the mission of the university. Tremendous effort must be given to constantly assessing the success of strategies. The president who is a vulnerable leader must work hard to stay on the road that leads to building a campus where a web of sociality exists. At times the web may become a safety net which protects the fall from the risky high wire walk of the spiritual journey. If the university, Christian or otherwise, is doing its job, then the web will be in place.

THE WEB OF SOCIALITY ON A COLLEGE CAMPUS

For an environment in which a healthy web of sociality can exist, there must be a leader committed to the concept of vulnerability. The leader must exhibit on a consistent basis the attributes and characteristics of vulnerability. Here is where the "what if" question comes into play: So what if the leader acts out of vulnerability? What are the concomitant results? At this point I can only offer the visions I see. The web of sociality on a college campus relies on a leader who is committed to being a vulnerable leader. The leader will facilitate an open environment of trust and service.

Grand Canyon University is located in Arizona, and I am very fortunate to have the privilege of working near two wonderful presidents who are willing to share their wisdom and guidance with me, Dr. Lattie Coor and Dr. Clara Lovitt.

Dr. Lattie Coor is the president of Arizona State University, a public school of over 40,000 students. Once a month Dr. Coor spends the entire day working alongside someone on the campus in customer service. A person on the ASU campus told me that "it sends an incredible message to see the president answering questions at the Student Union information booth." Being available is being vulnerable.

When the leader leads the campus it will reflect that person's style of leadership. The faculty will integrate service learning into the fabric of their curricula; student organizations will focus their energies on the needs of the community; staff members will see their role as one of modeling service to the students. At the center of the campus will be a sense of service and compassion.

Dr. Clara Lovitt is the president of Northern Arizona University, a residential state school of approximately 16,000 students. One of the university's goals is to create a "small private feel" on its campus, a goal which obviously starts with the president.

Four years ago several colleges and universities recruited my daughter. Each school had its own attractiveness for her. But the one thing that tipped the scale for her was a personal handwritten note from Dr. Lovitt. Personal notes send loud messages of openness, and openness is being vulnerable.

Dr. Coor and Dr. Lovitt are presidents at large public institutions. Grand Canyon University, where I am president, is a private Christian school that does not restrict its enrollment to only Christian students. We do, however, only hire Christian faculty and staff members. While it might be thought that the discussion of pluralism and spirituality would be foreign to our campus, they are at the heart of the discussion of how we can integrate our faith with our learning in a community that is religiously diverse.

At Grand Canyon University, we do not intend to indoctrinate. We are here to ask the primordial questions of life on a journey of discovery. Asking these questions should lead us as a university to deeper engagement with our community.

Service learning and community service are outcomes of our university's mission to be intimate with our community. Being an active agent in the community is a reflection of the web of sociality that exists on our campus. While we will never "arrive" at a successful conclusion, we see this as a process we are working through. It is a journey everyone on our campus is invited to join.

No matter whether a college is religious or secular, an environment of a web of sociality can empower its participants to make a difference on the campus and in the communities in which they reside. While one does not need to be a Christian to be a vulnerable leader, I would suggest that one find a role model like Jesus Christ, who emptied himself.

CONCLUSION

Within the first month of my presidency, the administrative team decided that we should sponsor a faculty and staff retreat. Sensing that the retreat could, in many ways, define my leadership, I asked for volunteers to serve on an ad hoc committee to plan the retreat. People from faculty, plant services, accounting, admissions, and financial aid worked together to create an event that drew all the varying perspectives of our campus together. The day was filled with prayer, laughter, camaraderie, and the development of community through relationships.

The committee worked independently with little administrative input, and they succeeded in giving birth to a marvelous retreat. That retreat has become a watershed event for me because I turned the entire planning over to these volunteers. By relying on our relationships, I could place the outcome of this important moment within the hands of the committee. I had to be vulnerable.

A vulnerable leader will have a theology that is dynamic, a theology that is growing and changing. This theology will include an openness that promotes and encourages a web of sociality. This web prompts us to move as a community. As a web, the participants can work together for the common good. The web will act out of an ethic of forgiveness and justice for the sake of the community.

Our responsibility as an educational community— and I include here faculty, administration, staff, and students— is to create an environment that supports the web of sociality.

As educators, we are responsible for equipping our students with relationship-building skills. The postmodern globally connected community forces its participants to interact on a personal basis. The world gets smaller and our web of sociality becomes more personal and yet broader in base. Diarmund O'Murchu says, "Our relationship with life— at both the micro and macro levels— is a learning process of mutual interdependence."[15]

ENDNOTES

1. Dietrich Bonhoeffer, *Sanctorum Communio: A Theological Study of the Sociology of the Church* (Minneapolis: Fortress Press, 1998), 65.
2. Henri J. Nouwen, *In the Name of Jesus: Reflections on Christian Leadership* (New York: Crossroads, 1995), 17.
3. Walter Brueggemann, *Theology of the Old Testament: Testimony, Dispute, Advocacy* (Minneapolis: Fortress Press, 1997), 731.
4. Clifford J. Green, *Bonhoeffer: A Theology of Sociality* (Grand Rapids: Eerdmans, 1999).
5. Eberhard Bethge, *Dietrich Bonhoeffer: A Biography* (Minneapolis: Fortress Press, 2000), 113.
6. Bonhoeffer, *Sanctorum*, 67.
7. Philippians 2:7
8. Sally Helgesen, *The Web of Inclusion: A New Architecture for Building Great Organizations* (New York: Currency/Doubleday, 1995), 16.
9. Margaret Wheatley, *Leadership and the New Science: Learning about Organization from an Orderly Universe* (San Francisco: Berret-Koehler, 1994), 34.
10. Cletus Wessels, *The Holy Web: Church and the New Universe Story* (New York: Maryknoll, 2000), 57.
11. Walter Brueggemann, *The Psalms of the Life of Faith* (Minneapolis: Fortress Press, 1995), 135–149.
12. Wheatley, *Leadership*, 21.
13. Matthew 18:21–22
14. Brueggemann, *Theology of the Old Testament,* 615.
15. Wessels, *Holy Web*, 23.

12.   Spirituality in Student Affairs: A Practitioner's Perspective

Margaret A. Jablonski

Where is God on a secular college campus? I saw God on our campus the other day in the eyes of the director of Hillel, as she explained "Who is God?" from her sermon delivered on Rosh Hoshanah. Debbie described God as a parent and the human race as a child/adolescent interacting throughout stages of development. Although she did not start out portraying God as a "mother" figure, our women and spirituality group discussed gender and the Divine for the next hour. The feminine face of God was reflected in the stories the six of us shared that day. I returned to work after that lunch gathering with strength of purpose, warmth in my heart, and an openness to accept what came my way for the afternoon. I was a much better dean of students that day because I had spent time thinking about my relationships with the Divine, with others, and with myself.

In this chapter I will describe the work of student affairs professionals on a college campus as a journey of spiritual growth. I will explore issues around spirit at work and how I have incorporated aspects of spirit into my role as supervisor, colleague, dean, and friend. I will share aspects of my spiritual development to illustrate how being female and feminist has affected how I do my work. After all, I believe that student affairs work is spiritual work. It involves connecting with individuals in a meaningful way and creating organizations that breathe with spirit and efficiency, balance and productivity, wholeness and success.

THE WORK OF STUDENT AFFAIRS

In the 1937 publication *The Student Personnel Point of View*, those of us who work with students were instructed to provide for the intellectual, emotional, occupational, physical, and spiritual development of students.[1] This emphasis on holistic development was congruent with the early trajectory of American higher education: almost all colleges, private and public, were founded in conjunction with a particular denomination. An explicit connection was made between spiritual exploration and growth and over-all adult human development. In the twentieth century, most public campuses distanced themselves from any expression of religion, including support of the spiritual development of their students.

In the past decade, however, deeper connections between religion and spirituality have been fostered on our public campuses. Students themselves appear eager to pose the big questions about the meaning of life and their place within it. A majority of students come to college already participating in community service projects in their local communities. National conferences such as the Education as Transformation conference at Wellesley College in 1998 and Going Public with Spirituality at the University of Massachusetts in 2000 have brought together spiritual and secular leaders to explore spirituality on our campuses and in society.

Yet we have lacked an understanding of human development that is grounded in human diversity. The developmental theory that supports the work of student affairs is based upon models of psychological development that used primarily white, male, middle- and upper-class subjects. Theorists such as Erikson and Chickering and Reesor describe adult development as an individual journey on a hierarchical ladder toward separation and autonomy.[2,3] Most of the student affairs programs across the country have been based on these identity development constructs. Over the past two decades, new models that take into consideration gender, ethnicity, race, sexual orientation, and religious affiliation have challenged the traditional notions of psychological growth and maturity. Feminist identity theorists such as Gilligan, Miller, and others have argued that women develop in relationship, use intuition and feeling, and reach maturity through connected experiences.[4,5]

As we continue to question the models upon which our student affairs programs and services are constructed, we enable feminist and multicultural perspectives on human development to inform our work. This exploration will force us to reconsider the fundamental tenets of the student affairs profession upon which our models for the organization of departments and programs have been built. What might result from such reconsideration? Ultimately, student affairs will grow to find new ways of including different voices and perspectives in designing our programs and services. These new ways of being and doing in student affairs will be both challenging and exciting.

GENDER AND RELIGION: FEMINIST INTERPRETATIONS

Over the past twenty-five years, many books have been written about the feminine aspect of the divine, arguing that the historical evolution of patriarchal religions has involved the exclusion or marginalization of women.[6] Studies in anthropology, archeology, history, and religion have uncovered civilizations where women were worshiped as creators and sustainers of the earth, fertility, life, and death. We are only beginning to explore the rich culture of centuries past, connecting theories of community, transforming social structures from one of a dominator model to a partnership model.[7] In this exploration, feminist religious/spiritual writers such as Daly, Borysenko, Estes, Christ and Plaskow, and others have developed models and theories to describe the "feminine face of god."[8,9,10,11]

Feminist spirituality, if we may refer to these ideas with this general term, explores a new consciousness that is communal, cooperative, respectful of nature, caring of all forms of labor, celebrative of feminine aspects of the divine, and ultimately transformational of both individuals and society.

The traditional hierarchical, technological, bureaucratic model of the academy is not welcoming to feminist perspectives on spirituality. One example is the misuse of power within the departmental system of hiring, promotion, and tenure which exalts conformity to the traditional forms and theories instead of welcoming alternative voices such as those of feminist or multicultural scholars. The time constraints placed on the tenure process (usually seven years, with a year leave for childbirth or adoption) are unrealistic given the demands of family life, either care for children or aging parents.

In seeking to understand the role of religious/spiritual life on college campuses, we must include the feminist perspective. Many of those in the academy who teach or work as administrators have been exposed to alternative interpretations of the traditional religions, and many have incorporated aspects of this new spirituality into their lives and their work. Embracing ecumenism has enabled the creation of shared religious centers on many campuses. The celebration of many faith traditions, and even pagan holy days such as the Solstice, are more common particularly on public campuses. As more women with feminist principles of work and organization assume positions of leadership in the academy, they may be able to affect some change. However, there are powerful forces at work to maintain things just the way they are: the dominance of the research paradigm;

the management of colleges by business-dominated boards of trustees; the continued separation of church and state; and the pervasive cultural norms of the higher education enterprise.

In my work on the leadership styles of women college presidents, I found that although the majority described themselves as participative and feminist leaders, their faculty did not view them this way. These women were mentored by men, had been leaders on campuses where they typically were the only woman, or one of a few women, in senior leadership roles. They also worked with primarily male boards of trustees. All of those factors contributed to their learned and practiced leadership style—a traditional, bureaucratic, hierarchical mode, rather than the feminist model they said they wanted to embody.

Personal Journey

Over the past twenty years, I have worked in student affairs on five campuses, both public and private. I have been on the staff or supervised the departments of residence life, dean of students, student activities, campus police, Greek life, judicial programs, orientation, counseling, and career services. I have been a liaison to the college chaplains and have worked on a variety of programs with them. By teaching both full-time and part-time in the School of Education at the University of Massachusetts, I help prepare all levels of teachers and administrators for work within the field of education. In all of these roles, I was usually one of the few women at the table or teaching in the classroom.

The field of student affairs has changed dramatically in the past twenty years, and it is now dominated by women in the entry and middle management ranks. Most of the students in graduate programs around the country are women. This shift has forced the reconsideration of aspects of the field, including salary, career paths, leadership styles, and the workplace itself.

I was brought up Roman Catholic, attending parochial schools until I went to a large public university. While at the University of Massachusetts, I discovered there were a variety of religious interpretations for any moral question. Although I remained anchored at the Newman Center on campus, I explored Judaism, feminist spirituality, and multiculturalism. Over the past twenty years, I have taken a circular route back toward my grounding in Catholicism, exploring feminist theology, goddesses, Benedictine principles, Eastern religions, Celtic spirituality, and "social justice" Catholicism. I find comfort in the rituals of the traditional church, and at the same time, remain uncomfortable with the hierarchy and patriarchy that pervades the institutional church. I continue to try to reconcile my past, present, and future connections to the church from a feminist spiritual perspective.

An avenue for incorporating the spiritual from my own experience into higher education involves designing graduate courses. In several courses I have developed, I have included discussion of spirituality, as well as the examination of policy and practice issues from the lens of gender. Last year, I developed a course entitled "Spirituality and Education," encountering skepticism from colleagues about incorporating the study of spirituality into an education course on a public campus. I approached the criticism from the perspective of multicultural education, arguing that we need to explore issues of educational pedagogy from various lenses, and that religion/spirituality have traditionally been left out of this examination. Although the course was limited to an enrollment of twenty, more than thirty students participated. They explored aspects of education and spirituality from theory to practice through different perspectives of gender, culture, social class, etc. Many students said the course was groundbreaking, inspirational, and provided the opportunity they were seeking for integrating their work with their self-identity.

SPIRIT AT WORK

How has the intersection of gender identity development and the spiritual reawakening among college students influenced our work in student affairs? I have always thought of my work as a female dean of students as an opportunity to guide, coach, or mentor students as well as the staff with whom I work. Role modeling ethical and inclusive behavior is one of the most important aspects of being a good supervisor and teacher. I seek to create a community of learners, where we all can challenge and support each other's growth and development. As a supervisor, I use the skills of intuition and listening (traditionally described as feminine) as much as I do analysis and planning (usually seen as masculine). Being empathetic in challenging situations allows for compassion to be a guiding principle of human interaction. The traditionally feminine qualities of intuition and empathy are integral to my daily interactions with both students and staff.

I am convinced that on the fast-paced campuses where we work, we need to create opportunities for people to be in relation with each other. In this way, they begin to touch each other's spirits. The pace of our work must be slowed to enable deep and personal connections with each other. Our priorities must be reordered to use technology to enhance relationships, not replace them. This seems to me to be connected to my feminist perspective on the nature and organization of work itself. In order for work to be more collaborative and transformational, it needs to be rooted, cared for, and harvested properly. Women have been doing such work for generations within the family, home, and environment.

Another aspect of honoring spirit on a college campus entails creating meaningful celebrations and traditions infused with spirit. When I was at the Massachusetts Institute of Technology, we provided structure to community service for entering students by having a full day of service projects during orientation. When students experience involvement in their community from the outset, they tend to stay actively engaged in public service throughout their time in college. At the University of Connecticut, we established a Midnight Breakfast before finals, where administrators and faculty serve students, creating community and connections.

GROUP WORK AND RETREATS

Earlier in this chapter I described a group of women exploring spirituality on a public college campus. On two campuses where I have worked, I have been part of such groups—sharing experiences, encouraging reflection, and honoring differing understandings of faith and practice. In each case, the women who came together were struggling with the male-dominated structure and model of the academy and their place within it. These women were spiritual seekers, and by coming together to explore feminine aspects of spirituality, answers to our long-standing questions were infused with new ideas and options. We prayed together, shared music and food, read spiritual works, created space for reflection and exploration, and deepened our faith. Each person shared responsibility for the maintenance of the group and its leadership. Based on this experience, I feel that providing space for reflection on who we are, in relation to the work we do, is vital to our human and spiritual development.

Typically, departmental retreats are looked upon with disdain as a wasted day away from campus. I have always relished the days of retreat from the regular pace and routine of work. When we are away from our meetings and constant office chatter, we share our stories and can be creative. Listening to each other's stories is a profoundly spiritual experience. Retreats should be more than goal setting and planning exercises. Time needs to be created to enhance relationships, share leadership, and explore new concepts of infusing spirit into work. Part of our time in retreats should be spent in silence to allow our minds to focus on the moment. Over the past decade, I have facilitated numerous retreats for staff in student affairs, and I have always tried to weave in spirit, intuition, and connections.

EXAMPLES OF SPIRIT AT WORK FROM A DEAN'S PERSPECTIVE

In thinking back over the past month (fall of 2000), I have had several opportunities to infuse spirit into my work and workplace. I believe that these examples are grounded in part in my feminist perspective on spirituality and work itself. Here are several illustrations:

1) In contract negotiations between employees and management, by asking open-ended questions, affirming the positions of others, seeking areas of agreement and supporting positions that enhance the quality of the workplace and the lives of employees, I seek to reach out and connect with others in collaboration instead of confrontation.

2) I seek to create connections that weave together community. For example, I took a new female staff member on a walk to see the horses on campus. The colors were changing, and the sun was setting at the end of the day. I could feel a sense of spirit flowing between us, as we practiced ways of being with colleagues that build a spiritual community.

3) In working with a colleague who was anxious about her position, I asked her what her inner spirit said about her dilemma. People need to have their stories heard, and we need to find time to listen. I think gender does play a role in the listening, sharing, and storytelling that women participate in with each other.

4) When role modeling ethical behavior in policymaking and decision making, I am setting an example for student government leaders and student affairs staff. I apologized to a staff member who felt hurt by my lack of support for him in a public meeting. Sometimes my own stress gets in the way of modeling ethical behavior. By recognizing the mistake, I can restore the relationship. By honoring the spirit of the person involved, we will be able to learn from this and do good work together in the future.

5) As the person who oversees the judicial system, I look at the outcome of cases from a spiritual viewpoint: how does this resolution influence the spirit of the individual, the group, or the campus? How can the development of character be central to those involved in this case? In the case of a sexual assault, can the female survivor and the male assailant learn and grow from discussions about issues of gender, power, sexuality, and violence? By caring for a sexual assault survivor through listening, sharing, and providing space for her to explore her feelings I am helping her heal and love herself. I encouraged her questions about why this happened to her, and how this connects to the larger picture of violence against women.

6) By participating in a bi-monthly spirituality group, I gain support for my own spiritual journey. I know I cannot go it alone, and want to support others in their exploration and development. As I stated earlier, the all-female composition of this group is a critical factor in providing the space for my spiritual journey.

Many of these examples may seem simple or obvious. However, each of them is an intentional act which takes time to initiate and carry out. Each example, for me, is also indicative of feminist spiritual perspectives influencing the workplace in a positive way. Through thoughtful examination of the questions "What is my role?" and "What must I do today to infuse spirit into my work?" we are better able to prioritize our time and energy.

DAILY PRACTICE

Cultivating spirituality in my life as a student affairs practitioner provides the energy I need to engage with my work in a mindful way. Having space for the exploration of gender in my work enables me to take advantage of underutilized aspects of my thinking and feeling self. There must be intentional examination of the intersection of spirit, gender, and work on a college campus.

One of my regular spiritual practices includes walking in nature every day, paying attention to the leaves on the trees, the wind, birds flying, and the flowers. This form of walking meditation focuses the mind, bringing clarity of thinking to everyday concerns. Yoga and massage are two other regular gifts to myself. Reconnecting the body, spirit, and mind are critical in an environment of the academy that has honored the separation of these unifying life forces. Over the past decade I have participated in both directed retreats (where I meet with a mentor or guide) and individual retreats where I spend time alone to think, pray, and rest. These retreats have often taken place at religious communities of women that model a caring community. Retreating completely from the world for several weekends a year allows you to reconnect with your soul, rejuvenate your body, and clear your mind.

Over the years, I have read dozens of spiritual books. I have moved from Catholicism to feminist theology, to exploration of Eastern religions, to Celtic spirituality, to Native American stories. This is very similar to many "seekers" described by Lesser in her book on the new American spirituality.[12] Another female dean in New England calls me every few months to talk about what we are reading, and to make the connections about spirituality and gender into our work and lives. Through a group of individuals in the Spiritual Life Network in New England, we have explored the connections between our faith and our work in student affairs, offering programs for others working in student affairs at our professional conferences.

We must find more ways such as these to continue to support our individual and collective explorations of spirit and work, and the connections between spirituality, gender, and student life. The future of our field depends on the full integration of mind, body, and spirit in the work that we do.

ENDNOTES

1. American Council on Education, *The Student Personnel Point of View* (Washington, DC: American Council on Education, 1937).
2. Erik Erikson, *Identity: Youth and Crisis* (New York: Norton, 1968).
3. Arthur Chickering and Linda Reesor, *Education and Identity,* 2nd ed. (San Francisco: Jossey-Bass, 1993).
4. Carol Gilligan, *In a Different Voice: Psychological Theory and Women's Development* (Cambridge, MA: Harvard University Press, 1992).
5. Jean Baker Miller, *Toward a New Psychology of Women* (Boston: Beacon Press, 1976).
6. See, for example, Riane Eisler, *The Chalice and the Blade: Our History, Our Future* (San Francisco: Harper & Row, 1987) and Merlin Stone, *When God Was a Woman* (New York: Dial Press, 1984).
7. Riane Eisler, *The Chalice.*

8. Mary Daly, *Gyn/Ecology* (London: The Women's Press, 1979) and *Beyond God the Father* (Boston: Beacon Press, 1973).

9. Joan Borysenko, *A Woman's Journey to God* (New York: Riverhead Books, 1999).

10. Clariss Pinkola Estes, *Women Who Run with the Wolves* (New York: Ballantine Books, 1992).

11. Carol Christ and Judith Plaskow, eds., *Womanspirit Rising: A Feminist Reader in Religion* (New York: Harper & Row, 1979).

12. Elizabeth Lesser, *The New American Spirituality* (New York: Random House, 2000).

13. Unpacking the Knapsack Is Not a Picnic

KATJA HAHN D'ERRICO

> You who want
> knowledge,
> seek the oneness
> within
>
> There you
> will find
> the clear mirror
> already waiting
> —Hadewijch of Antwerp, 13th century[1]

As an educator one brings to one's work who one is. I "am" the accumulation of my life experiences, they are "my knapsack," all that I have learned and taught. My joys and fears, my laughter and my tears assure me that I am alive. My life experiences are linked to the ever-evolving question: who am I?

In a small book of letters, which has accompanied me ever since my teenage years in Germany, the poet Rainer Marie Rilke advises a young writer not to search for life's questions, but rather to live the questions now. He goes on to say that someday in the future "you will gradually, without noticing it, live your way into the answer."[2] In the next few pages I shall talk about the contents of my knapsack and what effect my life experiences have had on my work as an educator and how I am trying to live my questions honestly and courageously.

Living on the edge of life has opened up a view beyond myself and taken me out of my inner isolation. Individuals like me make up organizations, including institutions of higher education. David K. Scott suggests that the prerequisite for organizational transformation lies in a change of beliefs and attitudes among individuals who are a part of those institutions.[3] He suggests that this process of change has already started and that a powerful movement has begun to change organizations of higher education. Integrative approaches help overcome fragmentation, specialization, and isolation in individuals and institutions. Through an understanding of my own journey I am able to be receptive to change in the classroom as well as in my daily work.

NOT YET READY TO LIVE THE QUESTION

Since 1983 I have been the director of student businesses, a position within campus activities at the University of Massachusetts Amherst. I returned to graduate school in mid-life and earned a master's degree in organizational development, followed by a doctorate in social justice education. I am currently an adjunct faculty member in the School of Education. For several years, I have been coteaching an undergraduate class in leadership and weekend seminars for graduate students on issues of social justice. I also work as a consultant and trainer on issues of social justice and the interconnectedness of body-mind-emotions-spirit.

The eight student businesses that I direct are unique in higher education. They were initiated and are still managed by full-time undergraduate students, thirty years after they were instituted at the University of Massachusetts Amherst. About 150 students are employed by these businesses and their annual revenue amounts to about $650,000. Students enjoy a unique opportunity to learn about leadership and teamwork, acquiring small business skills while serving the university community. As the director of these businesses, I am responsible for training and education, fiscal health, and the observance of university regulations. I see myself as a bridge between students and administration and as a resource when students need help.

When I started my job as the director of student businesses in 1983, I did not think of myself as a spiritual person. But over the years my work has become intricately interwoven with my spiritual journey: my work informs my spirituality; my spirituality informs my work. How did this transformation occur? Why is it important for my work? Let me tell you my story.

I came to my work with the "knapsack" of who I was in 1983: a white, forty-four-year-old woman of German extraction, who immigrated to the United States in 1962. I had just quit as a partner in a wholesale produce collective, Squash Trucking, where I played an active part in the second wave of the food cooperative movement in New England. As a single mother raising two sons and trying to share them with their father, I was dealing with bitterness and anger in the wake of my divorce. My curiosity was waning; I no longer felt alert in my work. It was high time to move on, to expand and explore different opportunities, but it was also necessary to look back.

LEAVING CHILDHOOD SAFETY FOR ADULT STRUGGLE

I grew up during World War II. I was educated in postwar Germany, where socialization was rigid. A certain narrowness of view proved especially difficult for me as a child. The German middle class strove for academic achievement as a path to a secure career. I could not understand that my parents, who had lived through the upheavals of two world wars, wanted nothing as much as to see their two daughters gain a stable footing in life. They wished for me to become a teacher with the prospect of a secure pension. Teaching was considered a "good" profession for girls. Only much later in life, when I had children of my own to be concerned about, did I grow to understand my parents' conservative stance and their keen desire for security. Going against their wishes, I chose medical research in order to please the love of my youth. From feeling beholden to my parents, I became "engaged" to another version of childhood dependency.

Only after I chose to join a collective, in the form of a wholesale cooperative, was I free to leave the authoritarian order of my childhood behind me and embrace a new norm of teamwork. Our cooperative grew to become the produce suppliers for all co-ops, small and large, in western Massachusetts. At the same time as we expanded we were caught up in a political struggle, advocating the "right agenda" of self-determination and care for the environment. We acted with passion, making up for our lack of skill and training. Soon enough our produce wholesale collective transformed itself into a commercial entity. We "solved" our problems by switching sides.

When I took up my current position at the University of Massachusetts Amherst, I was ready to embark on my third professional career. Having started out as a medical researcher—a skill that brought me to the United States in the first place—I became the co-owner in a business that didn't want to be one, before turning to education. I had not previously worked in an institution of higher education, but my six-year experience as a medical researcher in a laboratory at Yale University had given me a sense of management responsibility.

ENTERING HIGHER EDUCATION AS STAFF MEMBER AND GRADUATE STUDENT

Little did I know about the burden of participatory training in a highly defined, hierarchical, and bureaucratic system. Initially, I met with hostility from students who denied me access to their meetings, and from other staff whose perception of me was that of an "old hippie." In the eyes of students I was just an administrator, part of the power structure and therefore an "enemy," a spy who would usurp their power. I had neither been officially introduced to my job, nor trained in any way to perform it. I felt like a tofu burger between two stale buns. That sorry feeling still returns to haunt me from time to time, but my attitude has changed. Instead of allowing myself to feel hurt, I am now most of the time able to muster a sense of humor and ride out any tight situation.

The hostility that greeted me on arrival was further aggravated by my lack of familiarity with institutional practices. I lacked the tools to handle the issues. A colleague of mine later described my predicament: "in those days you were a dragon and I was afraid of you." For my part, I so much wanted to be liked that fear of failure became my constant companion. My childhood fears of not being good enough resurfaced and hamstrung my ability to act. As a child I countered those fears by rebellion, but that escape route was now closed. It quickly became clear to me that I needed to do two things: first, I must acquire the tools for a better understanding of business and group dynamics; second, I needed to know myself better, so as to understand my fears and break their hold over me. So far I had no sense of being "spirit" and was, therefore, unable to understand how my attitudes affected the people around me. Surrounded by all this negativity, I toyed with the idea of becoming a graduate student.

I applied as a master's student in organizational development under the auspices of the School of Education. I knew that I lacked skills and a sound theoretical basis. Only a better comprehension of my personal experience could restore my sense of creativity. During the first two semesters, I tested the waters as a nonmatriculated student. Before taking the plunge, I wanted to be sure that I could handle this challenge in a language and an educational system that were not native to me. I also needed confirmation that I was bright enough. I loved studying; I loved the process of learning, and I slowly overcame my fear of inadequacy. Finally, I dared to apply to the program as a full-time graduate student. My journey had restored my courage to grasp the circumstances and live the question, as the poet Rilke had advised the aspiring writer to do.[4] My curiosity for learning grew and I was rewarded with good grades and positive feedback. A new spark brought joy and fulfillment to my work.

In my personal life, however, things were not so bright. I still harbored a darkness within myself that engulfed me in sadness and depression, pushing me to the brink of suicidal ideas. Three people who were very important in my life died that same year: my mother, my surrogate American mother, and a close friend. I lost my German childhood home. It was sold and dissolved, leaving me with a sense of abandonment and drift. I felt like a plant with its roots exposed, dangling in mid-air. An important intimate relationship also unraveled in deceit and betrayal. The events in my life were disjointed, my emotions distraught, my work and my studies all separately compartmentalized. My knapsack was packed with ever more tightly wrapped packages, but their content remained secret and unknown to their very owner. I began therapy in order to find out what was happening to me and to begin unpacking my knapsack again.

THE BODY'S LAST RESORT

When I knew—for I could feel it—that I had a tumor growing in my left breast, I abruptly ended therapy out of fear that I would not be able to keep my secret from my therapist. My death wish overwhelmed and paralyzed me. Eight months into my ordeal the doctor assured me that it was nothing, just a normal calcification.

When I returned a few months later, the tumor had developed to the size of my breast. This time I went to see a physician I knew and trusted. He examined me, left the room, and returned to tell me that most probably I had a malignant tumor. A biopsy and mastectomy were ordered at once, in a single surgical intervention. Later on the physician shared his reaction with me, telling me that he had left the room to cry.

My simultaneous knowledge and denial proved shattering. For the first time I was able to confront my situation. My life felt empty, yet for the first time in many years I badly wanted it to continue. What was I going to tell my teenage sons?

With emptiness in my heart, I experienced a moment of synchronicity in which disjointed hopes and fears coalesced: I stopped at one of my professor's offices for a piece of advice. The hour we spent together was one of the most decisive of my life. Jack enabled me to see the difference between being tired and wanting to die. I wanted to live. When I left his office I was ready to fight for my life, to rest, to heal, and focus on myself. I felt the courage to learn about myself.

Today a colorful poster with a citation and a photograph of Audrey Lorde hangs over my office door: "When I dare to be powerful—to use my strength in the service of my vision, then it becomes less and less important whether I am afraid." I always want to remember this message of courage and perseverance. Once I gained the courage to face my fear, I was able to become fully alive.

In the week leading up to surgery I took control of my life. I resumed therapy, knowing that there was still a lot to work through. I made arrangements for my sons to stay with their father. Three women became my main source of emotional and practical support, my own "Red Cross" unit. They did research and accompanied me on all of my doctor's visits, helping me to understand the issues at hand.

When I returned from the hospital after my mastectomy, I found the notice of acceptance to the master's program in organizational development and a copy of the recommendation from one of my professors in my mailbox. It took a while to understand that this stellar recommendation spoke about me. My teacher's accompanying note read: "Katja, now more than ever." My operation having been scheduled during seminar time, the class had done a meditation and visualization for me. The professor left the tape of this session at my house so that I could listen to it upon my return. During the next few weeks he drove me to and from the university, understanding that learning was part of my recovery.

My medical prognosis was not good: I had only a 20 percent chance of survival. My breast cancer had reached stage three. There were still cancer cells on my chest wall because the cancer had grown too deep for them to be removed in surgery. The question I now had to face was, would I choose chemotherapy or radiation? I opted for both. My doctors were not happy with my decision. They thought it too risky. I knew that I had a healthy body and that I needed to take the strongest medicine possible in order to survive. For the first time in my life, I listened to and let myself be guided by my inner voice. For the first time I felt body and mind connected.

BECOMING FULLY ALIVE AND READY "TO LIVE THE QUESTIONS"

The first time I heard spirit speak to me was when I was in intensive care after waking up from surgery. A soft wind fanned across my chest.

My heart felt exposed and open. It no longer had the protection of the breast. I remember checking my covers and my bandage. They were all in place, but this gentle wind continued as a strong voice told me that this was all about love, about opening up my heart and allowing myself to be loved. The voice came from above and repeated this sentence several times. When the surgeon came to check on me, I told him about this experience and how it had moved me to the core. He grabbed the chart to see if I was overmedicated.

When I was out of the hospital, I made an appointment with Ellen, a spiritual clairvoyant counselor who has remained my teacher ever since. On the occasion of my first visit with her she told me about my journeys through many past lives. I listened in awe. I was too weak to assume my usual rebellious stance that had helped me survive the traumas of childhood. Instead I quietly listened. During the weeks that followed I replayed the tape recording of Ellen's comments and came to discover a familiarity with those distant lives and their recurring themes: I am worthy to be loved; I am love; I am good enough.

My spiritual journey brought me in contact with extraordinary healers, particularly Tom, who used his amethyst pendulum for diagnosis and sent his medication via an energy that was neither physical nor verbal. I would phone him and confirm the time I felt that he had sent the energy. His diagnosis of the state of my blood cells and my health was confirmed by Western medical tests and was never wrong in two years.

Healing became my opportunity to broaden and open up to other possibilities. I learned to let go and live in the present. Lying in the radiation chamber I spontaneously remembered the 23rd Psalm, which I had not thought of in thirty years. The lead doors of the radiation chamber would close and I started reciting the 23rd Psalm. With the last line, the chamber doors would open again and I felt calm and at peace. This is how I learned about compassion and gentleness. I learned that I am spirit always and, as in any other previous lifetime, I am learning to be human. "Despair and isolation are my greatest internal enemies"—these words by Audrey Lorde rang true for my life even before surgery.[5]

The question of "Why?" had made me passive, engendering the feeling of being a victim. Now I stopped asking why and started to wonder "What am I learning?" Pursuing this question has put me in charge of my life and allowed me to develop intuition and discernment, given me authority over my spirit, and moved me forward in understanding my condition. I know that this is an ongoing process, one that is never finished, but slowly bringing me closer to home, to the center of my being. The illness became my opportunity for change and the stimulus to excavate hidden dimensions of my childhood. I came to recognize the reality of energy, negative and positive. I gained balance in my doings and for the first time felt guided by love and spirit. With the help of my spiritual teacher I learned to value silence, engage in meditation and visualization. I learned to listen to my guides and to my spirit. My childhood pain did not need to remain in my knapsack any longer. I was able to turn my experiences into learning.

Paula, a fellow graduate student, worked with light and energy. She taught me how to visualize myself in a healthy body. It took me three weeks to learn to visualize my body in a healthy state. Before I acquired this ability, I thought I was lying, knowing that there were still cancer cells left on my chest wall, but now I realized that I was more than my breast and more than my hair, that there was a core of my being that needed my body to live in, and that my essence was not affected by cancer. Affirmations and visualizations are now regular tools of my work and teaching. Empowering individuals to positive thinking is an important part of my social justice work.

Two weeks after surgery I returned to work. Some of my colleagues, including the director of campus activities, could not deal with my grim prognosis or with me. Others among my colleagues became my "buddies," particularly my friend Margaret, with whom I have shared much of my inner life. We coteach the leadership class I previously mentioned; we train staff and students in teamwork and help them master total quality management; we share our joys and sorrows and most importantly we listen to each other with our hearts. A few of my colleagues remained uneasy with me: for them I was a constant reminder of instability and, perhaps, of death.

My students were fantastic in their steadfast support, my very own cheering section. They motivated me, gave me hope, made me laugh and truly believe that I would make it. I returned to work as fast as possible because I did not want to sit home and vainly ponder my fate.

My learning about spirituality had a profound effect on my life and work. I started to understand the simple, and yet profound, secret that the fox shared with the Little Prince shortly before his departure: "It is only with the heart that one can see rightly, what is essential is invisible to the eye."[6]

My love of social justice, which I have felt since childhood, gradually returned as my fear of life diminished. My graduate work, learning about family therapy and group dynamics, gave me an opportunity to use my newly acquired spiritual tools. I began listening in a different way. I learned, and still practice now, listening with my heart. I am working to leave judgmental attitudes behind. My attitude about life changed. I sorted out what was really important and what I could leave behind.

I continue to practice asking questions instead of pronouncing judgments. As I keep growing and changing, so does my work. I am less and less dependent on scripts. My heart is connected with academic learning and allows me to see students as whole beings, not just as personalities segmented into different components.

I am also learning to stand up for myself. Through the experience of interconnectedness with all things, I am able to recognize interconnectedness as an integral part of systems thinking. Recognizing that I am spirit urges me on to work for social justice. I am acutely aware that I can only change myself and live my life as honestly as possible. It is precisely this honesty that Parker Palmer considers an essential tool in the classroom.[7]

I started to love life when I was able to love myself (a constant process), my children, my work, and my studies. Learning to be frugal with my physical strength was a new challenge. Until recently I was the athletic person in our family, not the brainy one. In childhood, only intellect counted for something. As I developed a true appreciation for learning in graduate school, I began to see family, friends, colleagues, and people in general through a different lens. My concern about social justice was no longer fueled by my own hurt, but came out of a feeling of interconnectednesss and compassion for all. I am constantly learning that judgment separates and that I did not need to be liked in order to do a good job. Sometimes I have to make decisions that are disliked by some. I can now distinguish whether my decisions derive from my own desires or originate in a concern for the betterment of the whole, whatever that "whole" may be. Most of the time I can recognize my feelings without getting stuck in them. Parker Palmer describes a similar distinction when he speaks of how attention to familiar and unfamiliar feelings opens students to challenges and helps to create an honest learning space.[8]

MY DOCTORAL THESIS BECOMES AN INTEGRAL PART OF MY JOURNEY

I obtained my master's degree and decided to apply to the doctoral program. I wanted to explore spirit, its existence and nature, and its relationship to our lives. I was accepted and took many years to complete my thesis. My struggle with feelings of inadequacy were not yet over. I chose a topic which did not fit easily into the academic world, where all knowledge is rooted in the cognitive and rational. I interviewed organizational consultants about their beliefs about life, death, work, and spirituality. I engrossed myself in endless reading, studying organizational literature as well as spiritual literature from His Holiness the Dalai Lama, Hildegard von Bingen, Matthew Fox, and others.[9] I came to realize that what seemed to be new discoveries to me were, in fact, ancient and accepted truths in other cultures. And while none of the recent practitioners talked openly about spirituality, their action and work were guided by principles such as compassion, love, discernment, and a sense of interconnectedness.

I also learned about acupuncture. I read about gurus and saints, about parapsychology and ancient Buddhist texts on the human condition. My Native American friend, Faye, spoke with me about her nature philosophy and her beliefs. New doors of insight and understanding opened. My own spiritual practice developed under the guidance of my teacher. I can no longer imagine being without our Thursday night classes and the continuous unfolding of who I am.

My doctoral work led me on a wonderful journey of discovery: I'm living surrounded by books and in the midst of my space of meditation. As my life experiences change, I am finding my way into that answer of which the poet Rilke spoke.[10]

My intense new life as a graduate student was rudely interrupted one day when a policeman called at my house to give me news of my older son Julian and his friend Jeff. Both of them had just been killed in a car accident on their way home from a vacation in the Southwest. The very force of life (the chi) seemed to drain from my body, leaving me to collapse in grief. Now I really needed help. Everything I had read and learned was severely put to the test. I had to start all over again, seeking to understand beyond intellect, translating my knowledge of Julian from the physical into the spiritual realm.

Finally, I could locate him in nonphysical form and slowly, slowly learned that love is never lost. He is still my teacher, still present, even in his formless state. His spirit comes and goes. I learned that grieving over my loss has to do with my hopes and dreams for him. A friend of mine came and drummed to help me restore my life energy and get back into a conscious breathing pattern. I worked directly with the chakra system to regain balance and became alert to and unafraid of the messages Julian would send forth directly through his voice, or through owls and other animals, and through impressions. To his brother and other friends he comes in dreams.

Last August, around the anniversary of his death, I had breakfast with two of his very close friends from high school. They were astonished to discover that their dreams about their friend were very much alike, although they received different messages around the same time. This discovery came to us in conversation. They had never broached the subject with one another before.

After my son's death, I slowly returned to my academic work. My urge to complete my research was closely connected to Julian. In one of our last conversations he asked me if I was still interested in the project and, if so, that I needed to put my fear aside. "Get off the pity pot and do it," he said. He was loving, but he could also be stern. I dedicated my thesis to him and two close women friends who died of cancer a short time later.

LIVING THE QUESTIONS AT WORK

These experiences have profoundly affected my life and work. Living any question allows me to stay open, curious, and active. I remain a participant even in the midst of difficulty. For example, when faced with a supervisor who I felt did not respect me, I had two ways of addressing the problem. I could fall back on old patterns of rebellion, or I could go inside myself and find out if it was time to leave this job. My inner voice told me to stay, that it was not the time to leave. This took me by surprise. Meanwhile, I have learned to trust the process of meditation, reflection, listening to myself, making room to explore my inner voices in a quiet setting. What was needed was to change my attitude about my supervisor and about our relationship. I searched for other sources of validation for my work and concentrated on the job I love doing, educating and teaching on issues of leadership, participatory management, and social justice. I stopped criticizing and continued to ask questions in meetings rather than insisting on my judgment.

My spiritual belief that we are all connected naturally led to the question "what is my connection with my supervisor?" Slowly but surely small bridges were built. The situation has now become less charged for me. I am relaxed and do not feel any longer that I have to prove my "worth." There have been moments of laughter and agreement, learning to be compassionate and patient. I realized that my initially negative reactions would only have worsened the situation. Instead of avoiding my supervisor, I have enjoyed working with him on joint projects.

As a teacher, my spiritual journey has prepared me to recognize the importance of special "moments" that transform a classroom into a place of openness where it is acceptable to talk about difficult topics. I strive to create an atmosphere that leaves room for students to unpack their own "knapsacks" of experience. I no longer stand in the center, constantly needing to be liked. As long as I know that I am truthful, compassionate, and open to listening, the classroom can be a place where students feel free to share their dilemmas and ask questions. For all of us, learning becomes more meaningful if we find a connection between our lives and the subject matter at hand.

CONTEMPLATION AND SILENCE FACILITATE LEARNING IN STUDENTS AND TEACHERS ALIKE

The silence I need for myself, in order to be centered and able to hear my inner voice, Margaret and I also offer in our leadership class ("Leadership in Action with Spirit"), a two and one-half hour weekly seminar. Students from different majors, freshmen to seniors, join us. They come from very different cultural backgrounds, bringing diverse experiences and opinions to our conversation. One of the course objectives is to examine leadership with an awareness of spirituality and its connection to social justice. Readings, lectures, and self-explorations clarify differences and establish connections between spirituality and religion. Much confusion initially surrounds our conversations, but silence helps us to get to the heart of the matter. In fact, we start the semester talking about the meaning of silence. Initially, most students are hesitant, even uncomfortable, with silence. For beginners, silence means feeling uncomfortable, lost, and idle, fearful of what might be behind the silence, of what they might find out about themselves. After opening announcements, we agree to start with a minute of silence at the beginning of each class.

During the first few weeks, these silences are rather loud—shuffling, coughing, paper rustling, people moving. It sounds more like the concourse in Grand Central Station than a spell of silence. We guide the students with relaxation exercises and draw attention to their breathing. Not only does this period of silence become truly silent, its energy expands from week to week and creates a space of mutual experience. By the end of the semester, our time of reflection expands to nine minutes. We do not negotiate that length, we simply know when it is time to join again in silence or activity. We rejoin by looking around at each other in silence. Students grow to be aware of the positive energy in the room. This time of contemplation allows them to arrive and be fully present in class.

In their class evaluations, students strongly recommended continuing this period of reflection as an integral part of the curriculum. In last semester's evaluation, one student wrote: "This space allows me to leave the stressfulness of the day behind and to be more present." Another student said, "I can still see my to-do list but it does not bother me any longer." A third said, "I started sitting at home and am curious where this is bringing me."

In order to connect the classroom with the world outside of higher education we bring current issues that are important to students' lives into classroom discussion. During the 2000 spring semester, affirmative action was a topic of much debate and protest on our campus. We had noticed increasing tension and physical separation in class among white students and students of color, and a worrisome decrease of participation from students of color. This issue needed to be addressed. Although we are no experts on affirmative action, we informed ourselves and raised the issue.

A sharp division erupted between the perspectives of white students and students of color. A white student and an African American student ended up facing each other, sharing their life perspectives. One was raised in Maine in a white poverty-stricken town, where only three high school students went on to college. It was her opinion that ending affirmative action would give her peers a better chance for an education. The student of color had grown up in an inner-city tenement house. She feared that even the slim chances they had had would now disappear in the assault on affirmative action.

During this debate between the two women, the room was silent. The antagonists started out on opposite sides of the classroom. We asked them to move closer together and to face each other. We as teachers also moved closer and sat behind them. Slowly they began to listen to each other and to grasp each other's views. At the end, they could agree that they had learned something from each other, something they had never known in their own worlds. This conversation taught them to stay open, to listen, and to suspend judgment. The students of color felt more relaxed now that the issues that were so close to their hearts came out into the open. White students were grateful for this conversation. Teaching and learning could continue.

These critical exchanges are risky, yet they bring the everyday reality of students into the classroom. Learning and living closely connects students and teachers. Our experiences give me faith and help me avoid fear.

Seeing the whole person rather than just the "student" in his or her role also implies that I will recognize issues of health and safety. It means observing when somebody is out of "sync," that something is troubling them, and standing back until it is time to ask pertinent questions. I have found it important to curb my desire for a specific outcome and not to take things personally if the others are not yet ready to listen or share their concerns.

In my work with groups, paying attention to verbal as well as nonverbal communication is an important discipline. I have found that group observation and processing are spiritual activities, that paying attention to the invisible, yet palpable, dimension of energy is essential. It makes me strive for balance, for being rested. It is an inner process leading to external action, a challenge to understand the meaning and not just the words being spoken.

Some student groups have also embraced visualization. I have guided groups in visualization before facing an important decision. We visualize an outcome that serves the group best. Let me share an example: for years, my students and I have attended the National Association of Student Co-operatives. It was notoriously difficult to select the delegates from among the various student businesses because too many students wanted to participate. Leading a visualization exercise meant deepening this process of decision making for each individual. I ask the students to consider in silence the best decision for themselves and for the group, how they can serve themselves and the group. After mulling over these questions in silence, the decision fell into place. Instead of culminating in a power struggle, the ambitions of each gave way to the need of the group as a whole.

In my work with individuals I am able to gauge their energy. When I detect large imbalances over some time, I discuss it openly. For example, a student in one of the groups seemed very depressed recently, a marked change from the previous semester. I observed him and, when a quiet moment presented itself, asked if I could be of help. After a long silence, I learned that his mother was diagnosed with a critical illness and that her health was declining rapidly. He returned home every weekend and was, at that time, the most care-giving member of his family. I was able to put him in touch with the dean and arrange for a lighter academic load, as well as assist him in negotiating fewer working hours in his student business. I continued to support him with phone calls home and will be here for him when he returns to the area after his mother's recent death.

There are many similar stories about students diagnosed with cancer or facing other personal problems. When educating about teamwork, it is important to see a person as an integral whole. I try to be sensitive and honest, sensing the energy surrounding a person or an issue. I have gained a deeper understanding of the human condition and feel connected to life in a different way. Sometimes I accompany cancer patients as a support person during recovery, and at other times I lend my support to a student who is in the process of coming out as a same-sex loving person. I am now better able to let these situations evolve by listening patiently or speaking in metaphors, ready to encounter a person when the occasion arises. I speak less and listen more, trusting the moment to be my teacher.

I am writing about my personal experience because it has made me who I am. Who we are is what we bring to work in the classroom. My systems thinking springs from my experience of feeling interconnected with my surroundings. The love I am developing for myself is reflected in the compassion I have for others. The patience I am gaining comes from slowing down, from becoming more judicious about what I can take on.

Like most people I make decisions based on the intellectual knowledge I have accumulated over the years, drawing on my own data bank. But I must not neglect to listen to my intuition and inner guidance. Sometimes the decisions might run contrary to societal expectations, and then the risk has to be weighed by the importance of the decision itself. Silence is of paramount importance in this process, whereas noise and a hectic pace of life can make it difficult to heed the inner voice of being.

The responsibility I feel toward those I am teaching also obliges me to rest and eat well, so that I can be as balanced as possible. Audrey Lorde recognized that her political work was easier when she treated herself well.[11] It is quite common for students to fall asleep while watching a video in class. I have learned not to take this personally or simply as a sign of boredom, but as a common manifestation of the fact that undergraduate students do not get enough rest and sleep.

All of us come from distinctly different places and backgrounds, yet we also remain strongly connected to one another. As an educator and teacher it is my goal to lessen such binary divisions and move beyond linear thinking. I wish to open up other vistas and alert students to creativity as a natural part of their being. My skills and knowledge are only tools. Most of all I wish to affirm and challenge. To be sure, I have my own share of challenges: writing has been a personal struggle for me. My doubts about having something worthwhile to say continue to loom large. When my doubts threaten to overwhelm me, I hear my son's voice comforting and encouraging me. Like myself, I want students to welcome knowledge from beyond the rational realm, remembering the Little Prince's admonition "that words can be the source of great misunderstandings."[12]

As I get older my knapsack gets lighter, and I am able to view life's experiences through a more sharply focused lens. The growing recognition that I am more than my body gives me assurance and peace to live and strive to work in a balanced way. An intimation that events in our lives are not just haphazard and accidental, but that they work in synchronicity with one another inspires patience and a willingness to wait for insight.

> Tighten
> to nothing
> the circle
> that is
> the world's things
> Then the Naked
> circle
> can grow wide,
> enlarging, embracing all
>
> — Hadewich of Antwerp, 13th century [13]

ENDNOTES

1. Jane Hirschfield, *Women in Praise of the Sacred, Hadewijch of Antwerp* (New York: Harper Collins, 1993), 109.
2. Rainer Maria Rilke, *Letters to a Young Poet* (Boston: Harper Collins, 1993), 50.
3. David Scott, "Spirituality in an Integrative Age" in *Education as Transformation: Religious Pluralism, Spirituality and a New Vision for American Higher Education*, ed. Victor H. Kazanjian, Jr., and Peter L. Lawrence (New York: Peter Lang, 2000), 23–36.
4. Rainer Maria Rilke, *Letters*.
5. Audre Lorde, *A Burst of Light* (New York: Firebrand Books, 1988), 128.
6. Antoine de Saint-Exupery, *The Little Prince* (New York: Harvest Books, 1943), 87.
7. Parker Palmer, "A Vision of Education as Transformation," in *Education as Transformation: Religious Pluralism, Spirituality and a New Vision for American Higher Education*, ed. Victor H. Kazanjian, Jr., and Peter L. Lawrence (New York: Peter Lang, 2000).
8. Parker Palmer, *To Know As We Are Known* (San Francisco: Harper San Francisco, 1983), 87.

9. Katja Hahn d'Errico, *The Impact of Spirituality on the Work of Organization Development Consulting Practice* (unpublished thesis, 1998).
10. Rainer Maria Rilke, *Letters*.
11. Audre Lorde, *A Burst of Light*.
12. Antoine de Saint-Exupery, *The Little Prince,* 87.
13. Jane Hirschfield, *Women in Praise*, 109.

PART THREE

*Integrating Spirituality
into Learning
and Life on Campus*

14. *Innate Mental Health: Tapping the Divine Gift for Learning and Well-being*

JOEL GROSSMAN

Institutions of higher education are all about learning, with the expectation that learning will enable graduates to have an enhanced level of wellbeing in their lives. So much emphasis tends to be placed on the material to be learned that educators often forget to acknowledge the process of learning and what we are drawing upon that makes this process possible. Looking in this direction, we are delving into spiritual matters.

This chapter will describe how a program called Study Smarter, Not Harder, offered through a student affairs office, helps students become aware of the Divine gift of their mental health. By Divine gift, I simply mean a gift from G!d.[1] In acknowledging the ongoing presence of this gift, and understanding how to best make use of it, the learning process becomes richer, less stressful, and more effective.

I offer the Study Smarter, Not Harder program in my role as the coordinator of the Health Promotion Program of University Health Service at the University of Massachusetts Boston, an urban commuter campus with a large multicultural, multiethnic student population. At the Going Public with Spirituality in Work and Higher Education conference held in June of 2000, I copresented, with Adrian Haugabrook, assistant dean of students, a workshop titled "Speaking Spirituality Publicly: Voices from a Public University." I felt that the key question asked by a participant in the session was this: "How do you manage to address these spiritual matters in your positions?" I was struck by my response:

> There has been a recent shift in the definition of my work. I had described the mission of the Health Promotion Program as "helping students maintain and enhance their health and well-being, which includes their mental, physical, emotional and spiritual selves." I now say our mission is to "help students maintain and enhance their health and well-being, which includes their SPIRITUAL, mental, physical and emotional selves."

This shift in the emphasis on spirituality in my work has been the result of feeling strongly that the way to reach our dreams and goals, the way to deal with our concerns and dilemmas, is to be found in accessing the inner wisdom and guidance that is available to us all as a gift of the Divine. It has become clearer to me that the best way I can serve others is to help them to understand, acknowledge, open to, and utilize the inner knowing we all possess. I have found this orientation of helping students open to their wisdom to be applicable and effective regardless of the issue a student presents, whether it be academic performance, stress management, smoking cessation, weight management, career direction, grief, etc.

MENTAL LIFE FORCE

The gift of life provides mental capacities along with physical ones. We are familiar with our physical life force—breathing, the beating of our hearts, the flow of blood through our veins—all taking place without any effort on our part. In the same way, we have our mental life force working within us. Our mental life force provides a constant flow of thoughts and the ability to bring these thoughts to life so that they have meaning to us. This process of bringing thoughts to life is referred to here as "consciousness." It is the gifts of thought and consciousness that provide what we call "experience."

Thoughts come to us nonstop, as if rolling off of a conveyor belt running around the clock. As we pay attention to a particular thought, consciousness simultaneously helps us make sense of the thought, drawing upon the senses and memory. This results in our moment-to-moment experience. It is our "mental life force" at work.

THE DIVINE GIFT OF INNATE MENTAL HEALTH

The constant flow of thoughts that we receive range from being very helpful to being quite unhelpful. Fortunately, we all have mental health, used here to mean thinking that serves us well. This includes our common sense, clarity, insight, creativity, and intelligence—referring not to how smart we are, but to the retrieving of information we have gathered.

We are constantly moving into, out of, and back into thinking that is helpful to us in all aspects of life. Seeing how our thinking shapes our moment-to-moment experience provides greater freedom to use the gift of thought to our benefit, drawing on our mental health for a better approach when the way we are thinking is not working for us. This gift is what enables us to achieve academically; it is also what helps us to find the misplaced car keys. It is making use of our common sense, something we tend to take for granted. The Divine gift of innate mental health works for us all, regardless of age, sex, religion, race, level of education, or our socioeconomic status. It is a constant resource to draw on throughout our lives.

I have gained this understanding of innate mental health, and have developed the Study Smarter and other such programs to serve students, through my studies of a relatively new field of psychology, Psychology of Mind (POM). This body of work was developed by two psychologists, Dr. Roger Mills and Dr. George Pransky, based on the teachings of Syd Banks. Mills and Pransky were doing research on the key factors that underlie the effectiveness of various psychotherapeutic systems and came upon the teaching of Banks. A Scottish welder with a ninth grade education, Banks had an epiphany and began sharing the understanding of the spiritual nature of life that this experience brought him. Mills and Pransky found that his teaching offered a clear way to introduce to others the key elements that their research determined helped people have better lives.

Psychology of Mind is not drawn from, or tied to, any religion. Because it endeavors to describe basic truths, it is often identified with other belief systems that address the fundamentals of life. These identifications range from Buddhism to cognitive therapy. While POM shares views similar to these and other philosophies, it is not a part of any other belief system.

Psychology of Mind has proven to be effective in community work, education, business, health care, and social service settings. The community work aspect of POM, known as "Health Realization," has helped transform low-income housing projects in Dade County, Florida;[2] South Bronx; South Central Los Angeles; Oakland; Tampa, and other locations. All county social service providers in Santa Clara County, California, have been trained in the use of POM. Businesses ranging from a major California health care system to a billboard advertising agency in Georgia have used POM to enhance corporate performance. At the University of West Virginia, the Robert C. Byrd Health Sciences Center, which includes the Schools of Medicine, Dentistry, Nursing, and Pharmacy, has established the Sydney Banks Institute for Innate Health.[3] The stated goal of the Institute is to "awaken the innate wisdom within each faculty member, student and constituency served." The Institute is "committed to sharing the principle-based understanding of the spiritual essence of all things with interested individuals and institutions throughout the world."

The common thread in all the applications of POM is helping people understand that it is their thinking that is creating their moment-to-moment experience, and that if their thinking is not helpful, they can turn to their mental health to provide more helpful thinking. When we let go of unhelpful thinking and open our minds, we begin to access "free-flow thinking." Free-flow thinking refers to allowing a range of thoughts to pass through our minds versus paying attention to a certain train of thought. Free-flow thinking allows us to realize our innate mental health.

THE STUDY SMARTER, NOT HARDER PROGRAM

I have developed many formats for sharing this work with students, including individual consults; a seven-week, one credit stress management course; and a four-session, stress reduction/life enhancement program. The format that I have found to be most accessible is the Study Smarter, Not Harder program. I offer this forty-five to sixty minute seminar before midterm and final exams, in first-year seminar classes, for various student groups, and on an individual appointment basis.

The average age of UMass Boston students is twenty-seven. Many are the first ones in their family to attend college. Because they often have doubts about their academic capabilities, enhancing their belief in themselves and helping them develop faith in their inner guidance is essential to their success and sense of well-being. Most students are working twenty to forty hours a week and/or have family care responsibilities, bringing the added pressure of using their available study time as effectively as possible. Due to these issues, many students that I serve struggle with, or are anxious about, studying.

In the Study Smarter program we begin by examining some common experiences students face in studying. I discuss two basic study experiences: when our thinking is working for us, and when it is not. Sometimes we are present in the moment with the subject matter and we have thoughts that help us understand the material. Fresh ideas occur to us and all goes well. When our thinking serves us in this way, we tend to take our mental health for granted, so we are not aware of what is working for us. At other times, we become entangled in thinking that doesn't serve us well. We become distracted and ride on a train of thought that takes us away from the subject matter. Or, we get bogged down in one way of thinking about the material that stops the flow of creative thought. In response, we tend to bear down, to "study harder," trying to make our thinking work, resulting in tension and frustration. The unpleasantness of this experience can lead to anxiety about studying and to procrastination.

When we recognize we have become stuck in unhelpful thinking, we can help ourselves by letting go of this thinking and opening to our mental health. Sometimes it is simply a matter of returning to the material at hand, what we call concentration or focus. Sometimes it helps to step back from the material, open to free-flow thinking, ask the question "what would help now?" and open to the information our mental health provides us.

THE KEY PRINCIPLES OF THE PROGRAM

The program begins by identifying what study issues each student came to address. After discussing the presence of mental health in all of us, I then describe the three-step process of opening to, and making use of, our mental health:

- notice what you are thinking;
- assess if the thinking you are doing is helpful or not;
- if it is not, take steps to move to more helpful thinking.

Before presenting specifics on how to apply these three steps to studying, I discuss an important point that must be taken into account whenever we address thinking. It is the fact that we have no ability to choose what thoughts come to mind. A major aspect of the Divine gift of thought is that thoughts just appear without our having to do anything to bring them about. Once we are aware of what we are thinking, we have great control of what we do with what is on our minds.

To give students an experience of the capacity we have to observe our thinking, I ask them to take ten seconds to just notice what crosses their minds. When the ten seconds are over, I ask the students to share something they thought about. I then introduce the following points:

- to change the effect a thought is having on you, give it less time and/or meaning.

When we notice that we have become caught up in the type of thinking that is taking us away from effective studying, we can change the effect of what is on our minds by shifting our attention to something else (e.g., back on the study material), or by lessening the meaning we are giving the unhelpful thinking. An example of the latter is when we are involved in thinking "I just don't have time to get through all this reading." Instead, when we tell ourselves, "Well, I'll cover as much as I can" or "Let's see how it goes," we undercut the meaning we were giving the initial thought and move in a more positive direction.

- Concentration is not the absence of distraction. It is what we do when we are distracted.

More than any other difficulty, students present the challenge of not being able to concentrate. The problem usually involves an incorrect definition of concentration. Because most people think concentration is about not being distracted, when they repeatedly experience distraction, they feel they can't concentrate. I explain that concentration is the act of bringing attention back to the chosen subject matter when we notice we have become distracted. A little bit of distraction calls for a little concentration; a lot of distraction calls for a lot of concentration.

Concentration is what I am referring to by "Not Harder" in the program title. When our thinking is not serving us, we use concentration to get back on track. When we are spending more time thinking effectively than being distracted, this approach works fine. But when we are "spinning our wheels," being more consumed with distraction, tiredness, confusion, boredom, or frustration than with the study material, we need to find another, "smarter" approach to accomplishing our study goals.

- Use free flow thinking to access your innate mental health (i.e., common sense, intelligence, clarity, creativity, guidance)

When we step back from paying attention to the material at hand, it allows for an open flow of thinking to pass through our minds. In the more open mental space that this free flow of thoughts provides, we can access our innate mental health. This free flow thinking is a common state of mind; at all times we are either paying attention to something or we are in free flow thinking.

- Create a "Plan B" (how to study smarter) when concentrating (trying harder) isn't working—clear your mind a bit, brainstorm ideas, pick one, and go with it.

After having moved into free-flow thinking, we can ask ourselves, "What will help me get this studying done more effectively?" and then allow ideas to occur to us. It is important to gather a number of ideas before running with one idea. Our habits of thinking will present ideas that may not be the most helpful. If a habit of thinking is to procrastinate, the first thought we may receive is "I'll let it go for now and work on it tomorrow." If our tendency is to clean the desk when stuck, then that is one of the early thoughts that will enter our minds. By choosing among ideas, the likelihood of choosing an effective approach is heightened.

- Trust more in your mental health to provide what will help when you are struggling.

The main service of this program is to help students realize the clear, sensible thinking available to them from within. The more we trust our mental health, the more we will turn in that direction and make use of it. The less we appreciate the presence of our common sense, the more we tend to get discouraged, frustrated, or fearful when we are having a difficult time.

- Focus on your breath as a way to clear your mind.

After having explained to students about the ongoing presence of innate mental health and the richness of what it offers, I then make a shift from the theoretical to the experiential. I do this by offering students a way to experience and practice the three steps of moving from unhelpful to helpful thinking.

Studying is a joy when we are engaged by the ideas presented by a professor, the writing of an author, or by the ideas coming to us in writing a paper. When we are not particularly captivated by the material at hand, however, our minds drift. To simulate this experience, I ask students to attempt to keep their attention on something that is not very interesting, just following the flow of their breath in and out for three or four minutes. I explain that when our thinking is not interesting, we automatically start having thoughts about something that we find more interesting. In doing the exercise I ask them to notice when they are having thoughts other than of their breath, to accept this movement of thought as quite normal, and to gently return to following their breath, over and over again.

At the conclusion of the exercise, I ask students what they have experienced. Repeated responses are of feeling clearer and lighter, and everyone sees how they were able to follow the three steps, noticing what was on their minds, assessing if that is where they want their thinking to be (in the exercise, the choice is prescribed: to be back with their breath), and redirecting their attention.

I would imagine that most readers recognize what I just described as "meditation." I don't use this term in introducing the exercise because it can cause many expectations and reactions. Many people identify meditation with certain religious or spiritual practices. If they do not feel connected to or familiar with those practices, they can feel intimidated by the idea of meditating. Another complication to exploring meditation is the belief that to meditate means to clear one's mind and feel peaceful. When "trying" to meditate and not having these experiences, people tend to stay away from meditation.

I explain that meditation is like weight lifting: it is the repetitions that build muscles. Each time we notice that our attention has moved to something other than a given focus (in this case, the breath) and then return to the focus, we are strengthening our ability to move through the three steps of opening to our mental health: noticing what we are thinking, assessing if the thinking we are doing is helpful or not, and if it is not, taking steps to move to more helpful thinking. This nonsectarian approach helps students be more open to meditation and lessens the likelihood of it being seen as inappropriate for use in a public institution.

The majority of us who are interested in the spiritual aspects of life are aware of the benefits of meditation and/or of prayer. These are deep and complex topics about which many thousands of books have been written. A basic view of what meditation and prayer hold in common is that both provide a means of letting go of what else may be on our minds and opening to the guidance that enters our minds via thought. Making use of this guidance is a dynamic expression of our innate mental health at play.

Appreciation of our mental health and insight into how it works is a way of speaking about faith: faith in our G!d given mental capabilities, faith in the guidance which is made available to us as helpful thoughts, faith that there will always be another thought available to help us see things anew.

In presenting the program I do not emphasize the "Divine gift" of thought and mental health to the degree I have in this chapter, unless I feel the individuals are open to, and would benefit from, this input. Early in the program, when speaking about the constant flow of thoughts we receive and being able to make sense of these thoughts through consciousness, I do talk about thought and consciousness as being gifts of the Divine. Later in the program, when sharing how free-flow thinking enables us to access our mental health, I talk about mental health being a Divine gift we all have been given. I feel that these two references to the Divine are sufficient. Other than when I sense that a student has a religious or spiritual orientation, I believe that any further reference to the Divine may create blocks to opening to the concepts offered in the Study Smarter program.

PROGRAM EFFECTIVENESS

Students to whom I have presented this program have confirmed its effectiveness. I surveyed seventy-one students in seven first-year seminar classes. Eighty-seven percent of the responses stated that the material offered was "helpful" or "very helpful" four to six weeks after the session was given. I have also had the joy of receiving heartfelt thanks from students who were fearful of failing courses and/or suffering from high levels of tension and anxiety. They report the great relief this program provided them and how much improvement they experienced in their academic work.

One such expression of thanks came from a woman who only needed to pass chemistry in order to receive her degree in nursing. She had failed a previous chemistry course and was struggling in the present one she was taking. Despite many hours of study, participation in a study group, receiving tutoring and talking with the professor, she was terrified about failing the course.

After a couple of Study Smarter sessions she found she was able to notice when she started thinking negatively, quiet her mind, and then get helpful ideas of how to proceed and/or get insights about the chemistry material. She passed the midterm and came back for a refresher when she started having trouble understanding the course material as she approached the final. Using the same process of opening to her mental health to help deal with her fear and confusion, she passed the course and graduated. Another example comes from a note I received from a professor of a first-year seminar course in which I presented the program. She wrote that the

Study Smarter program helped her students "become more effective and efficient learners by enhancing (their) attention to learning."

The Role of Student Affairs in Students' Spiritual Lives

Student affairs programs often struggle with the issue of being seen as offering services that are secondary to the academic mission of the university. In not being confined to an area of academic specialization, and not being seen as biased by such specialization, I believe that student affairs personnel are in the best position to provide students with the deeper and broader, more spiritual, aspects of academic life. This viewpoint was strongly reinforced at a workshop I gave on "The Role Student Affairs Can Play in Students' Spiritual Lives" at the Education as Transformation Conference which took place at Wellesley College in 1998. Attendees at the workshop included staff members and administrators from athletics, housing, health services, student life, and other student affairs offices. Many participants spoke of their surprise at being asked religious or spiritually related questions by students. They shared their belief that they were being approached with these questions not because they had any recognized expertise in this area, but because they had, in some way, demonstrated their interest in the whole student, moving beyond the student's academic and career issues. Additionally, having no identified religious agenda, they were perceived as being someone who would be open and nonjudgmental.

Conclusion

The Study Smarter, Not Harder program focuses on the primary mission of the institution, i.e., to provide a beneficial learning experience. This orientation has made the sharing of these spiritually oriented concepts amenable and marketable. Though I offer this program at a public university, I have encountered no resistance. I have received numerous invitations from faculty across the academic spectrum to present the Study Smarter program in their classes. Other support service offices have invited me to present the program to their clients. I have also been successful in marketing the program directly to students.

By helping students appreciate the ability we all have to think in helpful ways and to access and use our inner knowing, we are not only assisting students in succeeding academically, but also in realizing the resources upon which they can draw to deal with any aspect of life. I have been so heartened by hearing from students who have participated in the Study Smarter program, and other related programs, that the notions they have learned have helped them deal with family and relationship matters, work issues, and in their thinking about their future.

ENDNOTES

1. A Jewish custom is to not write out the word "god" when used to describe the Divine, knowing that the paper will be discarded at some point. Traditionally, it is written G-d, but I recently found the G!d form and like the visual impact this form makes.
2. Jack Pransky, *Modello: A Story of Hope for the Inner City and Beyond* (Cabot, Vermont: North East Health Realization Institute Publications, 1998).
3. Please see the website: http://www.hsc.wvu.edu/sbi/

15. Creating a Learning Community and the Core Values of Spirituality

FAN YIHONG

> In closing, the NUANCE First-year Seminar was a great class. It helped me think about the world, and my community in a new light. I learned many new things whether they are about someone else's culture, or what they believe. Most importantly, I met a lot of really great people, and hopefully some friendships that will last into the future.

The above comment was from the final essay that one of the participants wrote about the NUANCE First-Year Seminar (NFYS) at the University of Massachusetts Amherst. It invites deeper exploration of the ways in which a learning community functions. How did the NFYS help students think about the world and their community in a new light? How can learning about others' cultures also support the creation of new friendships? And what do learning communities have to do with spirituality? This chapter will present the phenomenological case study I conducted of the NUANCE First-Year Seminar and describe how this student-initiated, student-designed, student-organized, and student-implemented program demonstrates core values of spirituality.

CORE VALUES OF SPIRITUALITY

People from different religious and cultural backgrounds have different understandings and definitions of spirituality. Therefore, it is important to reach a common understanding of the core values of spirituality. Levinger observes that people have an innate capacity and desire to transcend the bounds of self in search of a greater meaning and purpose of life.[1] This insight has been echoed and expanded, as Flake reports, by a group of eighty international holistic educators from different religious and ethnic backgrounds at a remarkable meeting in Chicago in 1990. They agreed that spirituality involves the following:

1) a deep connection to self and others;
2) a search of the larger meaning and purpose in daily life;
3) an experience of the wholeness and interdependence of life;
4) a desire to detach from a life too involved with material values;
5) an openness to creative experience; and
6) an appreciation of the mystery of life.[2]

These are clearly beautiful ideals, but how can we bring these core components of spirituality into practice in higher education? How can we transform the disconnected, fragmented, alienated academic world into a more caring, more nurturing, and more connecting environment so that students will enjoy their learning experience rather than dread it? How can we break away from what O'Banion calls the traditional college and university structure that limits learning, namely the structures that are *time-bound; place-bound; efficiency-bound; and role-bound*?[3] Does education have to be carried out in a 50-minute time period, confined within the classroom, only measured by scores and grades and by giving only teachers the expert role? These are the questions that O'Banion invites us to ask, as we develop more expanded modes of learning together.

Facing all these challenges, Brower and Dettinger have developed a "pyramid model" of a learning community.[4] This three-dimensional model demonstrates how academic, social, and physical components can interact to facilitate the development of professional, ethical, and civic responsibilities in students. They state that if a program can help students develop all three senses of responsibility, then it can be regarded as an ideal learning community.[5]

Parker Palmer writes, "We all know that what will transform education is not another theory, another book, or another formula but educators who are willing to seek transformed ways of being in the world."[6] Wesley Jacques, the student who initiated, planned, organized, and implemented the NUANCE First-Year Seminar, models how an individual can live all these core values of spirituality. The program he started broke away from the four bounds of time, place, efficiency, and role to create a loving, caring, and supportive learning community. As the result of his program, all participants in the 1998 and 1999 seminars developed *professional, ethical,* and *civic* responsibility that gave them a sense of a larger and deeper meaning of life, developed connections with the local community, and experienced powerful moments of openness and creativity.[7] The learning process undertaken in this community addressed the higher meaning and purpose of life; thus, it touched upon the core value of spirituality.

WESLEY JACQUES AND THE NUANCE FIRST-YEAR SEMINAR

I was very privileged to have known Wesley Jacques, an undergraduate student at the University of Massachusetts Amherst from 1996 to 2000, who initiated, designed, planned, and implemented the NUANCE First-Year Seminar for twenty students in 1998 and twenty-four students in 1999. I met him during a luncheon meeting of the university's Learning Community Network. As soon as I heard him introducing the NFYS and the way in which it addresses the crossing of racial, ethnic, and cultural boundaries through combining academic learning and community service, I was attracted to this program. This program particularly caught my attention because it was multidimensional and organized by student initiative. It was sheer luck that I sat right opposite Jacques at the lunch table so that I was able to ask more questions and schedule an interview.

From my in-depth interview with Jacques, I learned how and why he established the program. By studying the program documents I learned more about the NFYS and how much it meant to the participants. When I read their final essays for a mini-case study I was doing for my final project in a graduate course on spirituality and education in the spring semester of 2000, I was deeply impressed by how the seminar affected students' lives. Sometimes I was moved to tears by the participants' stories about how this program touched them and how it changed their understanding of themselves, others, the community, and society-at-large. Quite a few participants recommended that every first-year student should have a chance to enroll in this seminar. Based on the students' stories, it was clear that the seminar had powerful outcomes: it connected students with each other despite their cultural, ethnic, and racial differences; it combined academic study with community service; it built a strong mentoring system by connecting first-year students with seniors; it helped students smooth their transition from high school to college life; and it led students through the process of becoming aware of their own identities. In the following pages let us enjoy learning more about the beauty and joy of NFYS.

A STUDENT'S DREAM CAME TRUE

The night that I first learned about the program was when Wes came to my room to advocate "his dream," and sold me right there on the spot. With all of his work and determination, he produced his dream, and I am thankful that he did, because it has been the most valuable course that I've taken this semester.

As a first-year student starting his second semester at the University of Massachusetts in the beginning of 1997, Jacques was assigned to live in Gorman Hall. There he found that "despite the multicultural theme of the hall, social interaction across racial lines was minimal."[8] He told me in our interview that the cultural barriers between people were so great that he could see clearly how students grouped themselves by color, ethnicity, and other cultural traits. He was not happy with this situation. He believed that, as a multicultural residence hall, it should model a multicultural sense of life, and he was determined to do something to remedy the situation.

He heard about a program called NUANCE that had been active for some time, eight or nine years earlier. It had been initiated by an African American student who was uncomfortable with the way white students treated African American students. This student wanted to create more equitable living conditions for students from minority ethnic groups, and he started the NUANCE program. The title implied a fresh start, a program in which people of different social identities were brought together in order to better understand each other and to build a safe and supportive living environment. The original NUANCE program was active for a few years but ended after the student who started it graduated. Now Jacques wanted to revive the program and add new meaning and purpose to it.

First, Jacques wanted to restore the meaning of a multicultural residence hall by building bridges among students of different cultural, racial, and ethnic backgrounds. Second, he wanted to link academic work with community service. He explained his motivation:

> I worked in City Year Project in Boston after I graduated from high school. At that time, we had a dozen of young people from different ethnic, racial and cultural backgrounds working together for community service. I worked at an after school program. In our service we all put our heads together, despite of our cultural, ethnical and racial differences because we were working toward a common goal. We learned a lot from each other and learned to appreciate our differences and embrace our diversity. From our community service we also built a strong sense of responsibility and teamwork spirit. I would like more students to have this kind of experiences so that they could see their roles as young people in relation with the community they live in and be more conscious about the social issues real life involved.

Third, he wanted this program to be able to help students make a smooth transition, both academically and socially, from high school life to university life so they would have a successful college experience.

When reflecting on his first semester as a first-year student, Jacques could still remember a number of frustrating experiences. For example, in one class, the teacher kept talking about the syllabus, but Jacques did not know what a syllabus was. After class he asked around and found out that the syllabus was there in the handouts the teacher gave to the class. Jacques had also seen many first-year students who had no idea how to manage time and academic tasks without feeling overwhelmed. Because he wanted to see other first-year students freed from that kind of awkward experience, he thought a course covering all of these issues carried out right there inside the residence hall would be a good idea. He also wanted to design the program to provide community service to the Amherst area so that students could learn in the context of concrete life situations, serve the needs of local community, and create a sense of connection with the reality around them, all at the same time.

To begin acting on his vision, Jacques started to talk to the Residential Director (RD) and Assistant Residential Director (ARD) of his residence hall. He discussed with them how this program could help solve the problem of disconnection between students from different cultural, racial, and ethnic backgrounds and help students navigate their transition to college life. The RD and ARD said that it was a good idea, but at that time no one had any specific suggestions about how to start.

Jacques started to investigate the different areas of the university to find financial, human, and academic resources to run the program. He also contacted the director for community service in the town of Amherst to plan for the community service aspect of the course.

His first support came from the Counsel on Community, Diversity, and Social Justice, a group that provides grants for programs dedicated to strengthening the multiculturalism of the campus. Jacques wrote a proposal for his project and received a $1,000 grant to begin. Having won this grant, other offices realized he was serious about this project, and they were ready to offer more support. A professor from the sociology department agreed to work with the program, and support also came from the library, the Residential Academic Program, and Project Mosaik, a special project that focused on promoting intergroup dialogue.

By the fall of 1998, the NUANCE First-Year Seminar had taken shape, with twenty first-year students enrolled for three credits. Now after two years, the program has matured and become very successful, ready to pass on to future students.

Five Goals and Four Components of the NUANCE Seminar

Jacques established five goals for the NFYS program, which were clearly stated at the inception, so that all participants knew what they were working toward. The goals are the following:

1) to assist students in transition from high school to college;
2) to break down social barriers between students from different racial, cultural, and ethnic backgrounds and foster understanding of others;
3) to provide students with opportunities to learn through service to people in the local community;
4) to provide students with academic and ͜ ͜ͻial skills;
5) to create community in the residence hall.

To achieve these five goals, Jacques designed several major components of the program. The first component was an off-campus retreat that served as an icebreaker to initiate community building and to provide an opportunity for students to develop friendships with each other. The second component involved workshops designed to introduce students to the academic environment. The first half of the semester focused on information skills that the students would need to be socially responsible and academically successful. The students learned time management and study skills, as well as library skills. Later sessions focused on drug and alcohol awareness, AIDS, STDs, pregnancy, and relationship issues. The second set of workshops was geared toward social identity and intergroup dialogue. Through these dialogues, the students could develop an increased awareness of themselves as individuals and members of social groups, learn more about their own and other cultures, and explore commonalities and differences along social group boundaries. They also addressed the impact of various forms of oppression on their lives in the residence hall, at the university, and in the larger world.

Another important component of the program was service learning. Through task-oriented, team-based community service, people of different backgrounds could recognize commonalities and learn to appreciate the contributions of others. Social barriers such as race and gender were broken down through working toward common goals. With the help of the director of the Center for Community Service in the town of Amherst, Jacques developed six sites for students to participate for three hours each week in community service. The projects involved activities such as after school programming for youth, preparing meals for low-income members of the community, and facilitating gender issues workshops in local high schools. These service experiences provided vehicles for leadership development and practice in working with a socially diverse group. Students also felt more connected to the community and more concerned about local social issues.

Student Evaluations of the Program and Self-Evaluation

Perhaps the best way to appreciate the success of the NUANCE First-Year Seminar is to listen to the participants evaluating their own program. The key themes that emerged from studying students' evaluations of the NFYS are outlined below.

Successfully Broke Down Social Barriers

One of the goals of the seminar was to break down social barriers between students. One participant in the initial cohort named the countries where the participants of the program came from, including Sierra Leone, Brazil, Costa Rica, Jamaica, and the U.S. Then she commented that, despite the fact that most of the participants in the program were from different countries with different cultures, races, and social classes, this program brought them all together and made them one people and one family.

Another student particularly appreciated seeing some white participants in the program and remarked that he was happy that students from various backgrounds were actually making the step toward creating a unified educational and social setting. The value of intergroup dialogue was mentioned by another student, who felt that the willingness of her peers to share their experiences was inspiring. She commented on the necessity of establishing open lines of communication and sharing details about their lives because doing so promotes dialogue, communication, and understanding among all participants.

Another participant appreciated how he had benefited from the breakdown of social barriers: "I am aware of the social barriers now that exist between cultures, and even though it saddens me, I am fortunate that at least I now know how to be an ally instead of just a bystander." By this he meant that he would not keep silent when he witnessed oppressive situations involving people from different racial, cultural, and ethnic backgrounds.

More Healthy Attitude Toward One's Cultural Identity

A student of Asian origin reflected on how intergroup dialogue helped her to understand her identity development. Through the program, she realized that she could be different from the mainstream and still be accepted. She also learned that she could be friends with students from different ethnicities, learn about them, and still be herself. The program helped her to find peace with her identity and at the same time respect other people's identities. As she wrote in her final essay, "I always thought that in order to belong, I had to be the same. Never did I realize that if I educated myself about all the different races, and educate others about mine, I could still be a person with my own identity."

Enjoying Teamwork and Serving Community

A student in the second NFYS cohort gave an account of how he enjoyed teamwork in community service because tasks were done faster and in a more pleasant way. A student who helped children with terminal illnesses and worked at a homeless shelter established a strong sense of commitment to helping others. She said that both she and her friends realized how fortunate they were compared to people without homes and people with terminal illnesses. They were determined that they would go on volunteering their time at the homeless shelter even after the seminar ended. Another student expressed the same determination about continuing community service:

> Personally, I gained a lot from this service. I didn't really agree [at all times] with the situation and how we approach our mission in the service. But a sense of self-worth in myself and in the community did grow. Going back to my hometown, I am determined to give back and to be of any assistance where needed.

Supportive Mentoring Patterns and Easing Students' Transitions

The staff of the seminar were junior and senior students who lived in the same residence hall as the participants. Acting as mentors and peers, they assisted the first-year students in handling academic and personal issues. A 1998 NFYS student remembered how she had cried the first night of the weekend retreat and one of the staff members of the program, a senior student, came to comfort her so that she would not feel lonely and homesick. From that time on, she regarded that student as her mentor, and whenever she had problems in her life or at school she would turn to her mentor for help. An international student especially appreciated how the student staff of NFYS helped him in easing his transition to the university:

Both my team leader and program coordinator were not only leaders, but also mentors, and brother and sister. They were always there for me whenever I needed them. If they do not even have enough time, they will manage to listen to me and help me out as best they could. I can still remember when I had some problems with my biology class and got frustrated about it. My team leader told me about her own experience and helped me to get over it. My coordinator will always ask me about my progress in my other classes. These people were great contributors to my success through the first semester of my freshman year. For these reasons, I am grateful and thankful for them today, tomorrow, and forever.

A female student of the 1998 NFYS made similar comments:

S. was the team leader of my group, Shine. She has been a huge help to me over the past three months. She understands everything that I'm going through and I know that she will always be there for me to listen. Ever since the retreat when I was broken down crying one night at dinner because I was so homesick, she was right there, comforting and consoling and being my friend. Sasha is a great leader because she leads us without making us feel she is above us (even though she is, in years and position), and I think we all respect her for that. I think we all admire and look up to Sasha, and I know I greatly appreciate everything she has done for us as our leader.

Another female student appreciated how her team leader always helped her whenever she had difficulties. She also discussed how senior students served as role models, and how Jacques embodied the program goals:

[Jacques] is a model for breaking down social barriers. I can tell that he doesn't see things like race, and color. He is always interested to learn something new about someone else's culture, and he is one of the most accepting people that I have ever met.

From the students' evaluations we can see how NFYS touched their lives and how it had a great impact on their understanding of themselves, their roles in relation to others, to community, and to society-at-large. But how can we appreciate NFYS more at the level of spirituality and education? The following two sections will discuss this issue.

BREAKING THROUGH THE FOUR BOUNDS

Terry O'Banion criticizes the traditional college and university structure, namely the *time-bound, place-bound, efficiency-bound,* and *role-bound* elements, and calls for educational efforts to break away from the confinement of these four constrictions.[9] Because so few programs are able to break through these boundaries, the most remarkable aspect of NFYS is that, although it was initiated, designed, planned, organized, and implemented by one student, it succeeded in breaking through all of the four bounds to create a holistic learning community.

Regarding place, the program does not confine student learning within the classroom. It moved the site of learning from the classroom to the residence hall, thereby creating a more relaxed and friendly environment, nurturing more learning and creating a stronger feeling of community for the students. It also moved learning into the community, connecting students' academic studies to real-life issues and real community needs, thus moving beyond the exclusive use of grades and tests as measurement of knowledge acquisition. Regarding time, it moved far beyond the 50-minute classtime restriction, involving a retreat, workshops, and many other spaces with their own time parameters. Regarding role, Jacques was not a teacher or an expert in curriculum design. Nevertheless, he designed, organized, and implemented the program. He was not limited by the role of "student," with its attendant expectations of passive learning. If he had thought that designing curriculum was the business of professors, this program would never have happened.

He also created new roles for others, enlisting other students to be team leaders and staff members. They took on mentoring and teaching roles and provided support to the first-year students. By tapping all the available internal and external resources, the program went far beyond the boundary of efficiency. Even judging by the traditional efficiency criteria of student retention, this program was successful, achieving the highest retention rate of all programs on campus. All except one of the 44 participants in the first two years of the NFYS are still continuing their studies. The seminar's retention rate was 100 percent among students of color, compared to 78.4 percent for the university as a whole.[10]

This unique program succeeded in transforming a residence hall culture from division to integration, from separation to connection. It not only connected students from many different cultural, ethnic, and racial backgrounds, but it also integrated academic work with the students' daily lives and their community service.

This program demonstrates what an awakened individual can do and how much he can achieve as long as he has liberated himself from socially assumed and prescribed boundaries, constraints, and limitations. From a spiritual perspective, the boundaries educators usually place around learning are artificial. Once traditional boundaries are challenged through the formation of new learning communities such as the NFYS, the possibilities for integration open.

Based on students' evaluations, we can see that the program meets all of the features of the Brower and Dettinger model of an ideal learning community.[11] It was hosted in a residence hall, so that it has the *physical elements*. It included workshops related to information skills and social issues, which stresses the *academic elements*. It involves community service that provides many of the *social elements*. From their evaluations, we can see clearly that students developed *professional responsibility* through learning time management and other professional skills. Through community service, the students developed *civic responsibility*. The students' sense of social responsibility and community responsibility has been strongly enhanced through the community service projects. Also, due to the social issues the students discussed and their work in the intergroup seminar fueled by the diverse identities of the participants, the students developed greatly their sense of *ethical responsibility*. The remarks of Brower and Dettinger seem quite appropriate for the NUANCE First-Year Seminar, i.e., the NFYS offered an "integrated, comprehensive program in which transformative learning takes place through a community process as students develop professional, civic and ethical responsibility."[12]

HOW THE NFYS DEMONSTRATES THE CORE VALUES OF SPIRITUALITY

Writers who discuss the role of spirituality in education often illuminate the deeper purposes of learning, beyond the instrumental acquisition of skills or marketable knowledge. Parker Palmer maintains that "to educate is to guide students on an inner journey toward a more truthful way of seeing and being in the world."[13] He also calls for a spirituality of education that brings the "hidden-wholeness" to the surface of education.[14] In his discussions of education, the Indian philosopher Krishnamurti advocated an understanding of the fully developed human being as free from social conditioning, free from fear, free from self-centered ego so that she can be fully present, creative, and able to discern the essential in her experience.[15] Ron Miller, when proposing a constructive postmodern educational philosophy, describes the essence of holistic education as "concerned with the creative evolution of new consciousness rather than with the pursuit of personal success within the established cultural patterns."[16]

Looking back at the NFYS program, it is clear that Jacques was not pursuing academic success as most students do. When he arrived at Gorman Hall, he did not allow himself to turn a blind eye to what was going on there. He had an ideal of what human relationship could be, and he appreciated the power of community. Most importantly, he did not leave the problems he saw for other people to solve; instead, he thought first about what he could do and started doing it. The journeys he and the participants of the NFYS program have undergone have been so unique, so powerful, and so integrated that they have made a great impact on the students' understanding of themselves, of the world, and of their relationships with the world. In short, this program was able to bring the "hidden-wholeness" of life to the surface, and to enable all of the participants to become more conscious and fully developed human beings.

How can the traditional boundaries our institutions place around learning be broken open to make more room for the fullness of the human spirit and the interconnection of all things? If an undergraduate student, in two and a half years, can create a learning community that succeeded in nurturing students in the development of their *academic responsibility*, *civic responsibility*, and *ethical responsibility* all at once, then higher education professionals should consider how they might create dynamic, integrative learning environments on their campuses.

ENDNOTES

1. Beryl Levinger, "Why Are We Afraid of Spirituality in Political Debate," in *Proceedings of the 21st Century Learning Initiative Wingspread Conference*, Wisconsin, November 13, 1996.
2. Carol Flake, ed., *Holistic Education: Principles, Perspectives and Practices* (Brandon, VT: Psychology Press/Holistic Education Press, 1993).
3. Terry O'Banion, *A Learning College for the 21st Century* (Phoenix: Oryx Press, 1997).
4. Aaron M. Brower and Karen M. Dettinger, "What Is a Learning Community," *About Campus* (November–December, 1998): 15–21.
5. Ibid.
6. Parker Palmer, "The Grace of Great Things," in *The Heart of Learning*, ed. Steven Glazer (New York: Penguin Putnam, 1999): 15.
7. Brower and Dettinger, "What Is a Learning Community."
8. Wesley Jacques, "The NUANCE First-Year Seminar and Residential Learning Communities," unpublished article, 2000.
9. Terry O'Banion, *Learning College*.

10. Office of Institutional Research cited by Jacques, unpublished article, 2000.
11. Brower and Dettinger, "What Is a Learning Community," 18.
12. Ibid.
13. Parker Palmer, *The Courage to Teach* (San Francisco: Jossey Bass, 1998), 6.
14. Parker Palmer, *To Know as We Are Known: A Spirituality of Education* (San Francisco: Harper & Row, 1983), xiii.
15. Jiddu Krishnamurti, *Education and the Significance of Life* (New York: Harper Collins, 1981), 39.
16. Ron Miller, "Education and the Evolution of the Cosmos," *Encounter*, 12, no. 2 (Summer 1999): 22.

16. Approaches to Conflict from Spiritual and Religious Perspectives: Lessons for Student Affairs

PATRICIA E. MARTIN

As we enter the new millennium, we frequently read and hear about instances of interpersonal conflict, which sometime spill into violence. Higher education is not immune from such conflicts. The United States Department of Education, in a report to Congress, noted that hate crimes and violent conflicts increased exponentially on campuses from 1998 to 1999, and that one-third of these crimes took place in residence halls.[1] While these statistics are grim and reflect the violent end of the conflict continuum, conflicts less serious in nature, at least in terms of bodily or property harm, also affect students and workers on America's campuses. Personnel in student affairs are well acquainted with the judicial and dispute resolution remedies that are employed in these situations. These measures, however, may not be sufficient to mitigate the conflicts or to foster civil communities in the academy.

Additional resources for approaching conflict resolution in student affairs work may be useful. During the past decade, new interest has arisen in the use of religious and spiritual practices and techniques for the resolution of conflict. While the majority of these efforts have been focused on ethnic and religious conflict around the world, these practices and philosophies may also be useful to student affairs professionals in helping to resolve conflict on campus. A climate of openness toward spiritual matters among the general public, and among some in higher education, offers the opportunity to explore the application of these concepts in student affairs. Because student affairs professionals work with students in the realms of character development, teamwork, and interpersonal relationships, the profession is uniquely situated to offer assistance and insights regarding issues of conflict.

The question, however, is whether student affairs professionals are sufficiently prepared to deal with all of the conflicts they encounter and whether it might be useful to become more conversant with a wider range of strategies to use in conflict situations. In the following pages, I would like to suggest that personnel in student affairs explore religious/spiritual perspectives as another possibility in working with situations of conflict, as well as offer some thoughts on the use of these approaches.

CONFLICT SCENARIOS IN STUDENT AFFAIRS

Many professionals find that case studies or specific "real life" situations are helpful in the application of theory to practice. Below are two fictitious (though probably familiar) situations of conflict that may affect student affairs staff members. I will return to these scenarios when I describe approaches to conflict from religious/spiritual perspectives.

At a small midwestern liberal arts college, as Andrea and Joe, two resident assistants, make their evening rounds, they enter a common lounge area. Upon entering the lounge, they find a student tied to a chair, surrounded by a group of male students. It is immediately clear to the RAs that he is uncomfortable and embarrassed. The others standing around the student hold a can of shaving cream and glasses of water that they appear to be ready to pour over him. Andrea and Joe quickly recognize the restrained student as one who is known to be unpopular and eccentric. The staff members intervene by untying the student and by talking with him about the situation. The student indicates that he didn't like what was transpiring, told the others so, and asked them to stop. The other students retort that they are his friends, and that the antics were just spirited hi-jinks, a way to pass the time on a boring Sunday evening. The RAs tell the group that their behavior is inappropriate and must stop. They also indicate that the incident would be documented, forwarded to the resident coordinator and campus police, and would most likely be referred for judicial action.

Conflicts are found not only among students, but also within the faculty and staff. Higher education, while certainly enjoying an upturn in student enrollments and increased revenues since the mid-90s, still faces the mandate "to do more with less." The struggle for both increased status and resources on the part of the faculty and staff, along with the myriad family and personal issues that affect all workers, add to the tensions that can foment conflict. Additionally, increasingly consumption-oriented and litigious constituencies bring additional stress to strained institutional systems. What follows is one illustration of administrative conflict.

Dr. Marian Stead recently joined the student affairs staff at a large southeastern comprehensive university as vice president. As is the case with any new manager, she decided to make some changes that would meet the various needs of the institution. After a few months on the job, she developed a reorganization plan and presented it to the staff.

At that meeting, various camps immediately affirmed or opposed all or parts of her plan. Throughout the discussion, Stead indicated that the change was important since it promised to provide the best services to students within the division's fiscal constraints. Immediately, those who opposed the plan denounced Stead's statements as disingenuous and refused to cooperate. Those who supported the plan said that they believed that the plan was in the best interests of the students, and that the other staff members were selfishly guarding their turf. A nonviolent but vocal melee ensued. Stead wisely called the meeting to a close, but she asked that all parties review the plan in depth and be ready to return for a meeting the following week with ideas for carrying out the plan, as well as possible alternative options.

During the next week, the departments that believed they would benefit most from the proposed plan scheduled a meeting with the vice president and suggested working with her individually to carry it out. Although Stead did not agree to meet, the proposed meeting was immediately seen by the opposition parties as another example of the vice president's disingenuousness. Those departments then issued a joint memo to the vice president, refusing to engage in further meetings on this or any other topic. The opposing groups then met with members of the faculty and supporters from other divisions to discuss a possible meeting with the president to question the new vice president's competence.

CONFLICT IN THE ACADEMY

Conflict appears to be commonplace in many aspects of American society, and, as indicated in the scenarios, higher education is not immune from this contentiousness. A review of general and higher education publications, as well as anecdotal insights based on my conversations over the past ten years, indicates to me the great extent of conflict across campuses, as well as public concern with such conflict.[2] Faculty members have reported threats from students if they give poor grades, discharge students from class for rude behavior, or limit the numbers of students in a class.

Unfortunately frequent are instances of faculty and staff slayings, motivated by students' and staff members' dissatisfaction with grades or performance appraisals. Faculty and staff members have reported various kinds of rude and malicious behavior from colleagues, ranging from shoving, yelling, angry e-mails, and back-stabbing comments to supervisors and peers, to sexual and ethnic harassment.[3] Athletic departments are rife with stories of coach and student-athlete anger and violence, as well as postgame incidents by students, alumni, and townspeople. Trustee and alumni board meetings have reported contentious sessions, and students and staff members have vented anger with their presidents and others through the destruction of campus property. Clearly, higher education has experienced and continues to endure a series of conflict situations, including some with violent overtones.

SEARCHING FOR METHODOLOGIES FOR MITIGATING CONFLICT

Institutions of higher education may becoming more conscious of conflict and the importance of conflict resolution. Recent governmental requirements have mandated that students and parents have the ability to gather information about campus safety[4] and have relaxed some aspects of the Buckley (Privacy) Amendment.[5] On the proactive side, colleges are exploring their role as civic educators. As part of this process, college administrators, particularly in student affairs, have focused on training students in the peaceful resolution of conflict. Corporations and other hiring authorities[6] emphasize the value of these qualities in students, as they rank teamwork and the ability to get along with others (often in hangar-like work structures) as critical work skills.

Yet many institutions continue to struggle with the application of both appropriate and useful processes for conflict reduction. Although campus judicial systems are sophisticated and well utilized, government and media reports indicate that these mechanisms are not sufficiently reducing the number of incidents of conflict. Higher education administrators, especially those in student affairs, still struggle to find effective conflict management and resolution strategies.

At issue are the effectiveness and complexity of certain conflict resolution strategies. Generally, student affairs professionals possess the skills and abilities necessary for the effective resolution of most conflict situations, and they are often able to effect workable solutions for difficult problems. In recent years, however, I have had conversations with colleagues about, and have observed firsthand, some aversion to, or fear of, engaging with some conflicts. Several issues may be present in these situations. Although student affairs staff, particularly those in residence halls, receive training in conflict resolution (generally roommate concerns), the training often follows a prescribed pattern or focus. Staff members are often taught to resolve conflict individually, rather than in team settings, although working in teams might be more effective. It is imperative that student affairs professionals are comfortable working with groups in contentious contexts. As described later in the chapter, the very nature of group processing and strategizing for a common goal can help to mitigate conflict on all levels.

Although most staff members are well trained, they often are not taught that different conflict situations might require different methodologies. A corollary to this point is the challenge of dealing with conflict within a diverse population. While staff members may be trained to deal with diversity and conflict resolution separately, the interplay of the two areas is rarely discussed. Fried has noted that higher education administrators may need to seek out alternative ways of knowing when dealing with students and staff with nonmainstream or non-Western worldviews.[7] Alternative methods of conflict resolution might be useful with cross-cultural groups and situations. Additionally, staff members may not be aware of the pressures experienced by some individuals (especially adult students) from sources outside of the university. This is also an area often overlooked by coworkers when dealing with a troubled colleague. Often, coworkers are too polite or scared to confront someone or to seek help.

The United States also continues to be an increasingly litigious society. Staff members are loath to deal with difficult people, fearful of being sued or summoned to hearings. Some staff members may be fearful of engaging in conflict, due to political implications and constraints. Staff members speak often about their superiors giving in to demands to absolve perpetrators from fault if the administration is pressured by angry parents, legislators, the press, or donors. Others may still be uncomfortable in the dual roles of counselor and enforcer of rules, even though all student affairs training programs focus on the centrality of the educational focus in discipline. While student affairs staff have training that enables them to be successful in the majority of conflict resolution situations, it might be helpful to rethink approaches that are not working well in all types of situations.

Over the past several years, there has been an increasing awareness of the need to understand and support the ways in which spirituality and reli-

gion influence our personal and professional lives. There has been a growing body of work on spirituality and student affairs.[8] Additionally, many
professional staff members appear to be interested in exploring how faith
traditions influence engagement in the world and what lessons might be
gleaned from the wisdom of these traditions.

There is a conflict resolution theme in each of the faiths. In this century,
tenets of faith have been used to address conflict situations throughout the
world, most notably in colonial India and in the civil rights movement in
the United States. Broad applications of the philosophical principles of
religious faiths and specific spiritual practices can give student affairs practitioners new processes and practices which may more effectively meet the
challenges of complex conflict situations. Recognition that current practice is not wholly successful in all situations, coupled with escalating conflict on our campuses, calls for the consideration of alternative methods
and philosophies.

RELIGION AND SPIRITUALITY AS AN ALTERNATIVE WAY
TO RESOLVE CONFLICT IN THE ACADEMY

Although some writers have criticized religion as causing too many
conflicts rather than helping with their resolution, others have suggested
that conflict can be viewed as holy ground.[9] For believers in God, conflict
can be viewed positively, as a window into the ways in which God works.
For example, in her interpretation of the Genesis story in the Hebrew Bible,
Mendelson playfully suggests that God threw caution to the wind in creating almost unimaginable diversity, diversity in which conflict is inherent.
Difference is integral to God's overall plan, and the resulting conflict can
be healthy.[10] From this perspective, conflict balanced with peace supports
human development and growth. Diamond expands upon these ideas in
naming conflict as a creative and growth-producing process.[11] She also
links conflict with its opposite, peace, by suggesting that conflict binds the
community through involvement in the practice of democratic processes.
In other words, conflict and peace may be likened to the forces of yin and
yang, stretching and pulling each other in the process of disagreement,
discussion, and resolution, with a common goal of working out spaces of
agreement in the middle. The push and pull of opposition and agreement
underlies the engagement of all (ideally) in the democratic process. The
latter concept parallels the thoughts of Mendelson, in reference to the meta-

phor of equals working together rather than enemies fighting for victory. Finally, Diamond identifies this practice as one that is spiritual, further agreeing with Mendelson about the sacred nature of conflict.

These views regarding conflict as a spiritual process as well as a process that supports human development offer some guidance to those in student affairs. By identifying conflict as a natural, holy, and spiritual process, Mendelson encourages educators to facilitate learning through conflict. Additionally, by labeling conflict as a wholly human and God-given necessity, she allows those who have previously seen it as a negative force to be able to deal with it in a more accepting manner.

Earlier, we discussed some of the challenges that student affairs staff and others may face in dealing with feelings of fear and isolation in conflict situations. Following the concepts delineated by Mendelson and Diamond allows student affairs staff members to see conflict as necessary and positive. Additionally, by understanding conflict as a cooperative, democratic, and spiritual practice, staff members might be able to overcome their fears of those situations and enter conflict resolution efforts with an attitude of hope, rather than fatalism.

The history of conflict between faiths may indeed get in the way of using the tenets of faith to resolve conflict. Some people might think it laughable that religious faiths could bring any wisdom to the table. It is sadly true that many adherents of the various faiths are in violent conflict.

Recently, a new paradigm of a global ethic directed toward both the reduction of conflict and the enhancement of relationships has emerged.[12] Within the conceptual framework of the global ethic, Hans Küng, echoing the thoughts of Kant, suggests that all religious groups hold similar tenets in terms of ethics, namely respect for human dignity and values, thereby mitigating the differences among them.[13] Küng, a liberal Roman Catholic priest and theologian who has been active in world peace and conflict concerns academically and in governmental circles, views this commonality as a starting point for the dissipation of conflict, both within and outside of religious spheres.

This concept of a global religious ethic regarding the basic humanity and dignity of all persons could bring an enhanced meaning to conflict resolution. Generally, most conflict resolution scenarios focus on the issues of the dispute, not on the persons and the process. The spiritual or religious perspective emphasizes the persons and the process, rather than the issues. This emphasis may have a higher probability of long-range change, since there is concern about changing how the varying sides view each other and their interrelationships, rather than on resolving a particular disagreement, which generally is time-sensitive. Transformation on the levels of persons and processes, rather than on specific issues, is an integral tenet in all religions. Most faiths discuss movement toward the Transcendent as a goal.

While the mission of the academy is not the same as that of religious faiths, changes in how we see and handle conflict can create powerful changes within our institutions. For example, the major faith traditions view a preoccupation with winning and losing as detrimental to spiritual development. Rather, an emphasis on oneness with the other is highlighted. Perhaps if people saw themselves as part of a collective rather than mired in competitive conflict, organizations would be freer to engage in transformational activity. Hence, a focus on the unity of all persons would allow organizations to more effectively utilize their resources.

Central to Küng's approach are the concepts of *steadfastness* and *dialogue*. While appearing to be polarities and not vehicles for constructive conflict management, both concepts allow for unity, while valuing diversity at the same time. *Steadfastness* calls for all sides in a conflict to hold fast to their own viewpoint, as both an attitude and as a good or virtuous thing; each side must come to the realization that others will act similarly with regard to their own views. All persons in the conflict situation try to view all sides at all times as having equal merit—a challenging task.

In Küng's approach, the parties in a conflict would keep their own views but not regard those views as superior to others' views. Of course, one can believe (and Küng reiterates this) that her/his concept of God, philosophy, or politics is correct, yet that person respects the competing view as an equally valuable path for that other party. Allowing for one to hold fast and revere one's own position gives dignity to each person in a conflict and avoids win-lose scenarios. Underscoring this stance is the sense that all people of diverse viewpoints have dignity and worth. Understanding and believing the latter makes it difficult to see oneself as solely deserving of victory. Although not delineated here, legalistic conflict management methodologies foster some type of loss for one of the parties.

Küng completes his two-part conflict resolution strategy with the concept of dialogue.[14] A person in a conflict situation needs to understand and accept that her own position is important and vital to the overall discussion. Further, Küng urges all parties to see the relationships among all viewpoints, with a focus on similarities, not differences. This process allows each party dignity in their position and does not force them to give up their views.

Yet dialogue also demands an interplay between and among parties to form a "gray" or "center" area, one that is open for discussion. This center or middle zone is the area for the meshing and threshing of views. In most conflict resolution scenarios, the participants blend their demands, and they and/or a negotiator decide on a workable solution. The problem with this process is that all parties may not be represented equally in the discussion, and the decision may favor one more than others, or none at all.

Küng argues for a different type of center. He suggests that all viewpoints be woven together (synthesis), rather than blended (syncretism). This center of synthesis, or zone of synthesis, represents a new area of mutual agreement and work. Rather than taking pieces of each party's wants, each person participates in the creation of a new product, formulated by all members of the negotiation. In reality, the formerly disparate parties are engaged as members of a team creating a new program or process. Again, this type of dialogue offers each party their dignity and worth, but also creates a middle ground of interaction and new work, and, hopefully, more understanding and cooperation.

We can now return to the earlier scenario with the vice president and the various staff members. Instead of secular methodologies of conflict resolution, we can apply Küng's framework to the situation. A more secular approach, although urging the participants to be civil and calm, will generally pit one viewpoint against the other, and one viewpoint will probably gain more "goodies" at the end. Within Küng's paradigm, the first objective would be to create a sense of steadfastness on the part of each group or individual. The facilitation of a feeling and atmosphere of steadfastness would have two parts. First, all parties would need to be assured that they were safe, that their viewpoint was valuable, that they had the right to hold that viewpoint personally, and that the viewpoint could not be attacked. Secondly, the parties would need to become engaged in some hard work in order to understand the necessity and value of differences, as well as understand the importance of valuing their colleagues' viewpoints for this process.

After reaching some measure of safety and understanding, the facilitators can move to the dialogue phase, keeping an ear tuned to any breakdown in the steadfastness pact. Facilitators may need to harken back to the diversity theme in order to help participants to see their viewpoints as valuable, but just one of several possible and important viewpoints. The departments who supported the vice president may still agree with her but realize that all of the others may not. Using Küng's framework, the facilitators can help the participants to see the disparate viewpoints as equally valuable options, and just that: options. For example, the group vehemently opposing the vice president's restructuring plan has valid reasons for doing so, and other sides need to appreciate that validity, despite their disagreement. In the dialogue phase, parties are still allowed to hold their viewpoints, but they need to move toward the understanding of the interrelationships among the views and create a center. The facilitators work with the groups to fashion a synthesis of all viewpoints that is acceptable to all, not one that blends some views so that they are immersed and no longer visible. Rather, all of the views interrelate and become a new view in the center, a meshing of all of the standpoints.

Perhaps in this case, all parties might agree that each member of the student affairs team is needed for effective service to students, and that each member of the staff will reduce his or her work schedules so that all members can be retained. The parties might also resolve that all staff members would participate in cross-training, for the sake of better service to students. They might also agree that the vice president, along with all members of the team, work together to raise the status of student affairs and to garner more resources. This type of process ensures that all persons keep their dignity and worth, that all views are valued and valid, and that a new structure comes out of the process where all "win" on some level.

BRIEF LESSONS ON CONFLICT RESOLUTION FROM SELECTED FAITHS

As indicated earlier, all religious traditions offer some conflict resolution concepts and processes. A review of all faith-based strategies is beyond the scope of this chapter, however illuminating those might be. I have chosen, therefore, to focus on some of the conflict resolution practices and philosophies of two major world religions, Hinduism and Christianity. Although very different in their overarching theology and practice, both religions are well known for practical uses of their beliefs in the resolution of conflict, most notably through the work of Gandhi and Martin Luther King, Jr.

The Christian faith asks its adherents to act with love toward all others, since the faith purports that all human beings are created in God's image. Jesus Christ, believed by followers to be the son of God as well as the head of the Christian Church, has radical demands of his followers: to renounce their own rights in favor of others' rights, to renounce their power at their own expense, and to refuse to retaliate in case of injury. In one of the New Testament Gospels, the apostle Matthew[15] reports that Jesus requires his followers to "do unto others, as you would have them do to you," the so-called "Golden Rule." In another Gospel, that of Luke,[16] Jesus calls His followers to love and respect those who are different from themselves.

In the scenario of the residence hall students, the offending students were clearly seeing their fellow student as the "other." Rather than a contentious judicial hearing, the parties might be brought together in order to describe their differences, as well as their similarities. They can then be urged to respect differences as an integral and positive aspect of humanity, rather than responding to differences with hostile actions. A further goal of the session would be to enable the students to see each other as more similar than different and as part of a whole.

Similar to the tenets of the Christian religion, the Hindu faith promotes the philosophy and practice of *ahimsa*, of compassion to others, noninjury, and nonviolence. Two key principles of Hinduism are different from Christianity and give important guidance to different ways of viewing conflict. Important in the Hindu faith is the concept of the "other" being undifferentiated from one's self, at least on a spiritual plane.

A personal example might elucidate the discussion. Several years ago, I spent a good deal of time in a hospital bed tethered to various machines; I was unable to move out of the bed without nursing assistance. At the same time, the various painkilling drugs that I had been administered made me sleep and wake in two or three hour increments. As a result, I was often awake in the middle of the night. Not wanting to view the limited offerings on television or wake my roommate, and unable to concentrate on written material, I found myself staring out the window for many hours at what was a first quarter moon. I gazed at the moon and was soon in a meditative state. Next, I felt a connection to the moon, that it was part of me and I of it. Finally, the moon and I became one: we were undifferentiated.

Some may scoff at this notion, attributing it to medication or lack of sleep. However, this experience parallels the views of Gandhi and other Hindus that all matter (including humans) are undifferentiated on that spiritual plane; hence, one cannot be violent toward the other, since it would mean being violent toward one's self. Gandhi taught that when one is involved in a force against aggression, no hatred should be harbored against the aggressor; rather, one must try to convert that opponent to *ahimsa*.[17] In the case of the recalcitrant students, getting them to see themselves as integrally connected to the "other" may allow them to see the hurt to themselves that unhealthy conflict can foster. Facilitating this in a cognitive way may not meet the goal; we might need to work with the students on a meditative practice, similar to that which I experienced. Perhaps through that practice, the leap to a cognitive understanding might ensue.

Another tenet of Hinduism is that a person is a microcosm of the world. Following that, transcendence on all levels is necessary, since the true self is eternal and immortal and one with Ultimate Being. It stands to reason that if one is representing the entire world, then any action reflects on, and is connected to, the entire world. A person, therefore, needs to focus on goodwill and peace, since doing harm would be doing harm to oneself and to all of creation.[18]

With regard to our scenario with the professional staff, this concept could be used to help staff members to see themselves as part of a greater whole. This greater whole might be the mission of educating students, and hence, any harm coming from negative conflict would affect not only that particular group, but others engaged in higher education across the world.

This understanding appears to closely parallel some of Küng's precepts of steadfastness and dialogue in searching for the middle or common ground. Truly, it calls for the staff to go beyond themselves and to focus on the "center" or "holy ground" that all share in order to move from conflict to mutual understanding.

PRACTICAL IMPLICATIONS FOR STUDENT AFFAIRS PROFESSIONALS

Besides the reflections offered here on various religious tenets and practices applied to fictitious conflict scenarios, it might be helpful to offer some initial guidance for further exploration of the application of these themes to conflict reduction practices in student affairs. Staff members promoting these methodologies must attend to both diversity and the separation of church and state in public institutions. It also may be useful to follow Küng's lead here in naming any of these processes global ethics, in order to avoid the promotion of any particular beliefs. In discussing the linkage of all to a Transcendent Being, one might use the successful strategy utilized by 12-step groups in allowing participants to identify their own Higher Power: the latter might be humankind, God, freedom, nature, etc. This would allow all parties to engage deeply in the discussion.

One way to formulate some discussion, activity, and commitment to spiritual methodologies of conflict reduction on campus would be through the creation of a "global ethics" team. Much like campus crisis, mediation, or interdisciplinary student support teams, this group would draw disparate members of the campus together to not only promote and educate the members of the institution about the appropriate concepts and methodologies, but also to facilitate conflict resolution. Key members of the group would be members of student affairs, campus ministry, religious organizations, faculty members in the religion, philosophy, and mediation areas, and student leaders. Also included would be those personnel who work on issues of conduct, harassment, and violence. The diverse nature of the team would also facilitate some transformation of the campus in that it would bring together parties with differing views of campus issues.

This group would formulate structure, tenets, processes, and an agenda of education and outreach for the campus. The group would need to do some deep processing in order to ensure that all were committed to the concepts and practice of the global ethics construct. Imperative to the effective functioning of this team and program would be the blessing of the senior administration; in fact, it might be helpful if the group reported in an advisory capacity to the top executive, although it would be important that all processes be confidential.

Of utmost importance is that the group be seen as very different from other committees and administrative structures; the only way that it can do its work effectively would be if the group is allowed to question traditional methods. This issue may cause spots of contention and uncomfortable feelings of lack of power and control on the part of many. It is important, therefore, to have the overarching support of the campus community for the goals and processes of the team. This can only be achieved through a period of soul-searching and commitment to a more transformative institution. Professionals interested in attempting such a program will likely encounter many fears, anxieties, roadblocks, and (yes!) conflict. Utilizing the processes outlined earlier in this chapter may assist the team in overcoming these obstacles.

CONCLUDING COMMENTS

A theme in many faith traditions is the importance of compassion and understanding differences.[19] Acceptance and understanding of differences is also somewhat embedded in the traditional and secular methods of conflict resolution. It is the compassion and the deep accepting/understanding of the "other," as well as the notion that all creatures are part of a great whole or creation, that marks the differences between religious approaches to conflict resolution and secular approaches. Religious approaches invite us to not merely follow a process or procedure to change certain behaviors, but to become deeply empathic.

This task will not be easy, however. As delineated in the beginning of the chapter, two of the hallmarks of today's society are violence and litigiousness. People want what they want, and will often use (most) any means to get it. Yet, concurrently, there appears to be a new yearning among many people for a life that is more meaningful and more spiritual.

Many people may not consider how a faith tradition might inform their work with others. However, educators interested in the reduction of the negative aspects of conflict and perhaps in a spiritual journey as well may want to engage in a dialogue about how faith traditions and their diverse approaches to conflict resolution can assist us in our work with students and with each other.

ENDNOTES

1. Staff, "Campus Homicides Fall, But Some Crimes Rise." *The New York Times*. (New York: The New York Times Company, Inc., January 21, 2001), 25.
2. Peter Garland and Thomas Grace, *New Perspectives for Student Affairs Professionals: Evolving Realities, Responsibilities and Roles.* ASHE-ERIC Higher Education Reports, 22, no. 7 (Washington, DC: The George Washington University, 1993).
3. Staff, "Campus Homicides."
4. Campus Security Policy and Campus Crime Statistics Act. 20 USC §1092(f) as amended 1998.
5. Family Educational Rights and Privacy Act (FERPA) by the Higher Education Amendments of 1998. Pub.L. 105-244, §951, 105th Cong., 2nd Sess. (October 7, 1998).
6. Staff. *Recruitment Trends 2000* (East Lansing, MI: Michigan State University, 2000).
7. Jane Fried and Associates, *Shifting Paradigms in Student Affairs: Culture, Context, Teaching, and Learning* (Lanham, MD: University Press of America, 1995).
8. *National Association of Student Personnel Administrators National Conference Program* (Philadelphia, PA, March 1998; New Orleans, LA, March 1999; Indianapolis, IN, March 2000). Washington, DC: NASPA.
9. Bertrand Russell, *Why I Am Not a Christian and Other Essays on Religion or Related Subjects* (New York: Simon and Schuster, 1956).

10. Abby Mendelson, *Conflict as Opportunity. Conflict Resolution Notes,* 17, no. 4, April. (Washington, DC: Conflict Resolution Center International, 2000).

11. Rosalind Nagin Diamond, *Conflict Resolution and Democracy as a Spiritual Path* (Berkeley, CA: CRCI, 1991).

12. Hans Küng, *A Global Ethic for Global Politics and Economics* (New York: Oxford University Press, 1998).

13. Hans Küng, *Global Responsibility: In Search of a New World Ethic* (London: SCM Press, 1991).

14. Ibid.

15. Matthew 7:12.

16. Luke 6:23.

17. Hope Fitz, "Gandhi's Ethical/Religious Tradition," *Journal of Religious Studies* 27 (1996): 1 & 2, 97–106.

18. Bathika Mukerji, "The Foundations of Unity and Equality: A Hindu Understanding of Human Rights," in *Religion as a Source of Violence,* ed. Karl Josef Kuschel, Wim Beuken, and Aloysius Pieris, 70–78. Maryknoll, NY: SCM Press, 1997.

19. Hans Küng, *Paradigm Change in Theology: A Symposium for the Future* (New York: Crossroad, 1990).

17.   Civility and Spirituality

JANE FRIED

The next frontier is not in front of us; it is inside us.
—Senator Joseph Lieberman

Americans seem to expect educated people, particularly those who have graduated from college, to think rationally and behave reasonably, even in highly charged situations. This point was emphasized in a recent conversation about "trigger words" with a group of school counselors in a group dynamics class. Trigger words are the kind of words which can cause new professionals in counseling to lose their focus and mental clarity if they are used in a professional context. One student described a conversation in the faculty lounge of her school when one of her colleagues referred to another person as a "faggot." Another student in the class became incensed that such a word would be used by teachers, in any setting. For him there was a huge difference between hearing high school students use that type of derogatory word and hearing it from a college-educated person. His explanation was that younger students are generally ignorant of the history and implications of such language and that hearing them use such expletives can be turned into a "teachable moment." On the other hand, professionals, because of their education and role, should always know better than to dehumanize or stigmatize anyone. His belief, and mine, is that somehow education should involve helping people learn how to behave with civility and reason, even in uncomfortable situations.

Becoming well educated implies that a person can take the broad view in any situation and place the immediate events into a context that is both wider, from a social perspective, and deeper, from a historical or possibly spiritual perspective. The ability to be reasonable, prudent, and respectful of one's fellow human beings is one way to define civility. Although the ability to think and behave with civility may be a by-product of education, it rarely seems to be a part of any official curriculum. Educated people are expected to be civil, but nobody is expected to teach them how—a conundrum if ever there was one.

Civility implies a capacity for politeness and respect that supercedes the automatic "please and thank you's" of our daily life. It is the capacity to remain respectful in the face of differences that an individual finds difficult to tolerate.

Civility seems to be in short supply in our society. The postmodern era in the United States has generated a wave of consciousness and self-definition that includes ethnicity, gender, sexual orientation, age, religion, race, class and a range of other aspects of personal identity. People also seem to be changing their residence at a faster rate than ever, and continued immigration into the U.S. is adding new dimensions of diversity to our population. People often do not have, or take, the time to get to know one another or to understand the frames of reference that others use to interpret the world.

We don't know much about each other's codes of courtesy or civility, and one result of this situation is that our common understanding of what constitutes courteous or civil behavior seems to have disappeared. Behavior that is normal on public transportation in Athens or New York City, for example, might almost be considered assault in a rural area of the midwestern United States. Our population includes people whose ideas of voice tone, physical space, bodily hygiene, and interpersonal communication styles are so different that one person's intention to compliment might be construed by another as an insult. There is a serious need for us to articulate our notions of civility in everyday life and, by implication, to think about how expectations of civility translate into the various elements of our educational system. If educated people are supposed to behave with civility toward others, where and how will they learn about this increasingly complex area of human relationships?

On what basis can we learn to treat each other with civility if there is no cultural consensus about attitudes and behaviors that convey respect from one person to another? It seems as if there is a need to agree about what we all have in common, beyond differing cultural expectations and forms. We need a transcultural notion of civil behavior that addresses the fundamental rights we all seem to desire. Hughes has identified several universally held values that may provide a key to achieving this consensus. The primary value is "Personal development through spiritual freedom, educational opportunity and wellness,"[1] as well as a need to be treated with respect both individually and culturally, a need to resolve conflicts peacefully, and ultimately, the development of a global and life-enhancing code of ethics.[2] All of these values seem to converge on the notion that the ways people treat each other should minimize intrusion and maximize freedom for each, regardless of the ways that each person and each culture defines freedom and noninterference. The complexity of this task boggles the mind since, before one can respect another's freedom, one must understand what freedom, in all its forms, means to the other.

In most other countries of the world, personal development, education, and spirituality are not as strictly divided as they are in the United States. Personal and spiritual development may be considered almost synonymous in some cultures, and the vehicle for this development is education. In contrast, any discussion of spirituality and civility in the context of higher education in the United States is problematic. Separation of church and state makes thinking about spirituality in the context of public higher education difficult because of the fuzziness in the distinctions we draw between religion and spirituality.

Since spirituality is so closely associated with religion in the United States, it is necessary to draw some distinctions between the two in order to investigate the connections between spirituality and civility on our campuses. If we do not have a clear understanding of the differences between spirituality and religion, any discussion of civility and spirituality on campus will be confused, contentious, and truncated in our public institutions.

I offer some ideas about spirituality that are meaningful to me in the context of this chapter, recognizing that this is one of the most widely discussed topics on our planet. Spirituality, from my point of view, has to do with the experience of connection—connections between people, connections that one person makes between his or her knowledge and the wider meaning or application of that knowledge, connections that people experience between their own lives and all of life in either broader or deeper dimensions. A spiritual experience is one in which a person feels his or her connection to a much broader domain than is apparent in the minutiae of daily life. Faith, which is quite similar to spirituality in the way that I am describing it here, is defined by Fowler as always involving the perception and experience of relationship. It is described as "the relation of trust in, and loyalty to, the transcendent...an alignment of heart and will, a commitment of loyalty and trust."[3]

The Latin root of the word *spirit* is the same as the word for *breath*. It is connected to such other words as aspire, inspire, and expire. Aspiration and inspiration both imply hope, a looking up toward a greater good. Expiration implies the end of the presence of breath, the departure of the spirit from the body. In the Hebrew Bible, the word *ruach* is used for both breath and spirit in the statement in Genesis, "The Spirit of God hovered over the face of the waters; And God said, 'let there be light'…and God called the light day and the darkness night and there was evening and morning, one day."[4] Spirit is a nonmaterial sense of connection that lifts people's experience of themselves and their lives from the mundane to the transcendent, from the meaningless to the meaningful, from that which decays to that which sustains.

Spirituality also connects the various dimensions of our own awareness in order to allow us to find or create meaning in our lives. Zohar and Marshall define spirituality as the type of intelligence that allows us to "place our actions and our lives in a wider, richer, meaning-giving context."[5] An African proverb that illustrates this definition is this: "I am because we are." It suggests that "my life" has meaning only in the context of the lives of my people or my tribe. Spirituality involves the entire being as it is known in the broadest possible context. Spiritual experience involves the emotions, beliefs, and commitments to behave in the world in ways that are a consequence of those experiences and beliefs. Vaill describes spirituality as a personal process through which meaning is constructed as people attempt to transcend the values of materialism.[6] Materialism, as described later in this chapter, almost always implies competition and separation. Transcending materialism within the human community is a process of reestablishing connections on spiritual grounds, where no competition is necessary. The vehicle through which meaning often emerges is dialogue.

Spirituality and religion are often considered similar, if not synonymous terms. Since separation of church and state is a constitutional mandate in the United States, it is important to clarify the relationship between the two. I suggest that spirituality can be found in religion, particularly in the mystical traditions of all faiths, but that not all aspects of religious institutions can be considered spiritual. Spiritual experience provides the foundation for religion, but the institutions that have risen to proclaim the initial spiritual experience and insight are quite similar to other types of human institutions.

Organizations have many purposes, some of which may be spiritual. In order for an organization to exist, however, it also needs to attend to its economic, organizational, and political needs. For purposes of discussing spirituality and civility in higher education, I believe that spiritual concerns should be disengaged from the organizational aspects of the various faith communities that are involved, along with others, in discussions of spirituality and civility on campus. This is an idea that is easier to imagine in theory than in practice, but within the confines of constitutional mandates, I believe it is a viable approach.

AMERICAN VALUES AND BARRIERS TO CONNECTION

When spirituality is understood as awareness of multifaceted connection, spiritual experience and practice becomes quite a challenge for Americans. American culture is filled with barriers to connection and has precious little to support the idea that the actions of one person may have profound effects on the well-being of others. For example, grading systems in our colleges are almost universally based on individual achievement and often use the normal distribution curve, which places individuals in competition with each other for a limited number of good grades. The same approach prevails in many of our large corporations, where individuals may be on the "fast track" or not, depending on their achievement, presentation of self, and ability to manipulate organization politics. Although much work is done in teams, promotions are typically given to individuals. Advertising from rental car companies, copy services, and motels oriented to business travelers capitalize on the aspirations for upward mobility based on individual performance. Perhaps the most offensive of these ads is one in which one man is promoted over the other and the "loser" is shown licking and polishing the winner's shoes. Even the old American adage about "keeping up with the Joneses" implies that people want to connect with each other for purposes of maintaining personal advantage, rather than supporting each other. Our advertising is filled with examples of people glorifying in their ability to get the last one of an item or get the most of something, typically at the expense of the competition. In many circumstances, particularly within families and other affinity groups, people clearly support each other and cooperate for mutual benefit. However, the public attitude in this culture seems to emphasize competition rather than cooperation. There are two broad areas from which our self-protective national behavior seems to spring: political philosophy and national values.

Political Philosophy

The Constitution of the United States and most of our government structures are based on liberal assumptions and contract relationships. Each person is considered an autonomous entity that enters into contracts with other entities to form relationships that are precisely defined in terms of mutual obligations and benefits. Each party is presumed to act in his (sic) own self-interest and the derivative assumption is that the collective self-interests of the individuals will benefit the entire group. When a group enters into a mutual understanding of the benefits and responsibilities that should accrue to all members, this understanding is called a social contract. This approach to defining human relationships was first articulated by John Locke, who believed that "The individual is prior to society, which comes into existence only through the voluntary contracts of individuals trying to maximize their own self-interest."[7] One of the roles of law in the U.S. is to determine, in cases of conflicting interests, whose rights prevail in a particular situation. Our legal system is an adversarial one and is not designed to find compromise or connection. It is designed to determine who shall prevail.

Our civic decision making, as often as not, is shaped by conflicting or competing interests on a win/lose basis, each trying to gain advantage even at the expense of the interests of other groups. Do we give money back to people and lower taxes or do we use the tax surplus to provide services for people who can't afford to buy the services for themselves? Are Medicaid benefits more important than hiring more teachers and lowering class sizes in elementary schools? How often do we hear politicians talk about balance? Decisions are framed according to who wins and who loses, not how we address a range of complex issues with fairness.

National Values

An emphasis on individualism, materialism, and competition characterizes our national belief system.[8] Individualism is derived from the political philosophy discussed above, and it is a dominant value in this culture. We glorify individuals in sports, in space travel, and in all fields of achievement. We look for individual leaders who will help organizations achieve goals. We structure our entire educational system to reward individual achievement.

In our culture, the individual is clearly visible and the context, background, or support system is rarely noticed. However, our national and cultural emphasis on the individual to the exclusion of context is quite unusual.[9] From a global perspective, most cultures tend to emphasize the collectivist or communal approach to group life, in which the needs and values of individuals are typically placed in the context of the needs and values of the group. The contrast is encapsulated in two aphorisms—one is American: "Look out for number 1"; the other is Japanese: "The nail that sticks up gets beaten down."

Our belief in the value of material accumulation is also powerful. Reality in the United States has been defined as material reality. Having a lot means having a lot of things that can be counted, typically money and possessions that money can buy. People who are "doing well" are people who have a lot of money—not a lot of spiritual wisdom. In fact, being spiritually wise and being wealthy are often seen as contradictory. The activities necessary for the accumulation of personal wealth are thought to be at cross-purposes with the accumulation of wisdom.

When a very large textile factory burned to the ground in New England in the 1990s, the owner astounded the American public by announcing that he would rebuild the factory and keep all the workers on the payroll until they could go back to work. His workers were largely immigrants on relatively low hourly wages. They were not the sort of people who had money in the bank to get them through periods of unemployment. The owner was very wealthy and in his seventies. He could have retired and kept the insurance money for himself. When he did not do this, his explanation for his behavior was that he was a Jew and his religious ethics mandated that he care for his workers as members of the human family. There are certainly many Jewish businesspeople who would not have acted as this man did. The interesting thing about this incident is that the owner cited his Judaism, not his civic responsibility, as the reason for his actions. His behavior and thinking harkened back to an earlier phase of American society when the conflict between the public good and private benefit was not so clear, a time when faith traditions "placed individual autonomy in a context of moral and religious obligations that in some sense justified obedience as well as freedom."[10] In that context, wisdom and wealth do not contradict each other.

Competition can be understood as an aspect of the combined effects of individualism and materialism. One becomes materially wealthy by overcoming the competition in one's field and selling more than anybody else. Business leadership manuals and business metaphors use the language of sports and war to describe company policy and strategy. Business is always in competition, and winning competition leads to profits. Individuals are often placed in competition with each other, particularly in higher education. Norm-referenced grading practices, or grading on the curve, presume that the best students are those who can demonstrate that they have learned more than the rest by performance on tests or other assessment devices. Standard college admissions exams are norm referenced; class rank is norm referenced; admission to graduate schools of all kinds is norm referenced by other standardized tests and class rank. Getting where you want to go in life, as an American, is shaped more by the ability to compete and outperform your opponents than it is by collaborating and succeeding with your colleagues.

American colleges and universities typically create a competitive atmosphere within the institution and also exist in a very competitive environment among institutions. Faculty members compete for grants and publications with their colleagues around the world. Departments compete for resources. Administrators compete for promotions. Errors of judgment, performance, or mastery are embarrassing or harmful to one's career. Our models of teaching, learning, and working in universities set us against each other more than they place us in collaboration for the achievement of group goals. Parker Palmer has described the environment of most universities as a culture of fear.[11]

Spirituality and Civility on Campus

The competitive nature of academic life functions as a major barrier to both spirituality and civility. Spirituality can be understood as the ability to experience connections and to create meaning in one's life.[12,13] One makes meaning by connecting parts to the whole. The whole may be understood as "a vision of transcendent value and power, one's ultimate concern."[14] To the degree that people perceive others as their competitors, the logical goal is to try to dominate them, because their own self-interests exclude the interests of others or of the whole community. In order to maintain day-to-day civil relationships, people in college communities must avoid situations that set members of the community at odds with each other, including our tendency to zero-sum thinking.

On a very personal level, I have been guilty of this kind of perception and the resulting rather rude behavior. When a colleague I do not know well receives recognition for something that I believe I deserve (e.g., an award, a citation, a mention in a professional publication), I have great trouble being civil to that person for quite some time. It has taken me years to realize that if we are both working in the same area, recognition for one means advancing the cause to which we are both committed, not a slight to me. Incivility in this instance is a result of my failure to perceive our connections in a positive way and to see competition where a framework of cooperation would provide a greater benefit to both. Since my ultimate concern is justice, my efforts to overcome my own impulses to incivility have been rooted in a spiritual search for that which unites all of us as equals, worthy of respect from each to each.

Competition interferes with the perception of connection in many areas of campus life. For example, assessment techniques typically ask students for the right answer, setting up two categories, choosing one and excluding the other. People who are accustomed to seeing the world from one disciplinary perspective are not trained to appreciate other perspectives, particularly when those perspectives contradict or add more complexity to any topic. Institutions typically run on one dominant decision-making criterion: can we afford it?

The complexity of assessing the values on which decisions about affordability rest is easily seen as time consuming, unrealistic, or disruptive. For example, can a college afford to move to Division I athletics and support a football team when its classes are crowded, its part-time faculty is larger than its full-time faculty, and its residence halls are decaying and crowded? The answer is yes, if the president and the alumni want Division I athletics and no, if the faculty union successfully challenges the part-time to full-time faculty ratio. It all depends on funding sources, beliefs about outcomes for the college, and beliefs about teaching and learning. Conversations about this topic are rarely civil, but rather filled with suspicions about the motives and values of the opposing group. The decision is conceptualized as a conflict between the traditional intellectual values of academe and the populist values of athletic competition that ensure the loyalty and financial support of the nonintellectual alums. Zero-sum or dualistic thinking dominates the decision making process.

In the micro-environment of the classroom, the atmosphere is also typically competitive and divisive. If faculty members grade "on the curve," only a certain percentage of students can excel. Students compete for grades and some infer that it is appropriate to cut articles out of journals in order to gain the advantage over their peers. If the class is a seminar, students may believe that talking more is better than talking less and that listening is the least valuable form of participation. Skilled faculty members understand the techniques of helping students learn to listen to each other and to draw connections among various points of view. It takes even more training and experience to help students draw the connections between the topics being discussed and the rest of their lives in a way that the conversation becomes meaningful for them.

One of the most effective areas in which these kinds of connections can be made is in course-based service learning, where the connections between learning and life are most obvious. In the typical environment where we search for the right answer, learning to discuss complex topics across differences of perspective and values is very difficult to achieve. In a service learning environment where connections can be seen and made by both students and faculty members, academic improvement exceeds that which occurs in a traditional classroom. Students demonstrate significantly higher achievement in the academic skills of writing and critical thinking, while also improving their sense of self-efficacy, leadership, and interpersonal skills.[15]

If spirituality is based on the ability to make or see connections, how can it thrive in an atmosphere suffused with competition and separation? Although we have examples of circumstances in which cooperation enhances academic achievement, collaborative practices such as those involved in service learning fly beneath the radar screen of academic rigor as it is traditionally understood. Individual intellectual work is still considered the *summum bonum* of student performance, and helping students make personally meaningful connections in the classroom is still not part of the dominant paradigm of teaching and learning.

The domain in which collaboration and experiential learning is most generally used is in student affairs, an administrative area that is considered to fall outside the academic domain in most universities. While positivism governs traditional academic approaches to teaching and learning, constructivism and "connected knowing" dominate in the educational activities of student affairs.[16] Connected knowing emphasizes empathy, understanding the perceptions and thoughts of another person without judging. Two fundamental constructs of positivism, on the other hand, are that "reality is single, tangible and fragmentable" and that "knower and known are independent."[17] This approach discounts the value of empathy, since viewpoint is irrelevant and the knower and the known are expected to remain separate. These two perspectives conflict, and positivism inevitably dominates. From a positivist perspective, the educational activities of student affairs are, by definition, not academic, and by implication, not teaching and learning.

Efforts to support the creation of a civil environment on campus are almost certainly doomed to failure unless the conflicts between these two sets of values are made visible and placed in a dynamic relationship that does not require that one dominate the other. If efforts at campus civility are left to the student affairs side of the institution, the inherent tensions with the academic side will minimize the potential for success. Positivist approaches to teaching and learning privilege separation of the knower from the known and objectivity as a "way of knowing." Learning to distance oneself from that which one is studying minimizes the chances that new information will influence behavior or that students will perceive connections between information learned in a class and the real-life concerns and experiences of other students. In contrast, constructivist approaches so often used in student development education acknowledge the effect of viewpoint and life experience on constructing and interpreting knowledge. Student development approaches to helping students understand civility and the inherent connections between human beings are often hampered by the absence of the major positivist virtue, i.e., generalizeable information about the topic under discussion, information that is derived from research in the academic disciplines rather than from the unique experience of each person's life. The zero-sum thinking that dominates positivism, the notion of only one right answer or approach, also dominates the conversation about effective ways to develop a sense of civility on campus. In this case, zero-sum or dualistic thinking will not get us where we need to go—to a place where we understand that civility is an inevitable consequence of the deep perception of human connection, a place where we may all agree on "the facts," and still be able to respect different interpretations about what they mean.

The positivist/constructivist rift throws up an enormous barrier to connecting civility and spirituality on campus since civility and spirituality are both based on connection and the perception of common humanity, while academic norms are based on competition and distance. The positivist notion of objectivity devalues efforts to make connections between academic knowledge and personal perspective. The problem of individual achievement without consideration of the consequences for the group is not typically part of the classroom conversation. Within constructivism, the search for meaning across categories of experience is valued, but constructivist approaches are typically devalued as "soft," i.e., not worth academic credit.

Adherents of these two epistemological perspectives are as intellectually uncivil to each other as members of any other conflicting groups on campus. Nevertheless, enhancing perceptions of connection that result in greater spiritual appreciation and civil behavior depends on finding ways to overcome the rift.

As long as the positivist approach dominates our ideas of teaching and learning, this rift will divide thinking from feeling, living from learning, and knowing information from integrating that information into a system of beliefs that allows for the creation of personal meaning. This rift precludes the perception of spiritual connections between participants in any dialogue about civility because it is based on assumptions of separation.

We have at least two very effective models for bridging our great divide, but until this moment, we haven't paid enough attention to them: course-based service learning and ongoing group conversations about difference that are facilitated by teacher/trainers who are both well-versed in content and skilled as group facilitators, such as the "Intergroup Relations, Conflict and Community" program conducted at the University of Michigan and the University of Massachusetts.[18] In both approaches, the rift is overcome by requiring discussion of academic content while still acknowledging the validity of different approaches to understanding and interpretation. Yankelovitch has described dialogue as a kind of mutually respectful conversation that has three elements:[19]

- equality and the absence of coercive influences;
- listening with empathy;
- bringing assumptions into the open.

It is quite possible to create dialogic conversations in which students are required to listen carefully and speak clearly, to evaluate differences of opinion and simultaneously understand the experiential sources of those differences. It is quite possible to respect differences without demanding submission to a particular point of view. Cultures that operate from a consensus model, such as the Quakers and many Native American groups, use this approach. In the domain of civility and spirituality, understanding and respect seem far more important than deciding which point of view is correct. In fact, the notion of finding the right answer may be irrelevant. It is possible to have academically rigorous conversations that allow or even encourage different perspectives and interpretations based on both analysis and experience, and still maintain an overarching perception of common concern. It is simply an art that has not been practiced much on our modern American campuses.

SPIRITUALITY AND CIVILITY IN STUDENT AFFAIRS

If spirituality is a function of the experience of connection and the creation of meaning through dialogue, what types of changes might enhance our professional practice and graduate education? What we must do is first look at all the places in practice and preparation where we experience dysfunctional division—competition among staff members within departments, competition among departments for resources, competition between student affairs and the rest of the university for limited resources, competition between serving the administrative convenience of the institution and the educational needs of students. The list of competitions that sap resources is endless. It seems to me that people compete because they believe that accomplishing their individual goals is more valuable than accomplishing team or organizational goals. On a basketball team or on a professional staff, this behavior is fatal. It saps morale and impedes progress toward organizational goals.

In our professional work, a good first step to enhancing connections would be to create mission statements that are meaningful to all members of a staff, based on a sense of trust and respect among colleagues. Mission statements are notoriously irrelevant, and they are often imposed rather than developed out of a sense of shared purpose. Internally we need to overcome the traditional split between mind and heart by spending a significant amount of time discussing our personal sense of purpose for belonging to our profession.

Our willingness to share our most deeply held sense of professional purpose can emerge through dialogue. I am suggesting that we practice the same approach to dialogue in our staff meetings that we use in conversations with students about civility. We need practice in treating professional and personal differences respectfully and in focusing on our common humanity, our spiritual core. Dialogue demands that participants are willing to trust each other in areas where they feel vulnerable and would typically protect themselves. It means discussing what we really care about when it comes to student affairs because we are not worried that somebody else will ignore or demean our ideas. Mission statements that emerge through this kind of process reflect the deeply held beliefs of the staff and express a sense of joint purpose that uplifts everybody and gives them the energy to go on when things get very tense or tiring.

As a director of housing, I had a number of very aggravating problems to deal with, including students who wouldn't talk to their roommates, students who harassed each other mercilessly, staff members who had serious competition problems with each other and a limited sense of boundary setting with students, broken plumbing, angry parents, drug dealers, and a higher administration that cared more about public image than anything else. If I had not believed that my work was going to contribute to our students' education in a significant way, I could not have done that job. My higher purpose at the time was my belief that my entire staff was helping our students learn how to live responsibly and respectfully in a diverse community of their peers. We shared that sense of mission, and we were able to talk to each other, without disrupting our ability to work together, about ways in which we were not upholding our larger purpose. Even when we were angry with each other, we were able to discuss our conflicts respectfully. It was not easy, but it was worth the effort.

POSITIVISM: CONSEQUENCES AND CHALLENGES

A second means by which we can enhance our efforts at infusing civility and spirituality into student affairs is by becoming conscious of the ways that the positivist paradigm dominates campus life and thought outside the classroom as well as inside. This belief system emphasizes objectivity and separation and contradicts the engaged and connected values of the student affairs profession such as service, freedom, quality, justice, and community.[20] Whenever someone refers to student affairs work as "touchy-feely" or soft, that remark is an attempt to displace the engaged values of the student affairs profession with positivist values. These kinds of comments tend to stop those of us in the student affairs profession in our tracks. These phrases are intended as put-downs, and they typically have the intended effect. In the positivist paradigm, "touchy-feely" work has no place on campus.

Positivism translates into an approach to evaluating the various problems of campus life on the basis of things that can be counted: dollars, numbers of visits to an agency, numbers of majors, numbers of students in residence halls, numbers of arrests, costs of damage and so forth. Anyone who counsels students knows that a record of the numbers of visits students make to the counseling center, the career center, or the academic advising center is only one way to describe the quality of the work those centers do. Without qualitative information, descriptions of the types of problems students bring, their level of satisfaction with their visits, their enhanced sense of hope about the problems in their lives, we don't have the whole picture. But because of our cultural reliance on numbers to justify our value, we rarely have the courage to provide other data in support of our worth.

The dominance of the positivist paradigm is one of the reasons why civility and spirituality are so obviously absent from the heart of campus life. Students learn to think in "objective," or fragmented, and decontextualized ways in order to do well academically. Learning is defined and experienced as learning facts, or isolated bits of information, with very little sense of the impact that the existence of the facts might have on a person's life. Opportunities for students to develop relationships among themselves or to begin to understand how the differences in their frames of reference are directly related to the circumstances of their lives are not valued in this paradigm. Students rarely have the opportunity to struggle with the tensions that arise when they all know the same "facts," but interpret these facts differently. Denied the opportunity to *experience* both their similarities and their differences, students will inevitably have trouble mustering the energy to treat each other with civility. It is simply much easier to remain in one's own, unchallenged interpretation of the right way to live.

The student development approach to education makes the search for meaning and connection central, not peripheral, to the learning process. The values of the educator, as well as the processes by which she arrived at those values, are part of the learning dialogue. One of the most significant things we do with students in educational settings is to help them learn to think their way through complex problems and arrive at conclusions that are congruent with their values. At the same time, we want them to learn to understand and respect people for whom the same facts can lead to a different perspective on meaning. Crookston called this process "affective rationality," the ability to take one's feelings into account as one thinks about significant issues.[21]

Affective rationality presents a contrast to the positivist paradigm because it acknowledges the individuality and the emotionality of learning. Positivist learning contributes little to civility because it does not acknowledge differences in perspective or emotional reactions to "facts." We learn to behave civilly toward people who upset us when we realize that each of us may interpret the facts of a particular situation differently, but that when we hurt, we all feel pretty much the same. In order to enhance civility on campus and to place civility in a spiritual context, we must put ourselves into places where we can teach students to think, to feel, to listen, to empathize, and to develop their own sense of meaning and connection—all at the same time. Sometimes we are in these situations because we are facilitating a discussion among students in conflict. Then what we need to do is recognize the teachable moment. Other times we plan these conversations, knowing that conflict is valuable because it shows students the existence of ambiguity, differences in perspective, and the effect of listening carefully and respectfully. In our courses for resident assistants and student leaders, we should plan activities and discussions that will provoke constructive conflict so that students learn to manage their emotions and clarify their ideas at the same time. People do not think and feel independently of each other, but our traditional academic system is structured as if that were the case.

LEADERSHIP, CONSTRUCTION OF MEANING, AND SPIRITUALITY

Vaill describes organizations as "valuing systems" within which individuals learn to create meaning and value in their work lives. He posits a "five way bottom line" for organizations, focusing on the "economic, technical, communal, adaptive, and transcendent" dimensions.[22] All five streams of valuing are intertwined and every act is an act of creating or defining value. *Economic* refers to managing the material resources of the organization. *Technical* refers to the ways in which the organization conducts its business. *Communal* refers to the ways in which colleagues value each other, the spirit of the workplace. The *adaptive* dimension refers to the ways in which the organization is a citizen of its larger environment on both the material and interpersonal levels. Finally, *transcendent* refers to the ways in which the organization engages in acts of valuing that help people create their own sense of meaning as participants or gives them a sense of meaning in which they participate. Leadership, from this perspective, becomes a process by which leaders help members of their organization create meaning and engage in activities that are meaningful within the value system of the organization. The notion of the meaning of work as exclusively economic has been subsumed to a much broader definition. The process of creating value becomes conscious. The leader's role is to "create an ongoing process of ethical dialogue" with those they lead.[23]

The responsibility of leaders, and all student affairs professionals are leaders in some context, is to help those they lead create meaning in their worlds. For Crookston, "The manager-leader is concerned with *meaning*, not just with pseudo-objective truth, for it is in meaning that one's being-in-the-world-with-responsibility is discovered."[24] The creation of meaning is in part the perception of connections among the various segments or elements of a problem, a set of constituencies or the phases of a person's life. One overarching way that the student affairs profession can contribute to the enhancement of civility and spiritual awareness on campus is to continually raise issues of meaning in conversations about every area of their responsibility. This process would extend from the vice president, who asks those questions in cabinet meetings, to the newest student activities advisor who works with clubs to help them create programs and activities for their members. "Why are we doing this? What are the consequences of doing this? How are we doing this? How will our various constituencies react to and feel about what we are doing?" are some of the questions that need to be raised in order to exercise leadership in the area of civility as well as the other domains of campus life.

CONCLUSION

Spirituality, the creation of meaning, and the enhancement of civility on campus are all intertwined threads of a common issue: how shall we construct our humanity in this time and place? Vaill posits the creation of meaning as a basic human need. Maslow, in his description of "being values," implied the same thing many years before.[25] We need to discuss spirituality not because God exists, but because we exist and we need to create meaning for ourselves. We may choose to incorporate conversations about spirituality into our understanding of our educational roles as student affairs professionals because spiritual awareness enhances our ability to do good work with students and colleagues across campus. Most of all we need to remain aware of the connections between these three constructs, issues which are not often considered at the same time: spirituality, meaning, connection.

Recently in a cross-cultural counseling class I asked students how they defined themselves. I received three kinds of answers, "I am a child of God;" "I am a member of my family with responsibilities to other members;" and "I am a person who will contribute to the lives of others because of my achievements and my work with them." Each of these answers implied a different source of meaning in the lives of the speakers but they all involved a sense that each life is defined and shaped by its connections to other people and to transcendent purpose. Civility and spirituality are profoundly connected because we as humans are connected to each other and connected in a common search for meaning. One powerful purpose of the student affairs profession is to focus campus attention on these connections and help everyone remember how the most basic statement of connection affects each of us all the time, "do unto others as you would have them do unto you."

ENDNOTES

1. Jane Fried, *Ethics for Today's Campus, New Directions in Student Services #77* (San Francisco: Jossey Bass, 1997), 20.
2. Ibid.
3. James Fowler, *Stages of Faith* (New York: Harper Collins, 1981), 11.
4. Genesis, 1:2–5.
5. Danah Zohar and Ian Marshall, *Connecting with Our Spiritual Intelligence* (New York: Bloomsbury Publishing, 2000), 4.
6. Peter Vaill, *Spirited Leading and Learning* (New York: Simon and Schuster, 1999).
7. Robert Bellah, Richard Madsen, William Sullivan, Ann Swidler, and Steven Tipton, *Habits of the Heart* (New York: Harper and Row, 1985).
8. Jane Fried and Associates, *Shifting Paradigms in Student Affairs: Culture, Context, Teaching and Learning* (Lanham, MD: University Press of America/ American College Personnel Association, 1995).
9. Clifford Geertz, *Local Knowledge* (New York: Basic Books, 1983).
10. Bellah et.al., *Habits of the Heart,* 143.
11. Parker Palmer, *The Courage to Teach* (San Francisco: Jossey Bass, 1998).
12. Vaill, *Spirited Leading.*
13. Zohar and Marshall, *Connecting.*
14. Fowler, *Stages of Faith,* 14.
15. Alexander Astin, *How Service Learning Affects Students/Executive Summary* (Los Angeles, CA: University of California at Los Angeles, Higher Education Research Institute, 2000).
16. Fried, *Shifting Paradigms.*
17. Yvonna Lincoln and Egon Guba, *Naturalistic Inquiry* (Newbury Park, CA: Sage, 1985).
18. Richard Guarasci and Grant Cornwell and Associates, *Democratic Education in an Age of Difference* (San Francisco: Jossey Bass, 1997).
19. Daniel Yankelovitch, *The Magic of Dialogue: Transforming Conflict into Cooperation* (New York: Simon and Schuster, 1999), 41,43,44.
20. Robert Young, *No Neutral Ground* (San Francisco: Jossey Bass, 1997).

21. Burns Crookston, "Education for Human Development" in *New Directions for College Counselors,* ed. Charles Warner (San Francisco: Jossey Bass, 1973), 47.

22. Vaill, *Spirited Leading*, 199.

23. Ibid., 130.

24. Crookston, "Education for Human," 16.

25. Abraham Maslow, *The Farther Reaches of Human Nature* (New York: The Viking Press, 1971).

18. Higher Education and Eco-Justice

When the concept of the human spirit is understood as the mode of consciousness in which the individual feels connected to the cosmos as a whole, it becomes clear that ecological awareness is spiritual in its deepest essence.

—Fritjof Capra

The acquisition of knowledge and skills has been one of the most consistent reasons given for the pursuit of higher education. While many pursue it to obtain a well-paying job upon graduation, others do it for the sheer pleasure of learning something new, and still others to foster community well-being. These motivations do not exclude each other, and it is quite feasible to find someone who is interested in all three of them. This chapter, which focuses on the third motivation, will follow a definition given by J. Glenn Gray regarding the purpose of education: "The educated man...is one who has grasped the simple fact that his self is fully implicated in those beings around him, human and non-human, and who has learned to care deeply about them."[1] C. A. Bowers has called this new vision "eco-justice," a term that aptly encompasses the regeneration of both the natural and social environment.[2]

To understand the task ahead of colleges and universities, it is useful to enumerate some of the most pressing environmental and social problems affecting societies today. With regard to environmental calamities, we find the irreversible loss of at least one species of flora or fauna a day; the destruction of tropical rainforests at a rate of 1.3 acres per second; widespread soil erosion that leads to the removal of 75 billion metric tons of topsoil each year; a hole in the ozone layer roughly the size of the U.S.; and an unchecked population growth that adds about 254,000 people to the world's population each day.

And with respect to social problems and human rights violations? About 1.3 billion people worldwide struggle to survive on $1 daily, and another three billion people barely earn $2 a day; around 15 million die every year of preventable infectious and parasitic diseases, including tuberculosis and malaria; and the net worth of the ten richest people on the planet, just ten human beings, is greater than the national income of the forty-eight poorest countries combined. The system has reached such levels of absurdity that in the U.S. alone people spend $8 billion a year on cosmetics—$2 billion more than the estimated annual amount needed to provide basic education for all relevant-age children around the world.

I do not pretend that higher education is capable of solving most of these problems. However, as one of the few intellectual spaces vested with the responsibility for discussing these issues freely, universities have the moral responsibility for using their ingenuity and resources toward addressing them. Reevaluating the conventional purpose of higher education and redirecting it toward understanding that social and environmental concerns are intimately linked, and that students and faculty have a responsibility for minimizing these problems, becomes an imperative concern.

Destroying the Forest Again and Again

The Epic of Gilgamesh, one of the oldest extant stories in the world, narrates the life of a Sumerian king who probably lived between 2700 and 2500 B.C.E. Gilgamesh, the handsome ruler of the city-state of Uruk in southern Mesopotamia, was omniscient: "of him who knew all, the lord of wisdom, who knew everything, who saw things secret, opened the places hidden."[3] Despite this immense knowledge, which included the rare ability at the time of being literate, Gilgamesh oppressed his own people and displayed one of the most human of frailties: arrogance. To ensure that he would be respected and feared beyond the confines of his known world, Gilgamesh summoned his friend Enkido to destroy the magical cedar forest and its guardian, Humbada. "I will lift my hand and fell the cedars," said Gilgamesh. "I will make for myself a name that lasts."[4] This he accomplished, at a great social and environmental cost.

More than forty-five centuries would pass before the ecological damage caused by the likes of Gilgamesh was replicated on a planetary scale with a speed, complexity, and viciousness unparalleled in human history.[5] By the sixteenth and seventeenth centuries, a new mindset developed in Europe that was the result of scientific and technological discoveries, new geographic encounters, accumulation of unimaginable amounts of wealth, growing industrialization and consequent migration to the cities, and a slow but inexorable separation of humans from nature. Some scholars have called this period the birth of modernism,[6] which would have transcendental consequences for how Europeans viewed themselves in the universe and, for the purposes of this chapter, for how universities structured their purpose, content, and process. I will limit my comments to what was happening in Europe at the time, not because the university was a European invention (the closest equivalent to a modern university dates back to at least the fifth century C.E. with the founding of Nalanda University in India which had a single campus, student dormitories, libraries, and even an astronomical observatory), but because it was the European university that would be imitated and envied around the world.

A first tenet of modernism is the belief that Western science continuously advances, and with it technologies that allow individuals to dominate nature to the benefit of present and future generations. One of the most eloquent defenders of the rise of modernism was Francis Bacon. Although not himself a scientist, Bacon supported the inductive method of science—universal conclusions are drawn from particular understandings. The inductive approach had been used since antiquity, but he was perhaps the first to put it to a test as rigorous as the one employed by Aristotle in the deductive method. Bacon believed that Aristotle's logic, which dispensed of experimentation, could not advance knowledge in the field that occupied scholars at the time, the realm of nature; only scientific experimentation could unlock the mysteries of the universe and lead to social and political progress. This perspective eventually pushed for universalistic conceptions of life and marginalized non-Western, nonscientific viewpoints.

The second tenet of modernism was the rise of a manicheistic view of the world, an either/or approach. The intellectual foundations of this view are to be found in the work of Rene Descartes. In his *Discourse on Method* (published in 1637), Descartes affirmed the independence and the preeminence of the mind. His famous dictum *cogito ergo sum* embodied the assumption of mind existing prior to, and autonomous from, matter. It was assumed that the mind, enjoying greater import than the body, contained all the operations of sensation, intuition, and feeling that allow humans to reach knowledge. With these dichotomous beliefs, Descartes was much more categorical and explicit than Bacon. His separation of and irreconcilability between mind and body led to a "bifurcation of nature," as Alfred North Whitehead wrote, and with it nefarious dualisms that included the severance of humans from nature, science from spirituality, and facts from values. These understandings stress the absolute, the unchanging, and the predictable.

A third tenet was the fragmentation of knowledge. A clear expression of this fragmentation was found in Bacon's utopia *New Atlantis* (published in 1626), in which knowledge was subdivided into several disciplines, including mathematics, biology, chemistry, hydrology, and mechanics. He wanted to use his method of inquiry to reach a mechanical and reliable formula for the orderly acquisition of knowledge, which would be all-comprehensive and encyclopedic in scope. His ultimate purpose was to use scientific knowledge to control the whole of nature to benefit humankind.[7] These ideas influenced Descartes' analytic method. He would take a segment of reality and break it apart until he reached its most basic components. This strategy became essential in modern science, and has made it possible to advance most scientific theories. Taken to an extreme, Cartesianism leads to a fragmented and reductionist view of reality. It compartamentalizes knowledge by focusing on the particular, while preventing the individual from perceiving the picture in its entirety.

A fourth tenet was the development of a mechanistic view of nature. Nature came to be seen as a soulless, perfect machine governed by exact mathematical laws. In Descartes' work we witness the mechanistic view extended to all living matter, including plants, animals, and humans. For instance, he gave a detailed explanation of the flow of blood through the heart, veins, and arteries, and he concluded that the same mechanical principles that determined this motion dictated the mechanical behavior of the whole body and even the whole of nature. A logical consequence of referring to nature and humans as machines was that both could be manipulated, controlled, and exploited at will. Isaac Newton, deeply influenced by the works of his predecessors, provided a synthesis between the Cartesian view (truth can be deduced from ideas) and the Baconian view (truth can be arrived at through observation and experimentation), a synthesis spelled out in his *Mathematical Principles of Natural Philosophy* (published in 1687). Newton's famous metaphor of God as a giant clockmaker and the universe as a clock machine influenced not just the natural sciences, but also the social sciences in the nineteenth century.

A fifth and final tenet of modernity is an atomistic understanding of life that stresses isolation, separateness, and individuality. Newton's universalistic and totalizing vision answered a question that had puzzled philosophers for ages: What is reality composed of? What is the "stuff" that makes up the universe? Twenty centuries before Newton's time, Democritus answered that same question by saying that everything in nature was comprised of material particles that were disconnected, invisible, and unalterable. He called these particles *atomos*. During the Middle Ages and the Renaissance this idea cropped up on several occasions, but it was only with Newton's mechanical science that philosophical atomism became physical atomism. Swayed by Descartes' ideas that reality could be understood only by breaking it up into the smallest fractions possible, Newton also argued that all matter was made of small, indestructible, solid particles. These particles differed in size and form, but they were all made from the same substance. As Zohar and Marshall have pointed out, atomism has led to an extreme form of individualism that has delivered fatal blows to communal responsibility. This atomism has also created "the modern cult of the expert [in which] he is alienated from the situation or community in which he practices his expertise."[8]

This brief description of the intellectual origins of modernism serves as a backdrop for understanding the mechanistic and reductionistic paradigm that has influenced the West for the past four centuries. This paradigm prevented alternative worldviews from having a rightful place, and everything that could not be quantified lost validity and importance. The imposition of one single standard regardless of particularistic differences owes much to the mechanistic paradigm. It also led to the fanatical pursuit of correct and objective answers, preventing paradoxes, contradictions, and ambiguities from entering the halls of academia. Myths, legends, and magic lost all credence, and only knowledge that could be tested and verified was granted legitimacy. Through new scientific discoveries, humans were granted awesome powers to reveal the secrets of the universe. Nature finally ceased to be a living entity that was full of mystery and enchantment, and instead became a lifeless machine that could be dissected, manipulated, and exploited. Individuals started to have an enormous faith in their ability to control their destinies. No longer were they subject to the whims of nature or the arbitrariness of religious interpretation. Humans were finally placed at the center of the universe.

THE UNIVERSITY AS A MODERNIST EXPRESSION

While the university as an institution predates the rise of modernism by at least six centuries, it was nevertheless greatly influenced by the new modernist ethos during the nineteenth and twentieth centuries. The extreme pursuit of objectivity and rationality in both the natural and social sciences, the vehement attacks against forms of knowledge that could not be quantified and tested with the rigor required by Western rationality, the compartmentalization of knowledge so that individuals understand only a small (and often inconsequential) part of a much larger whole, the expert scholar working in isolation from others, were all part and parcel of the new industrial university. As Stan Rowe writes,

> Years ago the university shaped itself to an industrial ideal—the knowledge factory. Now it is overloaded and top-heavy with expertness and information. Its goal [still unfulfilled] should be deliverance from the crushing weight of unevaluated facts, from bare bones cognition or ignorant knowledge: knowledge in fragments, knowing without direction, knowledge without commitment.[9]

One of the manifestations of modernism in the universities has been the implementation of a single point of view for widely different circumstances. Universalistic truths became the norm, and instead of coming up with unique answers for unique problems, one-answer-fits-all became the rule. Modern methods of agriculture are a clear example of this. Characterized by the widespread usage of synthetic pesticides and fertilizers, heavy machinery, and dependency on a few crops, modern agriculture did away with small-scale, labor intensive, and poli-cultural practices that were more suitable to each ecosystem. These innovations, many of which were created and perfected at universities (and private corporations), were exported worldwide during the Green Revolution of the 1950s and 1960s. While modern agriculture did increase crop yields exponentially, it led peasant farmers to become dependent on only one or two crops while millions of other peasants became unemployed due to the usage of heavy machinery. Other negative consequences included soil impoverishment, erosion, and a reduction of genetic diversity in plants, making them more vulnerable to new diseases and pests. Even more, a proclivity for universal answers has led to a loss of ancestral agricultural knowledge, knowledge that had been transmitted from generation to generation for centuries but that modern agriculture has placed in an extremely vulnerable situation.

Within the modern university accuracy and objectivity have become the *sine qua non* for all research, often at the expense of social and environmental justice. A case in point was the nineteenth-century field of craniometry, a "science" that measured the size and shape of the skull according to race, gender, intelligence, criminal temperament, etc. Based on these studies, the most brilliant British and French intellectuals of the time concluded that women and nonwhites were less intelligent than white men. There are two important lessons here: first, precision and accuracy in scientific measurement is no guarantee of improving the social good; second, science is deeply influenced by the cultural mores of the time. In this case, racism and sexism became legitimated through the tools of science. These mores colored their views so much that scientists dismissed evidence that was contrary to their conclusions. When French researchers found that some skulls of French men were smaller than that of Germans, they did not conclude that Germans were more intelligent. They simply discounted the finding as an anomaly.[10]

A related problem has been an obsession with using the scientific method at the exclusion of alternative forms of knowing and feeling. Folk knowledge, oral traditions, personal stories, and feelings seldom receive the same sense of deference and importance. Only knowledge that can be objectively measured and quantified is granted legitimacy. Here, I am not arguing for the dismissal of the scientific method. Rather, I am defending a pluralistic conception for determining theories and ultimately truth. As affirmative postmodernists would claim, academics must reject the search for the Grand Theory, and instead defend the "petite histoires" (small stories): community-based narratives that focus on the ordinary lives of ordinary people, local memories that are richly descriptive, and fragments of wisdom that are an integral part of every community.

Take planning and organization theory, for instance. Modern versions presuppose rationality, a centralized system for making decisions, top-down input, efficiency, and objectivity. While not abandoning rationality, postmodern planning would start with a participatory, bottom-up approach. It would include as many divergent views as possible and attempt to find commonalities among them. It would integrate various disciplines (administration, sociology, psychology, and environmental studies), and emphasize interactive adaptation. It would reject universal, singular, global planning, and adapt each planning strategy to the unique context in which it will be executed. Learning to share responsibility and deciding important questions communally would constitute a hallmark of the postmodern administrator.[11]

As mentioned previously, the general trend is to divide the disciplines into smaller subdomains to the point where each specialty becomes a triflingly small field, unconnected from the rest. Knowledge is broken down into small, fragmented pieces, and each piece becomes a discipline unto itself. In the modern university a single disciplinary lens is used to study complex issues, which ultimately leads to a simplification and distortion of the whole. While more and more professors and administrators are cognizant of the problems associated with the fragmentation of knowledge, few are the schools involved in establishing a truly interdisciplinary academic environment.

One of the fields where an interdisciplinary approach is needed is economics. Social systems and ecosystems are in constant exchange, albeit in the contemporary world these interconnections are too often neglected and even violated. The modern economic system, arguably the preeminent social system that conditions the interconnections between social systems and natural systems, acts as a parasite on ecosystems by extracting natural resources in a ceaseless, linear fashion, and by dumping back into them all the resulting waste. This can only be tolerated by an ecosystem for so long until it eventually breaks down along with the social systems it supports, in part because the goods and services that are consumed by human groups to guarantee their survival all originate directly or indirectly in the natural environment. A diseased or terminally ill ecosystem endangers the constant supply of these goods and services and with it the viability of the economic system and that of the human groups it supports.

An additional problem has been the extreme isolation that researchers feel in academia. The most pressing economic, social, political, and environmental problems cannot be solved by single individuals but by people working in close association. The problems are so complex and of such magnitude—unemployment, inter-ethnic and religious rivalry, nations battling over natural resources, the depletion of the ozone layer, just to mention a few—that a continuous rehearsal of the all-knowing sage scholar invariably leads to a dead end.

Unfortunately, this reality has not changed much. Academic journals (and the language they use) are ever more specialized and hermetic. As a result, researchers in biology, economy, and sociology, and so on, only read their respective journals, and they very seldom interact with their colleagues in other disciplines. Whatever collaboration there does exist is generally limited to scholars in the same field. The Ph.D. thesis, the most complex writing piece that doctoral students need to deliver, cannot be written collaboratively. Faculty members are not given incentives to work with colleagues in other fields. All in all, academia is set up in such a way as to encourage isolation and individual work.[12] As with the other characteristics of modernism, isolation in and of itself is not necessarily negative. It becomes negative when it precludes the possibility of working in collaboration with others.

To introduce the following section, the story of Sir Albert Howard, author of *An Agricultural Testament* (1940), will serve quite well.[13] Howard was an agronomist sent by the British to India to teach Indians about the benefits of Western agriculture. Before leaving Britain, Howard suffered from the hubris typical of the expert Westerner who would teach natives about his universalistic knowledge. When he arrived in India he observed how the native people used their cows and their straw and how they restored the soil constantly through composting. Over time he recognized that they knew more about agriculture than he did. Howard changed his cosmovision and began to understand that the natural cycles were being worked in a way that was attuned to local culture and nature. Today, history remembers Howard as one of the most influential thinkers in the organic agriculture movement in the industrialized world.

A New Eco-Justice Vision for Universities

In the last decade several books have been published that explicate the arguments and strategies needed to transform the university toward an eco-justice vision.[14] Perhaps the main foundation is to reestablish the connection between the individual with the social and natural systems with which that person interacts. I will develop five main areas in which universities can change some of their ways to accomplish this goal: (1) using the environment as a unifying theme; (2) developing an ethic of care and acceptance; (3) contextualizing lessons through service learning and other community-oriented activities; (4) supporting a pro-social and pro-green research agenda; and (5) using the campus as a pedagogical tool.

First, universities could use the relationship between social systems and ecosystems as the main unifying theme for all disciplines. Fields as dissimilar as economics, religion, anthropology, and literature all stand to benefit from using the environment as the main topic around which the syllabus can be structured. Here I am proposing not just to provide an interdisciplinary lens, which is essential to curtail the fragmentation of the modern curriculum, but to do so by using the relationship between communities and environment at its core.

This theme was highlighted in the historic meeting "Joint Appeal by Religion and Science for the Environment" that convened in Washington, D.C., in 1992. More than 150 spiritual leaders and scientists issued a declaration to undertake bold action to cherish and protect the environment and affirmed a deep sense of common purpose. Using the relationship between people and the environment as a key organizing principle may seem out of tune to postmodernists who believe that it would represent a direct affront on intellectual pluralism. Far from it.

Just as there is a large number of ecosystems worldwide hosting an immensely large number of species of flora and fauna, each requiring unique answers, so do disciplines need to thrive with a multiplicity of viewpoints to address complex social and environmental phenomena. While the modernist ethos stressed a single, either/or, true/false point of view, an ecological vision allows for nuance, paradox, and difference. Learning to live with multiple and at times contradictory perspectives is one of the greatest challenges faced by societies today. Moreover, the idea of using the environment as a unifying category reminds us that all human groups on this planet, from Australian Aborigines to Wall Street executives, are completely dependent on the land for survival. If there is one point in common among all cultures, it is that if a group does not develop a land ethic that protects the integrity of the ecosystem, it will not survive in the long run. As David Ehrenfeld commented,

> The environment is one subject about which there is a clear and overriding need for all students to be informed. There is no right that grants students and teachers the freedom to be ignorant of the central concern that affects human civilization in this, its greatest struggle for life.[15]

Second, universities must develop an ethic of care and acceptance. As mentioned previously, the modern university became a preeminent site for the transmission of knowledge in a mechanistic fashion that disregarded feeling and empathy. The new ecological and social vision cannot be forged with the mere acquisition of knowledge, regardless of how accurate that knowledge may be. Knowledge is a necessary but insufficient ingredient to bring about eco-justice. How often have we encountered individuals who, while being extremely well informed, are selfish, cruel, or indifferent? One must first get to know the object of study intimately, and this cannot be done solely through intellectual stimulation. It needs a sense of physical and emotional attachment as well. One cannot love what one does not know through firsthand experience. In the craniometry example, I am convinced that had the researchers met their subjects as human beings, and not as guinea pigs for scientific research, they would have arrived at vastly different conclusions. As often as possible, opportunities need to be provided for students to have direct contact with the natural environment. If we expect students to care for the forests, rivers, lakes, and mountains, they need to become affectionately connected with them. They must spend ample time sleeping, laughing, dancing, studying, walking, and in contemplative silence surrounded by nature. Only then will they feel something akin to caring.

Since most formal education takes place inside a classroom, students are unable to develop an ethic of care. When I ask my students what are some of the most enjoyable and important experiences in their lives, invariably they all mention something related to being in nature. Not a single student has ever mentioned being in the classroom as an enjoyable or important experience, despite the fact that all students will have spent well over 15,000 hours inside one by the time they reach college. Thus, universities need to devise more strategies to reconnect students with the natural world.

Having said this, it is certainly possible to find a human group that displays a sense of wisdom as caretakers of the earth while simultaneously ignoring social problems and exploitation. Problems of poverty, homelessness, and discrimination cannot be adequately addressed if students have never met individuals who are victims of these circumstances. If they have never spoken to, sat down with, or shared a meal with a homeless person, the likelihood that they care about the problem is minimal. Developing an ethic of care for others comes only after a prolonged and intimate contact. That contact must also be coupled with a new spiritual vision that transcends tolerance and openly embraces acceptance and respect. As Zygmunt Bauman has written, tolerance as mere tolerance is not enough for solving the social problems that affect us all.[16] Tolerance is not acceptance, it is closer to resignation: "I tolerate him because I have no choice." It ultimately thrives on the mechanistic and atomistic view of modernism by erecting concrete walls between individuals. What is needed is a new conception of relationships, one that accepts the "either" and the "or" of the proposition, that respects the "I" and the "you" simultaneously. It is easy to accept people who are similar to us, who think, speak, dress, eat, and socialize like us. The real challenge is to learn to accept those who are different from us, who have a different ethnicity, speak a different language, profess a different religion, and belong to a different social class. We need to create a philosophy that celebrates diversity and ensures that the dignity of all peoples (which includes their material, emotional, and spiritual well-being) is secured.

Third, universities should push for service learning and participation in community projects. Efforts by universities to provide a service component through which students obtain credit for doing community work should be applauded. However, they are generally add-on programs that not all students take advantage of. Moreover, given that universities have generally privileged mental activities over manual ones, whenever possible service learning ought to combine both. The famous Deweyan maxim of "learning by doing" is applicable not just to K-12 learning but also to higher education. As Smith and Williams have written, students

> who learn how to renovate deteriorated homes, replant damaged riparian zones with appropriate species, grow food, create parks, or set up businesses that meet previously unfulfilled community needs discover their own capacity to contribute to beneficial projects.[17]

There are many activities that university students can engage in that have highly positive social and environmental consequences. Researching renewable alternatives to fossil fuels, participating in sustainable projects of agriculture and forestry, learning about the micro-credit industry that provides low-interest loans to poor families, tutoring poor children to encourage them to love nature, and renovating homes for the elderly are all activities that teach university students important skills.

Through these activities students also learn that collaborating with peers and other adults is an indispensable prerequisite for doing the job well. The individualism characteristic of many courses should give way to an understanding that the most urgent problems faced by our planet cannot be solved by single individuals, but by groups of people joining forces and sharing skills.

An important aspect of building competencies involves preparing students for political life. Students should be allowed to develop the necessary skills to negotiate within local and national institutions to protect human rights and the environment. Student political activism is a well-known legacy from the 1960s that constituted one of the most important lessons learned by many students during their academic career. Universities ought to recognize those experiences and grant them the legitimacy they deserve. Active participation in organizations inside and outside of campus (e.g., a local environmental group, shelter for battered women, student government body) is a valuable experience that allows students to contextualize classroom lessons in a manner that serves a larger good.

Fourth, universities should encourage a pro-social and pro-green research agenda. Given that research is occupying a larger and larger universe of the faculty's time, establishing some tentative guidelines would appear to be a small and welcome start. In their busy lives and in their eagerness to obtain new grants and fellowships to advance their professional careers, too often questions of social and environmental utility become displaced. In a virulent attack on university research with little or no social value, Page Smith wrote:

> the vast majority of the so-called research turned out in the modern university is essentially worthless. It does not result in any measurable benefit to anything or anyone. It does not *in the main* result in greater health or happiness among the general populace or any particular segment of it (emphasis in original).[18]

Usefulness can be measured in many different ways, and I do not propose here that universities should engage in the act of measuring the worthiness of any given project. That may lead to socioecological McCarthyism. Rather, I believe it is the responsibility of each individual researcher (or group of researchers) to see to it that their research does some good to the world in the short or long run. Too often, however, researchers turn a blind eye to the ethical considerations of their research in order to guarantee continued grant assistance. Some of the more glaring examples are the growing alliances of universities with the Department of Defense and mega-corporations that too often do not have the public interest at heart. In a piercing indictment on the lack of moral responsibility in higher education, Franklin Littell asked, "What kind of medical school trained Mengele? What departments of anthropology prepared the staff of Strasbourg University's 'Institute of Ancestral Heredity'?"[19]

While Littell asked those questions in the context of the Holocaust, an unmistakable modern creation, universities today are not immune from collaborating in highly ethically questionable research. Researchers should ask themselves if their work improves our deteriorated social and natural habitats, if it makes our cities more beautiful and habitable, if it brings nations in dispute to the table of negotiations, if it dreams up an economic system that places more value on human well-being than on profit, if it helps individuals to become more humble, more generous, more compassionate, more courageous. If it does, then it is research worth pursuing. Research, just as the pursuit of knowledge, is justified only if it seeks a larger and nobler purpose than the mere advancing of an academician's career.

Fifth, and the last element I will mention to bring about a new eco-justice vision to higher education, is using the university campus as a pedagogical tool. The most obvious starting point for universities is the one least considered. The campus is one of the most ignored pedagogical resources, and yet it represents the most accessible and rich opportunity to apply classroom lessons to real life.

Take, for instance, a campus assessment of its environmental impact. The professor and students engage in an analysis of resource flows to determine what energy and matter enters and leaves the institution. A comprehensive environmental audit would uncover the amount of water, electricity, natural gas, paper, and other materials used per capita. With that information in hand, staff, teachers, and students can come up with realistic strategies to minimize consumption and cost. An audit would also show university policies regarding procurement, recycling, landscaping, energy use, transportation, building construction, and institutional investment. Green procurement, for instance, is one of the least developed areas in institutions of higher education, yet one that shows great promise in terms of economic savings and environmental protection. To consider the market's potential, in 1993 U.S. institutions of higher education spent over $186 billion dollars. As Keniry has written,

> Through careful purchasing, university procurement staff can support a range of environmental practices, including source reduction (buying less of what eventually will become waste), waste stream diversion (assuring that what was once discarded is now used longer, recycled, or reused), recycling (an approach that now reaches far beyond paper, bottles, and cans), and closing the loop by buying goods made from recycled materials.[20]

These strategies should be coupled with policies that support local producers and farmers to protect local economies, buy organic foods to promote healthy diets, purchase energy-efficient appliances, avoid buying tropical hardwoods that are raised unsustainably, and encourage suppliers to eliminate unnecessary packaging. Through these strategies, U.S. colleges and universities would be able to earn substantial long-term savings while influencing the university population to be more aware of the consequences of their own purchasing power.

The fiscal clout of universities is also manifest in their corporate investments that, if used wisely, can promote socially and environmentally sound practices. Since the 1970s, Hampshire College in Massachusetts has developed a portfolio that supports socially responsible companies. It was the first college in the U.S. to divest from South Africa, and in 1991 it divested itself from companies that contracted with the U.S. Department of Defense. In recent years, the college has also invested in companies involved in renewable and safe energy development, sustainable agriculture and forestry, manufacturing of products made from recycled materials, and waste reduction techniques.[21]

As part of the practice of using the campus as a pedagogical tool, some institutions of higher education have mustered the vision and financial resources to retrofit an old building along ecological principles, or even to build from the ground up an entirely new structure employing the most recent advances in eco-architecture. An example of this latter case is the Center for Environmental Studies at Oberlin College in Ohio.[22] The building, considered one of the best examples in the U.S. of low environmental impact, included input from about 250 students, faculty, and local community members. The building followed the strictest guidelines for environmental protection, some of which were to generate more electricity than it uses; discharge wastewater at least as pure as the water it takes in; use materials that conserve energy; meet requirements for full-cost accounting; and use products and materials grown or manufactured sustainably. To meet these guidelines, the architectural innovations included special photovoltaic panels covering the roof to power the building; a graywater treatment system full of bacteria, algae, snails, fish, and plants to purify water for irrigation purposes; highly efficient window panes to stop heat loss; data panels at the entrance displaying the building's energy and water use; and timber used in the construction of the building grown from local sustainable forests.

Numerous lessons are derived from this building. Students discover that what they learn is as important as where they learn it. They learn to be more mindful of resource consumption, to take the local environment less for granted. And they also learn about the origin and cost of construction materials, and about the interconnections between the places they inhabit and the homes and buildings where they spend most of their time.

WHAT IS IMPORTANT, AFTER ALL?

Throughout history, human societies have experienced the reenactment of the Epic of Gilgamesh again and again. As king, Gilgamesh first dominated his subjects, then he dominated nature. Gilgamesh's erudition did not prevent him from destroying the magical forest or being indifferent to the ensuing ecological calamities. There was a spiritual void that his quest for immortality could not fill. The modern university, with its stress on acquiring knowledge and cultivating the mind at the expense of other important forms of knowing, feeling, and acting, has also suffered from this spiritual void. While it is true that through a fragmented and detached approach to discovery, science and technology have advanced society in some respects, this same approach has been instrumental in undermining it in many other respects. The cultivation of the mind under the aegis of divorcing science from values has led in many instances to an utter negligence in building an ethical, just, and spiritual society. Rebuilding the purpose of the university would require doing away with the high degree of specialization that prevents an awareness of how the different elements hold together in real life, developing an ethic of care in each student and teacher, reducing what Page Smith calls "the meretriciousness of most academic research," and integrating classroom lessons toward improving campus and community life.

Knowledge, care, and competence in the direction of protecting and enhancing our communities and natural habitats must become a major concern for higher education. Blaise Pascal motivated us to think as people of action and act as people of thought. Thought, feeling, and action cannot be separated one from the other. They are all vertices of the same triangle. These elements must be combined in a certain direction, one that was eloquently chosen by Robert Bellah and his colleagues when they said, "However pluralistic its forms, education can never merely be for the sake of individual self-enhancement. [Education] pulls us into the common world or it fails altogether."[23]

ENDNOTES

1. J. Glenn Gray, *The Promise of Wisdom: An Introduction to Philosophy of Education* (Philadelphia: J. B. Lippincott Company, 1968), 67.
2. C. A. Bowers, *The Practice of an Eco-Justice Pedagogy,* in press.
3. John Gardner and John Maier, *Gilgamesh: Translated from the Sîn-leqi-unninnî version* (New York: Alfred A. Knopf, 1984), 57.
4. Gardner and Maier, *Gilgamesh,* 109.
5. Prior to the rise of modernism there were clear examples of ecological catastrophes caused by the human hand, including the damage brought about during the Sumerian civilization about 300 years prior to Gilgamesh's reign when the topsoil of southern Mesopotamia was oversalinized due to excessive irri-

gation. However, these catastrophes were restricted to specific geographic areas, damage occurred over a long period of time, and there were only one or two factors that accounted for the devastation. In contrast, the environmental destruction witnessed today involves a scale, speed, and complexity that has left no corner of the world unharmed, the same problem affects vastly different regions, and few possibilities for responding adequately to the problems are available. For an extensive treatment of this topic, read Clive Ponting's *A Green History of the World: The Environment and the Collapse of Great Civilizations* (New York: St. Martin's Press, 1992).

6. See, for instance, Fritjof Capra, *The Turning Point: Science, Society and the Rising of Culture* (Toronto: Bantam Books, 1988); Richard Norgaard, *Development Betrayed: The End of Progress and a Coevolutionary Revisioning of the Future* (London and New York: Routledge, 1994); John Herman Jr. Randall, *The Making of the Modern Mind: A Survey of the Intellectual Background of the Present Age* (New York: Columbia University Press, 1976); Danah Zohar and Ian Marshall, *The Quantum Society: Mind, Physics and a New Social Vision* (New York: William Morrow and Company, Inc., 1994).

7. James Bowen, *A History of Western Education, Vol. III.* (New York: St. Martin's Press, 1981), 43.

8. Zohar and Marshall, *The Quantum Society,* 27.

9. Stan J. Rowe, *Home Place: Essays on Ecology* (Edmonton, Canada: NeWest Books, 1990), 129.

10. Ernest R. House, "Methodology and Justice." In *Evaluation and Social Justice: Issues in Public Education,* ed. Kenneth A. Sirotnik (San Francisco: Jossey-Bass Inc., 1990).

11. Pauline Marie Rosenau, *Post-Modernism and the Social Sciences: Insights, Inroads and Intrusions* (Princeton, New Jersey: Princeton University Press, 1992), 82–89.

12. There are a few exceptions to the cult of the expert. In capital-intensive fields (physics, archeology, biology, and others), where research is extremely expensive and minute measurements are required, teams of scholars work and publish together. This strategy ought to be adopted in other fields and enhanced with the introduction of scholars from various disciplines.

13. Sir Albert Howard, *An Agricultural Testament* (London: Oxford University Press, 1940).

14. See, for instance, Jonathan Collett and Stephen Karakashian, eds., *Greening the College Curriculum: A Guide to Environmental Teaching in the Liberal Arts* (Washington, D.C.: Island Press, 1996); Julian Keniry, *Ecodemia: Campus Environmental Stewardship at the Turn of the 21st Century* (Washington, D.C.: National Wildlife Federation, 1995); Walter Leal Filho, ed., *Sustainability and University Life* (Frankfurt: Peter Lang, 1999); David W. Orr, *Ecological Literacy: Education and the Transition to a Postmodern World* (Albany: State

University of New York Press, 1992); April Smith and the Student Environmental Action Coalition, *Campus Ecology: A Guide to Assessing Environmental Quality and Creating Strategies for Change* (Los Angeles: Living Planet Press, 1993).

15. David Ehrenfeld, "Foreword" in Jonathan Collett and Stephen Karakashian eds., *Greening the College Curriculum: A Guide to Environmental Teaching in the Liberal Arts* (Washington, D.C.: Island Press, 1996), x.

16. Zygmunt Bauman, *Modernity and the Holocaust* (Ithaca, New York: Cornell University Press, 1989).

17. Gregory A. Smith and Dilafruz R. Williams, eds., *Ecological Education in Action: On Weaving Education, Culture, and the Environment* (Albany: State University of New York Press, 1999), 10.

18. Page Smith, *Killing the Spirit: Higher Education in America* (New York: Penguin Books, 1991), 7.

19. Bauman, *Modernity and the Holocaust*, 29.

20. Keniry, *Ecodemia*, 5.

21. April Smith and the Student Environmental Action Coalition, *Campus Ecology*, 89.

22. Donella Meadows, "A Building Can Be a Teacher," *The Global Citizen*, October 20, 1997.

23. Robert Bellah, et al., *The Good Society* (New York: Alfred A. Knopf, 1991), 176.

19. Transforming Campus Life: Conclusions and Other Questions

Vachel W. Miller

I would like to organize my summary comments around a set of questions inspired by the essays collected in this book. Zohar and Marshall believe that spiritual intelligence—that dimension of our intelligence concerned with meaning, purpose, and value—manifests in the persistent questions we ask.[1] In this concluding chapter, I would like to revisit several of the questions raised by the contributors, introduce additional perspectives, and ask other questions.

Asking questions about religious pluralism and spirituality can enable us to imagine new possibilities for revitalizing campus life on multiple levels. The purpose of this book is to advocate broad thinking about religious pluralism and spirituality on campus in ways that help us connect concern for students' holistic development with creative programming for the campus community; connect the desire for personal meaning to organizational change; and connect epistemological critique to a critique of larger economic, political, and cultural forces at play in the world.

Spirituality involves exploration of the multiple manifestations of that which has enduring meaning; exploration of the sacred dimension of our being, our work, our relationships. From this perspective, spiritual issues are everywhere: the amount of waste produced on campus is a spiritual issue; the extent of alcohol abuse is a spiritual issue; conflict between colleagues is a spiritual issue; leadership is a spiritual issue; learning is a spiritual issue. Spirituality is not something special—not bounded to a place of worship or practices of certain traditions—but involves the whole of what we do in higher education.

Our effort here is to assert that there is a spiritual dimension to the entirety of campus life, diverse ways of articulating that spiritual dimension, and diverse ways of responding to it. This is not to say that these issues are exclusively spiritual—obviously not—or to claim them as the exclusive domain of spiritual interventions in order to give greater power to religious organizations. None of the authors seek a revival of religion for

for the sake of that religion, i.e., as a covert effort to reclaim lost power, assert absolute truths, or redeem the unenlightened. Living in postmodern times, when all beliefs have been exposed as the particular constructions of particular people, it would be naive to believe anyone could hold a copyright on truth.

Nevertheless, we each have particular lives, particular histories, and particular beliefs. Even in a postmodern world, belief and spiritual sensitivity remain a vital part of our lives. The contributors to this book express, from different religious traditions and institutional positions, dissatisfaction with the exclusion of religious identity and spirituality from campus. Such exclusion has made religion a dimension of social identity that remains hidden from view and unwelcome in public. Consequently, religious ideas, questions, and commitments cannot enter into dialogue with other ideas, questions, and commitments arising in our own lives and the lives of our communities. Such exclusion has reduced spiritual sensibilities to seem, in an academic environment, an odd, even embarrassing, nonintellectual concern for mystery, for beauty, for justice, for meaning, for the fullness of being and inter-being. With this book we hope to reclaim the legitimacy of that concern.

The exclusion of religious and spiritual perspectives from our conversations about living and working and learning together does not serve us well. It thwarts the integration necessary for building a wiser world.[2] It bifurcates lives, separating our holy days from our working days, our scholarly lives from our spiritual lives. It keeps us spinning in cultural patterns that we often sense to be out of attunement with deeper harmonies of life.

With this book, we seek to enrich and support conversations about integration and wisdom that have engaged ever wider audiences at conferences, workshops, and discussion groups across the country. This book contributes to the movement of spirituality and religious pluralism from the margins of campus life to the heart of renewal in higher education.

How Do We Talk about Spirituality and Religion on Campus?

New conversations nurture transformation. The contributors to this book offer insight into how such conversations might begin. Raper reminds us of the big questions—Who am I? What is my work in the world?—and their value for integrative conversation. Fried suggests that dialogue about mission can serve as an entry into deeper understanding of purpose, values, and aspiration. From her work at Michigan, Walters notes how fully students engaged in interfaith conversations when asked to discuss their experience together. She also points to the importance of personal reflection as a starting point: "It is in the particularity of our own experience that we most deeply connect with others." Based on her research, Stockton suggests that faculty and administrators would be interested in discussing spiritual and religious concerns, provided there is a comfortable container and safeguards against the manipulation of dialogue for purposes of marketing faith—especially a faith that already has cultural dominance.

There are a thousand ways, great and small, to begin new conversations about religious pluralism and spirituality. Many of the contributors to this book are leading the way. As an initiative organized by students, the Self Knowledge Symposium offers a model that links spiritual questions with practical activities on campus. It encourages students to reflect on their growth in terms of everyday work, thereby overcoming the compartmentalization of "spiritual growth" as separate from courage, compassion, and openness in other dimensions of life. At Brandeis University, the Religious Pluralism and Spirituality (RPS) group has organized a number of structures for spiritual engagement, from casual conversations to community ritual. The Festival of Lights, for example, provides a rich model of joyful and reflective observance welcoming to multiple religious traditions. Events at Wellesley College, such as Flower Sunday, also offer new forms of gathering for shared celebration. Such events can create moments of collective meaning on campus, the stuff of new conversations about how we want to live and learn and work together. Manhattanville College has developed an integrative model that places religion in the context of political, cultural, and economic issues. It brings faculty members, staff members, students, and community members together for conversations across lines of division. Importantly, public conversations are not treated as end points, but as touchstones for ongoing informal conversations that nurture the slow opening of mind and heart to the worlds of others.

All of these approaches illuminate the possibilities for invigorating campus life. Whether supported by campus leadership, as at Manhattanville and Wellesley, or as a student-driven initiative such as the Self Knowledge Symposium, they all attempt to open space for creative and critical reflection on deep personal questions and their relationship to issues of community and social well-being. In all of these cases, the effort is not driven by sectarian interests, but rather by an interest in creating a richly textured learning community large enough to hold all of our questions.

One of the most profound needs of our time is learning how to build community across difference. As bell hooks points out, a culture of domination doesn't teach us how to live in community. It is an art that must be practiced, against the grain of our socialization. It is especially challenging to develop what hooks calls "intimacy with otherness."[3] Several of the contributors to this book ask, how do we bring ourselves into community with those who are not typically present in our familiar gatherings? A question at the heart of pluralism.

The challenge of religious pluralism has resulted in imaginative responses from institutions of diverse backgrounds. As discussed by Kazanjian and Laurence, several colleges have found new ways to configure resources and worship spaces to welcome the various observances of religiously diverse students. New worship spaces send important messages about equal membership in the academic community and encourage exchange across traditions. The development of such spaces, of course, will hinge on the quality and depth of conversations about the meaning of "education as transformation" throughout campus.

Of course, transformation of any kind is not easy. Efforts to animate spirituality and religious pluralism on campus raise prickly questions about the orthodoxy of tradition—both secular and religious. There are many reasons for ignoring or avoiding this conversation. Some institutions have no interest in such issues, preoccupied with solidifying rankings and raising money; some institutions avoid religious issues through narrow interpretations of the Constitution; other institutions and their constituencies may be wedded to the symbols and identity of a founding religious tradition and feel anxious about losing that identity if it is challenged to change. The movement toward openness and pluralism can raise hard questions of identity, membership, and power. Embracing difference can create new divisions: Burrows' reflection on the Ecumenical Christian Church at Smith College offers a telling illustration of how the inclusion of members of socially marginalized groups in worship can create tensions and may lead those who felt safe within traditional structures to worship elsewhere.

The reflections on leadership gathered here provide insight into new possibilities for conversations about spirituality and religious meaning in organizational life. Stafford's use of the "web of sociality" offers a vivid metaphor for the value of connection and mutuality for effective action. Creating such a web, as Stafford and others point out, calls for leaders to be reflective, open, and honest—habits of being which most institutions rarely nurture. Institutions of higher education tend to place punishing demands on the time and energy of their leaders. On campuses of all kinds, leaders often feel drained, emptied. From a spiritual perspective, we might ask, what is the difference between the emptiness that results from overwhelming work and the self-emptying described by Stafford?

Several contributors encourage leaders to be sensitive to the spiritual journeys of their colleagues. Being quiet, sitting in silence, walking with an anxious friend, taking time to write a card to a grieving employee—such moments of spiritual sensitivity are also moments of profound effectiveness, in terms of building a caring and connective human community.

To affirm those who practice such sensitivity, we need to affirm an expanded conversation about what work is, what learning is, and what organizations could be. How might insight and compassion, rather than mere busyness, become valid criteria for excellence? Can we move beyond the limited notion that sharpening skills/knowledge is the singular bottom line of professional development? Calming the breath and enlarging the heart are profound dimensions of professional development that we must begin to affirm. As Allen and Kellom suggest, we need to be more deliberate about what habits are rewarded, as well as be more aware of the inhibitors to spiritual development in our work lives. Further, as Jablonski asks, what are the structures created by gendered assumptions about organizational life and scholarly work? In the sense that we are all leaders, these essays challenge our conventional habits of being in the academy. They invite us to ask, how can we practice vulnerability, openness, calm, and compassion amid systems that often push us in other directions?

DO WE NEED TO TALK ABOUT SPIRITUALITY AT ALL?

A challenge facing those concerned with spirituality is finding the secular cognates of traditional religious and spiritual language so that the terms can become more available for broader community conversation. To facilitate public conversation on matters of the spirit, we may need to let go of some of the language that we hold dear in our traditions in exchange for a vocabulary that is more accessible and comfortable for others. Terms such as meaning, purpose, and connection, as used by the Education as Transformation Project, hold great promise here, as do terms such as integration and care. Grossman's work with students on innate mental health provides another example of how spiritual notions and practices can be articulated for a secular academic environment.

But is a larger conversation about spirituality only an issue of finding new words? During the Going Public with Spirituality conference held at the University of Massachusetts Amherst in June of 2000, the question that kept returning to me was this: how do we talk about spirituality in education with people who don't share an interest in spirituality? How can the conversation about spirituality and religious pluralism move beyond the circle of those who already gravitate toward it? At the closing session of the conference, I asked Peter Senge this question. He responded by questioning why I wanted to talk about spirituality with colleagues. Why reify spirituality? Why use the term at all? Could people itching to bring spirituality into public conversation be driven by the desire for a more subtle form of proselytizing, preaching the gospel of meaning and connection? How might such conversations generate more alienation than connection?

Based on their inquiries, Stockton and Raper both note how the academy functions as a neutral territory in which some students and staff members are grateful to escape religiously charged conversations, emotion-laden dialogue, or subtle tests of faith. Allegiance to established creeds was often required in the early American academy, and some people fear a return to denominational control or pressure to participate in rituals not of one's choosing. And then, for others, higher education is simply a work site, not a place where they desire emotional bonds or transformative conversations with others. They may find plenty of meaning and connection elsewhere. In that light, could "going public" with spirituality be a new intrusion or imposition? After all, there can be much wisdom in maintaining certain boundaries around the tender life of the soul.

Such questions, at moments, have quieted my enthusiasm for this topic. I have continued to wonder, should we talk about spirituality at all? Instead of talking directly about spirituality, Senge suggested that we talk about our lives. Everyone is interested in their lives, he pointed out, and what we need to do is connect the events of our lives to larger social and global issues. We do not necessarily need to talk about spirituality explicitly to have meaning-rich dialogue. As we talk about families, diseases, elections, racism, taxes, environmental problems, globalization, stress, and organizational politics; as we talk about what bothers us, what we struggle to do better, and what we hope to build together in our communities and the world—isn't that enough? Perhaps using the word "spirituality" can create a fog around the experiences we want to talk about together and stand in the way of creating the more integrative, just world we seek.

WHAT DOES SPIRITUALITY HAVE TO DO WITH TEACHING AND LEARNING?

The spiritual concern about community is, at heart, a concern about the quality of the learning environment. Recent thinking in the cognitive sciences and other areas of educational research has led to the appreciation that learning is fundamentally social. We learn to participate in communities we care to join, communities that affirm and expand our sense of meaning and identity.[4] To build connections, to build community, is to create the relational infrastructure that supports powerful learning. Fresh ideas, controversial books, friendly critiques, invitations to join inquiries—all these currents of learning swirl more fluidly in communities of shared activity, and the more diverse those communities, the richer the exchange. Learning will go deeper, the more it is not merely about exchange, but about being changed by our encounters. This perspective on learning echoes what Parker Palmer has long taught: truth is communal, and to teach is to create a space in which the community of truth is practiced.[5]

Understanding learning as social and communal helps us appreciate that human connection, as highlighted by Stafford's discussion of the "web of sociality," is an issue that goes to the heart of the mission of our institutions of higher education, i.e., to create an effective environment for learning. Amid concern about the quality of student achievement, rather than looking to new assessment mechanisms to gauge learning on campus, perhaps the more important pedagogical question is this: how does the institution nurture and frustrate relationship, across barriers of difference?

The issue of spirituality and learning, at root, calls for an engagement with the epistemological challenges of positivism. Positivism, the dominant mode of knowing in the modern university, has led to dispirited, instrumental, exploitative relationships with the social and natural world. As Arenas points out, it has led to a level of professional specialization and faith in controlling nature that may create comfort for the privileged few, but, in global terms, has contributed to terrible injustice for the many. In the words of educational theorist David Purpel, "we find ourselves without serious competition to a system that is killing us with its popularity."[6]

The dominant Western mode of knowledge, like a genetically modified plant, crowds out alternative epistemologies and modes of meaning-making. Intuition, imagination, contemplation, revelation, and the knowledges of the somatic self have little room in our professional conversations. Worldviews that emphasize connection, mutuality, harmony, responsibility, and care have been displaced as Western science leads the march of "progress." Saying this is not intended to demonize science, but to suggest that our fascination with technological change has obscured deeper issues. For a new kind of progress, we must begin to ask ourselves, where is the dialogue among epistemological systems? Where is there space for empirical and contemplative modes of knowing to share their insights? Where are the institutions grounded in nondualistic, relational cosmologies? A few exist, and more may be on the way.

Spirituality has the potential to be a richly transformative force in higher education. In their book, *The University in Transformation*, Gidley and Inayatullah include several chapters on alternative teaching/learning approaches informed by wisdom traditions.[7] They argue that modernity and its attendant faith in progress and technological control of nature has outlived its usefulness. Higher education must begin to take alternative cosmologies more seriously as the basis for rethinking their purpose and organization. What would a college look like, if constructed from Buddhist or Tantric principles about knowing and being? What of a feminist university? How might the professoriate be re-envisioned, were it based on integrative meaning-making and community partnership, rather than simple mastery of a fragmented sub-field of knowledge? Gidley suggests that some universities will metamorphosize into "humaniversities" which liberate themselves from service to the global economy and value human development over the production of knowledge workers.[8] In the face of the deep malaise that young people feel, these new institutions will support the recreation of meaning. Those faculty members acknowledged as meaning-makers—the equivalent of today's full professor—will have broad experience in intellectual, aesthetic, and practical domains, in addition to deep familiarity with at least two wisdom traditions. Such a vision acknowledges that, ultimately, we learn each other: students' development into complete human beings requires the company of people moving toward their own completeness.

Moving slowly toward the radical possibilities offered by Gidley and Inayatullah, hopeful forms of pedagogy are taking hold on campus, especially service learning and the formation of learning communities. These efforts, as Yihong, Arenas, Stafford, Raper and others in this volume note, are a promising approach for bringing greater meaning and connection into academic life. Alongside their academic content, service learning courses offer students lessons in civility, collaboration, social justice, and community building. Service learning breaks down the walls around the insular academic experience, engages students with people they might not otherwise encounter, and encourages an intimacy with the curriculum that goes far deeper than exams would ever reveal. In developing a more spiritually mature form of higher education, such practices should not be considered "alternative." Learning that feels healthy and whole should not be so strange; rather, we should begin to point out how the organizational and pedagogical structures which separate students from each other, the university from the ecology of its communities, action from reflection, and the rational from the affective are an artifice. The walls between the academic and the rest of life, in a more integrative future, will be seen as antiquated barriers to learning.

AND WHAT OF LOVE?

In the end, perhaps, the transformation of campus life is the work of love. Love is a word used casually, immaturely in higher education: fans love the football team; students love a popular course, etc. Love is often used to mark affection or infatuation, but we tend to avoid talking about love in deeper ways. A challenge of our time is to find a vocabulary of love in education that is not sentimental or silly or commercial, that honors the light and dark texture of our pedagogical and organizational experiences. Doing so will require richer approaches to conflict, as Martin explores, since conflict tends to accompany deep engagement.

Questions abound: how can we find ways to talk about the love that called us to our work? How can we talk together about the moments when that love has been betrayed? How do we talk about the barriers to love in our work, and ways to create institutions worthy of being loved? How can our institutions act out of love for social and ecological well-being? How do our institutions support loving work—work that is more gift than transaction? Transactional relationships are convenient, but typically plastic. Especially as highly integrated technologies enable student services to operate with greater convenience, how do we creatively choose inconvenience, i.e., processes that foster mutuality and interdependency?

When we talk about going public with spirituality, we can begin to critique ways in which the dominant culture has privatized spirituality. In the United States, spirituality has become rather individualized and commodified. With books on spirituality usually found next to the self-help section in bookstores, it has become easy for academics to dismiss spirituality as fluffy feel-goodism. Spirituality has come to be associated with products, from Zen safus to energy crystals. (There must be a master database somewhere in cyberland that keeps track of spiritual seekers. Once you order one thing, the catalogs multiply like loaves and fishes!)

Certainly, these products can support spiritual growth and healing. Yet there is also the danger that spirituality can be mined commercially, uprooted from its cultural moorings, and treated as another social marker of sophisticated consumption. In a time when everything is packaged for individual consumption, spirituality must be re-appropriated for collective use. The transformation of campus life demands a spirituality that is concerned with individual wellness as well as social wellness, a spirituality that helps us heal individually and culturally.

Over the past year, I have begun to wonder how the need to "go public with spirituality" is a white issue. As Arenas reminds us, the divorce of spirituality from science and rationality is a heritage of the European enlightenment. The Western cultural tradition has created institutions that follow Enlightenment logic, elevating rationality above all other modes of knowing, and separating matters of spirit from research and productive life. Sometimes I wonder if those of us European Americans who seek more meaning and connection in institutions are trying to heal the wounds inflicted by our own cultural systems. Non-European traditions may not need to "go public with spirituality" in the way whites seem to do, because spirituality is, and long has been, public. Not all public institutions of higher education disconnect themselves from religion and spirituality. As Jackson, McDemmond, and Curtis explain, HBCU's have retained spiritual development as an important emphasis in campus life.

As white people talk about bringing spirituality back into their institutions, there should be some caution about "white love." As discussed by Spring, "white love" refers to the self-proclaimed noble goals of explorers, colonists, and missionaries to bring civilization and liberation to less enlightened people on the margins of Western culture.[9]

In our conversations about spirituality on campus, the desire for universal meaning can carry the temptation of "white love." People seeking common ground between religious traditions, or more creative expressions outside traditions, have welcomed the notion of spirituality as the space where we can finally all come together. Spirituality is often articulated as dogma-free, as universal. Spirituality, from this perspective, transcends the limitations of particular traditions or social identities. If the concepts are universal, then the color or background of the person speaking about spirituality can be considered irrelevant.

One of the privileges of membership in a majority culture is seeing one's own identity and values as universal. By positioning spirituality as universal, beyond social identity, European Americans and Christians can gloss over the powerful ways in which social identity does matter.

In other words, European Americans talking about universal spirituality risk being the only ones who show up at the revival meeting. Speaking at a 1997 conference on spirituality in education held at the Naropa Institute in Boulder, Colorado, Vincent Harding asked why the participants were predominantly white: "What is the source of this great absence of color?"[10] That absence occurred again at the Going Public with Spirituality conference, raising difficult questions about the pluralistic nature of the spirituality conversation. Stockton's study touches on these questions and, as the field matures, further exploration will be possible. Expanding the pluralism in the movement for spirituality and religious pluralism requires more careful attention to differences in the historical, political, economic, and other experiences of different groups.

RECLAIMING VALUE

What is often forgotten in the discussion of religion and education is that faith traditions are not merely concerned with theology; they are profoundly concerned with the stuff of life—with the foods we eat, with our behavior toward one another, with the way we handle money, etc. Religious traditions carry powerful aesthetic, moral, and economic values. Exiling religion from campus life, we also exorcise their perspectives on living compassionately and wisely together. The values of the market fill the vacuum.

Academic capitalism is inching, sometimes yanking, higher education closer to corporate modes of organizing. While new partnerships between corporations and universities are promising at the pedagogical level, and certainly financially attractive, they can be constrictive in promoting a single bottom line rather than the multiple bottom lines suggested by Arenas and Fried. In the absence of competing logic, dictates of rational management and the market can structure community life for us. Colleges and universities, like other institutions of social maintenance, can become trapped in modes of narrow economic valuing. Talking about spirituality and religious ideals enables us to assert alternative benchmarks of meaning in our work and learning together as we challenge what counts and reclaim a role in the social negotiation of values.

How do we bring religious and spiritual concerns into our systems of institutional valuing? In strategic planning conversations, for example, what would it mean to include an analysis of the threats and opportunities to the spiritual health of the campus community? If that topic sounds too fuzzy, it can be easily concretized. The contributors to this book suggest that we already have many meaningful indicators for the spiritual health of our academic communities, including the following: the level of substance abuse, the extent of partnerships with community organizations, the number of spaces for silence on campus, the consumption of natural resources, and the level of collaboration between academic and student affairs in creating learning communities. In the end, transforming campus life involves inter-religious and trans-religious thinking about new forms of institutional reflection that speak, in ordinary terms, to higher levels of meaning and value.

In spite of perennial budget problems and exasperations, American higher education is incredibly wealthy, from a global perspective. How can we regain a sense of simplicity and abundance? Instead of always looking to build what is bigger and more elaborate, what if we began to think about building—whether in terms of physical construction or programmatic initiatives—that which is simpler, more elegant, more enduring, and less taxing on the local ecology, be that physical or social? Further, how can the roles of those who work in campus life take on a more expansive, transformative dimension? How might those who care for the quality of campus life be understood as educators in the fullest sense: as "social leaders, cultural advocates, moral visionaries, spiritual directors"?[11]

Transforming campus life is not only what this book is about. That phrase is not meant to imply an ending, as if the campus itself were the boundary for our work. There is no boundary. Ultimately, the transformation of campus life is about the transformation of community life, of cultural life, and of global systems. Spiritual work, at a personal level, can help us move "upward and outward," as Allen and Kellom note, and become more critical of the ways in which economic and social conditions limit human freedom and justice. At the same time, we can become more creative and bolder, in our imagination of alternatives. Educators need to do whatever we need to do—meditation, prayer, chanting, vision quests, retreats, going to church—that enables us to reclaim what Gidley calls "inspired human agency."[12] Although local efforts on campus may not directly affect larger transformations in and of themselves, they stimulate the imagination and expand our vocabulary of possibility.[13]

The transformation of campus life demands turning a critical eye and creative spirit toward overcoming our epistemological limitations, affirming religious identities as a resource for learning, and revitalizing dialogue. The transformation of campus life is an invitation, ever gently, ever more courageously, to talk about what matters to us and welcome what spirit may emerge.

ENDNOTES

1. Danah Zohar and Ian Marshall, *SQ: Connecting with Our Spiritual Intelligence* (New York: Bloomsbury, 2000).
2. David K. Scott, "Spirituality in an Integrative Age," in *Education as Transformation: Religious Pluralism, Spirituality, and a New Vision for Higher Education in America,* ed. Victor H. Kazanjian, Jr., and Peter L. Laurence (New York: Peter Lang, 2000).
3. bell hooks, "Embracing Freedom: Spirituality and Liberation," in *The Heart of Learning: Spirituality in Education,* ed. Steven Glazer (New York: Jeremy P. Tarcher/Putnam, 1999).
4. This approach to learning is richly articulated by Etienne Wenger in *Communities of Practice: Learning, Meaning, and Identity* (Cambridge: Cambridge University Press, 1998).
5. This idea has been elaborated by Parker Palmer in several publications and most fully in his book, *To Know as We Are Known: Education as a Spiritual Journey* (San Francisco: HarperSanFrancisco, 1983).
6. David Purpel, "Social Transformation and Holistic Education: Limitations and Possibilities," in *Critical Social Issues in American Education: Transformation in a Postmodern World,* ed. David Purpel and Svi Shapiro (Mahweh, NJ: Laurence Erlbaum Associates, 1998), 360.
7. Sohail Inayatullah and Jennifer Gidley, eds., *The University in Transformation: Global Perspectives on the Futures of the University* (Westport, CT: Bergin and Garvey, 2000).
8. Jennifer Gidley, "Unveiling the Human Face of University Futures" in *The University in Transformation: Global Perspectives on the Futures of the University,* ed. Sohail Inayatullah and Jennifer Gidley (Westport, CT: Bergin and Garvey, 2000).
9. Joel Spring, *Education and the Rise of the Global Economy* (Mahwah, NJ: Lawrence Erlbaum Associates, 1998). Spring borrows the term "white love" from Vicente Rafael's essay, "White Love: Surveillance and Nationalist Resistance in the U. S. Colonization of the Philippines" in *Cultures of United States Imperialism,* ed. Amy Kaplan and Donald Pease (Durham: Duke University, 1993).

10. Vincent Harding, "Where Do We Go from Here?" in *The Heart of Learning: Spirituality in Education,* ed. Steven Glazer (New York: Jeremy P. Tarcher/ Putnam, 1999), 238.
11. Purpel, "Social Transformation," 361.
12. Gidley, "Unveiling the Human Face," 236.
13. Purpel, "Social Transformation."

Contributors

Kathleen E. Allen is an Associate Professor in the Department of Educational Leadership, School of Education, at the University of St. Thomas in St. Paul, Minnesota. In addition, she is principle in her own consulting firm, Allen Associates, which specializes in leadership coaching and organizational change.

Alberto Arenas is an Assistant Professor in the School of Education and Center for International Education at the University of Massachusetts Amherst.

Richard A. Berman is Manhattanville College's tenth president. He has been the driving force behind the college's transformation. Under Berman's leadership, enrollment has doubled, finances have vastly improved and academic facilities have been restored to meet the needs of the diverse student body. Prior to his appointment at Manhattanville, Berman had a distinguished record in the private sector, government, health care, education and housing. He is very active in the local community.

Georg Buehler is an associate director of the Self Knowledge Symposium Foundation, and one of the original founding members of the student organization at North Carolina State University. He has spent the last eleven years working with college students as a facilitator and writing instructor for the SKSF. Professionally, Buehler is a senior systems analyst with the software corporation MuTek Solutions.

Leon Tilson Burrows is Chaplain to Smith College and Protestant Religious Advisor at Amherst College. He holds degrees from the University of Hartford, Yale University School of Music and Divinity School and the Lutheran Theological Seminary at Philadelphia. Prior to assuming his current positions he was a pastor, for eight years, of an American Baptist congregation in Philadelphia.

Margaret L. Causey, RSCJ, is Assistant Professor of World Religions and Founder and Director of the Duchesne Center for Religion and Social Justice at Manhattanville College. Prior to her appointment at Manhattanville, Sr. Causey was a Visiting Assistant Professor of Religion at Georgetown University and spent fifteen years in secondary school administration.

Jacqueline A. Curtis is a naturalized citizen of the United States from Guyana, South America. She has more than thirty years' experience in higher education at private and public institutions. She is active in her church and graduated from Central State University. She is a wife and mother of three grown children and the grandmother of Janae.

Katja Hahn d'Errico, Ed.D., is the Director of Student Businesses and Adjunct Faculty in the School of Education at the University of Massachusetts Amherst. In an experiental learning community she trains students in participatory management, teamwork, and leadership. Her teaching focuses on issues of diversity, leadership, and spirituality. Critical illness and loss have prepared her to include spiritual practice in her life.

Kenny Felder has been a member of the Self Knowledge Symposium for ten years. He lives in Chapel Hill, North Carolina, with his wife and three children. He has taught classes, given many lectures, and appeared on the radio, always discussing the theme of how college students can begin to build their lives around their spiritual goals.

Jane Fried earned her doctorate from the Union of Experimenting Colleges and Universities after studying at the University of Connecticut. She is currently coordinator of the master's degree program in student development in higher education at Central Connecticut State University. Integrating the search for meaning, particularly spiritual meaning, with higher education has been her lifelong work.

Ora Gladstone is the co-coordinator of the Religious Pluralism and Spirituality (RPS) group at Brandeis University. Despite her master's in Community Mental Health Counseling and a License in Music Therapy, her professional life has been spent working primarily with Jewish students as Associate Director of Brandeis Hillel. Her interest in helping bridge the gulf between groups from diverse religions, cultures, and socioeconomic backgrounds is a primary motivation for her activism in groups such as the RPS.

Rev. Joel Grossman, M.Ed., L.C.S.W., is the Coordinator of the Health Promotion Program at the University of Massachusetts Boston, where he has been since 1990. Joel has maintained a private practice as a spiritually oriented psychotherapist since 1975, working full-time from 1982 to 1988 at the New England Center for Holistic Medicine in Newbury, Massachusetts. He was ordained as an interfaith minister in October 2000.

Margaret A. Jablonski currently serves as the Dean for Campus Life at Brown University. For the past twenty years, she has held positions in student affairs on five campuses in New England. She continues to teach in the School of Education at the University of Massachusetts Amherst, weaving spiritual issues into the graduate curriculum.

Arthur R. Jackson is currently the Vice President of Student Affairs and Visiting Associate Professor at Westfield State College, Westfield, Massachusetts. Prior to this position he was Vice President for Student Affairs at Norfolk State University and Associate Dean of Student Affairs at Eastern Connecticut University. He received his doctorate of education at the University of Massachusetts Amherst.

Victor H. Kazanjian, Jr., is the Dean of Religious and Spiritual Life and co-director of the Peace and Justice Studies Program at Wellesley College as well as the co-founder and Senior Advisor of the Education as Transformation Project. He is the author of numerous articles and a lecturer and workshop leader on issues of religious pluralism, spirituality, interreligious/intercultural dialogue and conflict resolution, and principles of peacemaking and social justice.

Gar Kellom is the Vice President for Student Development at St. John's University in Collegeville, Minnesota, which is one of the four men's colleges remaining in American higher education. He holds a doctorate from the Joint Ph.D. program offered by the University California, Berkeley and the Graduate Theological Union. His passions are Asian studies, men's development and increasing the quality of adult interaction in the lives of young people.

Peter Laurence, Ed.D., is Director of the Education as Transformation Project at Wellesley College. He has been a consultant in interfaith education for many years, having served as Chair of the Board of the North American Interfaith Network and a member of the Assembly for the Parliament of the World's Religions.

Patricia E. Martin, Ph.D., is Dean of Career Development at Mt. Hood Community College in Gresham, Oregon. She is particularly interested in issues of spirituality on the college campus and how this area can be considered a new area of diversity. She served on the inaugural spiritual studies task force in Region I NASPA, the first such group in the country.

Marie V. McDemmond is President of Norfolk State University, the fifth largest Historically Black University in the U.S. She is the university's first female president and the first woman to serve as the chief executive officer of a four-year, state-supported university in Virginia. She teaches in Wellesley and Bryn Mawr Colleges' Project HERS and speaks on topics ranging from financial management to leadership. She received her undergraduate degree from Xavier University and completed here doctoral degree at the University of Massachusetts Amherst.

Vachel W. Miller is a doctoral candidate at the Center for International Education at the University of Massachusetts Amherst and former assistant to the Provost for Academic Affairs at the College of St. Benedict/St. John's University in Minnesota. He is interested in new possibilities for the transformation of educational institutions internationally to nurture human learning and community collaboration.

Judy Raper is the Assistant Dean of Campus Life at Lyndon State College. She received her bachelor's degree from Indiana University. She received her master's and doctoral degrees from the University of Vermont.

Merle M. Ryan, Ed.D., is currently Assistant Dean of Students at the University of Massachusetts Amherst. Among her various responsibilities, she chairs the Religious Affairs Committee. Recently, Merle worked closely on the "Going Public with Spirituality in Work and Higher Education" conference. She is also an Adjunct Assistant Professor in the Higher Education graduate program at the university.

Mary Alice Scott is the Executive Director of the Self Knowledge Symposium Foundation and has been involved with the organization since 1996. A recent graduate of Duke University in Women's Studies, she has been involved with several not-for-profit organizations dedicated to both social change and personal transformation including Caminamos Juntos Para Salud Y Desarrollo in Tlamacazapa, Guerrero, Mexico, Youth Voice Radio in Durham, North Carolina, and Empty the Shelters in Atlanta, Georgia.

Gil Stafford is the President of Grand Canyon University in Phoenix, Arizona. He has served the university for twenty-one years as baseball coach, Athletic Director, Dean of Students, Vice President of Student Life, Executive Vice President, and now President.

Sarah Stockton, M.A., is a freelance editor and writer. She is also an intern at the Spiritual Director's Institute at the Mercy Center in Burlingame, California.

Jennifer L. Walters is the Dean of Religious Life at Smith College and formerly the University of Michigan's ombuds for student affairs. She is also a mediator and an Episcopal priest. She holds master's degrees from Boston College and Michigan State University and a doctorate in ministry from the Episcopal Divinity School.

Fan Yihong is currently a doctoral candidate at the School of Education, University of Massachusetts Amherst and has been an Associate Professor at Southwest Jiaotong University, Chengdu, China. Having successfully changed campus culture and brought out students' creativity and potentiality at her university in China, she focuses her research on how to create self-organizing learning communities.